TURN RIGHT FOR JAPAN

Cycling the Silk Road to the Orient

TALLON, STEVE ANTHONY

Stantopia Press

Cover Design by Stewart J. Cowlishaw

For Kellan

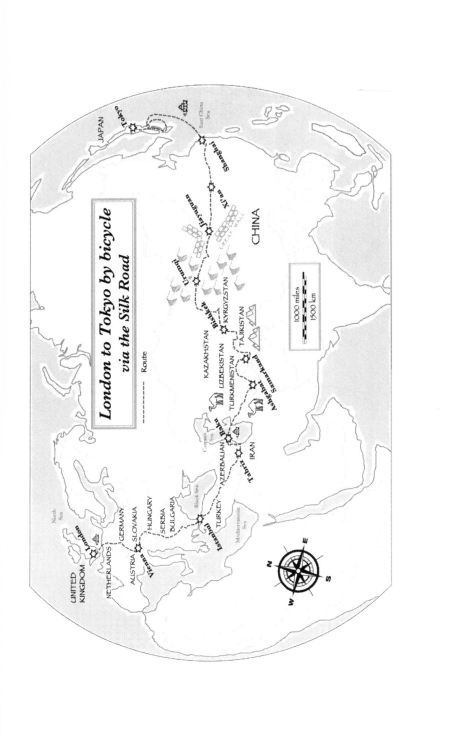

London to Tokyo by bicycle via the Silk Road

CONTENTS

INTRODUCTION

The nurse was Russian and looked very determined; she came into the doctor's waiting room wielding a long, fat plunger type instrument, and I had a fearful premonition of where that might be going. She towered above my chair and growled some unintelligible commands, translated by an English-speaker drafted in from the foreign ministry next door.

"Pants down!" she said.

"What?" I said. "WHAT?"

"Pants down... please", he repeated.

Things were not going well. I was in Bishkek, the capital of Kyrgyzstan, on my way to Japan. I had left London over four months earlier on a plan to cycle to Tokyo, via the northern route of the ancient Silk Road. Twice I had tried to leave, and twice I had collapsed in a heap, neutralised by the re-emergence of the stomach bug that had last tried to finish me off in Uzbekistan. So I had decided to find a hospital, to get checked out once and for all.

I looked around: there were three or four other patients here, a couple of whom were starting to take an interest. The nurse grabbed my arms and manhandled me to my feet, gesturing to the wall at the front of the room. She spun me around and kicked my legs apart, so I was spread-eagled against it, with my back facing everyone.

"Pants DOWN!"

She said it much more belligerently this time, tugging roughly at my belt, and for some unfathomable reason I complied. There were now over half a dozen people in the room and I had the full attention of every one of them.

"Spread wide!"

Today I was learning Russian I prayed to heaven I would never have to hear again. The ministry man was struggling to communicate the next directive issued by the nurse as I heard the elastic snap of rubber gloves behind me, and another couple of people entered the room, to be met with a view of my bare backside. It was all happening so fast.

"Please pull apart your... your..."

The vocabulary evaded him, and he fanned out his hands, joining the tips of his fingers together and pulled them apart slowly and deliberately. He shrugged his shoulders and looked at me apologetically.

"*Cheeks...?*" I asked, in a very tiny voice.

At least nobody was streaming this to the Internet - this was 2005, two years before the first iPhone. Facebook was still unknown to 99% of the population and forget Twitter - the best option for on-the-move news updates (like this?) was a bulky shortwave radio.

There were now at least a dozen people in the room, many of whom it seemed had just popped in off the street for the entertainment. The nurse was getting impatient now, repeating the same angry words again and again, clenching and unclenching her gloved hands, and the spectators were murmuring excitedly.

"Yes! That's right!" the ministry man said, relieved. "Please pull apart your *cheeks!*"

There was no Google Maps or bike GPS either - I had navigated my way from London to Central Asia with just paper maps and a compass: seven thousand miles on a leather saddle, and now I was subjecting my bum to new horrors.

The procedure was mercifully quick; a brief poke, an adept twist and an involuntary gasp (that was me, not the nurse), and the sample was withdrawn, test thankfully completed. I may have imagined the round of applause.

When I went back for the results a couple of days later, they had found nothing, and I was none the wiser about my repeated bouts of sickness. The only useful thing I'd learnt was never again to seek medical attention within a hundred miles of this place. Four months later I finished what I'd started, and after traversing the expanse of China, then taking a boat from Shanghai, finally rolled into Tokyo, admirably still in one piece.

Fourteen years on, I'm still here.

The region has transformed enormously since then. Presidents and dictators have come and gone, some nations have changed for the better, whilst others continue to bear the brunt of Central Asia's colourful politics. The scattered construction projects that I witnessed through China's far west will now have only accelerated toward its ambitious goal: to create a modern Silk Road of high-speed rail and road links back to Beijing. The empty miles of desert and savanna that I write about here will quite possibly be lost forever.

The world progresses, and in the intervening years I have found it all too easy to become wrapped up in the daily routines of life. To start taking everything far too seriously, and more often dwell on what could go wrong, rather than what could go right.

So why not write a book, I thought, and remind myself that I had once cycled halfway round the world - ten-thousand hard-earned miles through countries I could once barely pronounce. Chronicle the stories from all those years ago, and rediscover the optimism of a slightly younger me, one who didn't need to be told that anything really *is* possible.

And this time, at least, there would be no ex-Soviet nurses shoving a plunger up my bum.

CHAPTER 1
EARTHQUAKES IN ESSEX

W hile I had plotted my route across rough and rocky roads in far-away Chinese deserts, hidden hundred-dollar bills in my bicycle frame and startled myself regularly at the latest travel warnings on the British Home Office homepage, the thought of cycling through London on my first day was, quite simply, horrifying. I had decided it was a much better idea to start from somewhere quiet, familiar, and with a high proportion of unthreatening old-age pensioners: Wallingford, where my mother lives.

There were some last-minute jitters; a visit to the doctors for an imaginary sore throat, and a strange foreboding that the blue skies and 20-degree temperatures would turn into snow and hail by the afternoon, with the possibility of earthquakes in Essex. But unable to come up with a good excuse to call the whole thing off, I found myself mounting my heavy touring bike in the forecourt of our block of flats. My mother questioned me worryingly about the excessive load on the bike, as I swayed unsteadily from side to side on a warm-up lap around the carpark. In all it came to almost 50 kilos and I explained again that I needed to be prepared: warm clothes, camping gear, cooking utensils, maps, guidebooks, spare bike parts, a range of medicines and emergency food rations - none of which did anything to reassure her. After a few tears, she finally let me prise myself away; I did a final victory-be-mine lap of the carpark, fist in the air, and headed out from the cul-de-sac, turning right towards the Orient!

I came back five minutes later for my pump.

St. Albans was today's modest goal, and it was my first experience of cycling in England since I was a teenager. It felt like a lazy Sunday afternoon, the scent of freshly cut grass in the air, rolling fields dotted with sheep and cows, and endless views of meadows spilling over with dandelions. Many of these views were from the top of some challenging hills; this was my first time on the bike in three months, and I was feeling it. Not only were my legs struggling at the slightest incline, but in my enthusiasm to do things properly, I had opted for a classic Brooks touring saddle – a flap of hardened leather stretched over a steel skeleton and hammered in place by a dozen bronze rivets. Over the course of a thousand miles it would mould itself perfectly into the shape of my nether regions, but until then I had better be prepared for some tender moments. Today my manhood would be further bruised - metaphorically speaking - by a party of young women who cycled past me effortlessly while I struggled, panting and wheezing, up the final hill of the day.

Arriving in St. Albans, I found myself with enough time for some sightseeing. I had completed 82 kilometres, not bad for a first day I thought, and wanted to mark the occasion with a photo of the cathedral. So I stopped in at the local tourist information office to ask where it was.

"Don't bother, it's complete rubbish" grunted the old man behind the counter.

A moment later, the harried-looking tourist information lady returned, shooing the old boy away from behind the counter.

"Oh Trevor, I really wish you'd stop saying that" she gently scolded him, "it is our number one tourist attraction after all."

PASTEL PINK WALLS, PADDED LEATHER DRINK COASTERS AND ROSE scented toilet paper. I had chosen a pleasant bed and breakfast for my first night, and I knew all too well that it was hardly the choice for a nomad of the road. The blue skies of yesterday had been drained of their colour and most of the day was spent under dark clouds, with long periods of drizzle. I was headed through the commuter towns north of London, towards the curiously named town of Braintree. More traffic, more urban landscape, and frequent downpours turned the day into a bit of a slog, and I rejected the notion of pitching my tent, instead choosing to check in to a dreary motel complex.

The following morning, my bike started to waver all over the busy road of its own accord and shudder violently at certain speeds. In heavy rain, I unloaded the bags and started following rain-sodden instructions on how to adjust the headset. It didn't help. I loosened the handlebars and realigned them again. That didn't help either. So, I called the bike shop and breathlessly explained the symptoms, whining that I had to get to Asia on this machine and I hadn't even made it past bloody Essex.

"Alright mate, calm down" said the guy on the other end of the line with a tired sigh. "Have you actually tried balancing the panniers?"

I redistributed the contents of the front panniers - a BLT sandwich and a book, portentously called "It's Not About The Bike" - angrily moving them from the left to the right bag, remounted and continued down the main road without incident. How on earth did I believe that I could cycle all the way to Tokyo? I couldn't even pack properly! Almost as if my biking incompetence had been broadcast over national radio, two different drivers in the space of thirty minutes slowed down beside me and shouted if I needed a lift.

The rain stopped and the day was brightening up. Instead of the main roads and conurbations of the morning, I was soon riding on quiet country lanes, catching generous glimpses of the ocean beyond the trees and could already taste the salt in the air. All too soon I arrived in Harwich, and made my way to the port; I rolled up to the front of my row, waiting for the evening ferry bound for Holland. It was approaching dusk and I could already see the distant lights of ships in the North Sea. A car pulled up beside me, and the driver asked where I was headed.

"Tokyo!" I replied, and for the first time realised the enormity of what I was doing.

Yet it felt right, like the whole plan had finally clicked into place.

I was thirty-six years old, and most of my working life had been spent in Japan. I had become quite comfortable living over there, but also complacent. Routinely manhandled into crowded commuter trains, face pressed up against the glass and someone else's sweat soaked through to my back. Twelve-hour days stuck in a tiny, airless office cubicle. A cascade of spreadsheets plastered across my computer that I could never hope to complete. Every year when I flew home for Christmas, I would gaze out the window over stark, snow-covered peaks, increasingly fascinated at the small clusters of lights appearing in lonely valleys 35,000 feet below. I was in awe of whoever lived down there... mystified as to what on earth they did. On one of those flights I had wondered: would it be possible to travel back to Japan by bike?

And now, implausibly, I was on the point of finding out.

Neglected splendours of Eastern European capitals, extravagant Turkish mosques, and the lonely deserts of Iran... exotic images razed my imagination. Ancient forts and citadels, a chain of mythical Silk Road towns through to China and, of course, the Great Wall itself. I was standing on the dock of Harwich ferry port with my bike and a few belongings, and I was planning to cycle halfway across the world to Japan!

The driver next to me hurriedly wound up his window and with a look of disbelief, stared straight ahead.

WHEN I STARTED PLANNING THIS VENTURE, I HAD PINNED A world map to the wall and drawn a simple line from west to east. It passed worryingly through Iran then half-a-dozen countries ending ominously in -*stan*. Most of these I had never heard of, but in mapping an overland route between Europe and the Far East, it became evident that I was retracing a network of ancient caravan trade routes, better known as the Silk Road.

Stretching from the Mediterranean through Central Asia, India and into China, the Silk Road had been a conduit for goods like tea, porcelain, spices, weapons and slaves since 130 B.C. Marco Polo had famously documented his own journey in the 13th century, providing the first glimpse, for Europeans at least, into middle Asia and the wonders of China. Marco was one of last to witness the Silk Road in all its glory; it fell into disuse as more practical sea routes became established, and the once thriving cities were swallowed up by the sands of the desert, much of the area reverting to a perilous land of lawless and brutally governed khanates.

It wasn't until the 18th century that the region found itself in the spotlight again, in a hundred years of subterfuge between the Russian and British empires that would become known as the Great Game, popularised in Rudyard Kipling's famous novel *Kim*. In its efforts to protect imperial India from Russian ambitions, the British army sent young officers, disguised as traders or pilgrims, to map the land and take notes of fortifications in the still medieval caravan towns of the old Silk Road. Inevitably many would pay with their lives. Russia eventually brought the region under its control, splitting it into a number of satellite states (the various *stans*) where they remained until the breakup in 1991 of the Soviet Union.

It was certainly an entertaining part of the world and it was lucky that I found myself lost in the details of planning. The alternative would have been to muse over all manner of horrible ways to meet my end.

WE DOCKED AT THE HOOK OF HOLLAND SIX HOURS LATER AND I could tick off a minor milestone - my first change of time zone. The first night was to be spent in the Hotel America by the docks; pushing my bike into the dimly lit lobby I saw a corridor of red lights leading into a bar, from where raucous sailor-like laughter and singing could be heard. This was, funnily enough, exactly how I had imagined a dockside hotel in Holland to be. Tired, and a little wary of all manner of liberal activities that might be taking place on the other side of those double doors, I waited until a barman came back and showed me to my room, at the top of several narrow creaking wooden staircases.

The Netherlands is famous for its cycle-friendly society and with 13 million bicycles, there are twice as many bikes as cars and nearly as many bicycles as people. An 11,000-mile system of bike paths criss-crosses the nation, but it was a system designed for locals who had no intention of cycling further than a couple of miles from home, and I would inevitably end up at the bottom of a cul-de-sac or in somebody's garage.

In towns I hit bicycle traffic jams, starting and stopping my behemoth of a machine every fifty yards for a traffic light, or pulling the bike left and right to avoid pedestrians. The first word to learn in a new country: "Excuse me". The second: "Move!". I once ventured out on to the road and how people loathed that, shouting and gesturing at me to get back onto the path. And I'd thought this country was meant to be laid-back.

After an exhausting day of near collisions, manhandling my bike through throngs of pedestrians and calling out "excuse me" in a language that I wasn't entirely sure was Dutch, I found myself in Shoonhaven, a picturesque town of cobbled streets and pretty pastel-coloured curio shops. The hotel was expensive, and at the breakfast buffet the next morning, I felt obliged to tip all the bread-rolls and three plates of cheese into my backpack.

My last full day in Holland was a cold, wet and rainy one, heading south-east through Tiel, a town which had the worn look of an early Seventies television drama. I was given directions to a hotel by the elderly town mayor, dressed in full officiating regalia (at least I thought he was the mayor), but it had been long closed and eventually I found a campsite out of town, well after it had turned dark. The old lady who ran the place kept refilling my cup with hot coffee, and it took an hour before I realised that she was patiently waiting for me to pay. I set up my tent for the first time and with boyish excitement, settled down for the night.

In the morning I looked out at the miserable scene before me, listening to the tap-tap-tap of rain on the flysheet and watching water splash up from the waterlogged ground; I decided to race straight through to Kleve in Germany, so I could at least salvage something from this day by making it into my next country. And with a very real sense of relief, I finally got myself a photograph of a windmill – I had lost sleep over the last couple of nights worrying that I might actually pass through the Netherlands without managing even this.

The road to Kleve opened out with long lines of trees on either side and the rain made the colours of the surrounding forest shine. I hadn't travelled in Europe for almost fifteen years and I was expecting a proper border post, a clear physical presence marking the different territories, and hopefully a bit of barbed wire and a few jack-booted soldiers sucking on cheroots and demanding my travel papers - but there was nothing to mark where Holland stopped, and Germany started. I had my first puncture of the trip on the same road when I ran over a broken beer bottle, and wasn't even sure which country to swear at.

A still chubby author and his pretentiously clean bicycle

CHAPTER 2

A RANT FROM THE RHINE

LONDON · {Germany} · Rothenburg · Regensburg · {Austria} · Passau · Vienna · TOKYO

The Rhine starts in Switzerland and winds its way north west for 1,300 kilometres, eventually emptying into the North Sea. My imagination had conjured up images of mediaeval castles, cathedrals and dark menacing forests, but what actually got my attention were the increasing numbers of corpulent middle-aged cyclists on the road (myself included). Attired in fluorescent tops and astonishingly tight lycra shorts, this was perhaps the "great German romantic tradition" that I had read so much about in the tourist brochures.

I delayed in Cologne long enough to take a brief look at the imposing Dom Cathedral and it felt satisfying to cycle through the tourist hordes, as I realised that I had made my first European landmark by bike. I continued on to Bonn along the pleasant riverside path reaching it in fading light with 120 kilometres on the clock; it had been a long day for my still unfit body.

The hotels and guesthouses seemed far too clean for me and my bike, so I headed south out of the city towards the futuristically named Venusberg where, I'd gathered from my map, there was a youth hostel. The location was superb, set on the edge of the deeply forested Kottenforst Nature Reserve, although the hostel itself had the ambience of a gulag, with bare cell-like rooms, a narrow bed and strip-lighting. On the other hand, it did have a bar, and I wandered down there for a little creature comfort. Techno music was pumping out, young noisy chatter permeated the room, and drunken teenagers were running around the place or fondling each other in various corners of the building - I suddenly felt about eighty years old. And a little lonely I realised, thinking I could do with a bit of fondling myself. Suppressing that thought, I retired to a local pub, a large steak and several large German beers.

~

IT WAS A RAINY DAY IN KOBLENZ, AND IT FELT LIKE IT SOUNDS.

Ignoring a mild hangover, I headed out onto the Rhine bike-path under lashings of heavy rain. Today I didn't have to worry about other bikes, pedestrians, pushchairs or dogs, but the rain was relentless and cold, and the route was becoming rougher, muddier and more waterlogged. I stopped in a bus-shelter as I pointlessly tried to wring out my wet clothes, and dry my freezing torso with a towel, which caused some finger-pointing and looks of disapproval from the grey-haired occupants of a large house nearby. So I shocked them once again with a much more directed display of vigorous towelling.

When blue skies eventually appeared a few days later, I couldn't contain myself - like a pet dog locked up all day and then taunted with the word "Walkies!", I leapt on the bike and shot off madly down the hill in the direction of the river, panting hard, tail wagging and tongue hanging out. It was wonderful - the Rhine really *is* beautiful, the towns and villages pristinely kept, very pretty, and every new bend in the river offering yet another brooding castle high up in the hills. I passed the Rock of Loreley; a huge rock on the corner of one of the tightest and most dangerous bends in the river. Local legend holds that the Loreley was a beautiful young mermaid, who had been betrayed in her previous life by an unfaithful lover. Here she now sits at the Rhine's narrowest point, combing her long blonde hair, and luring sailors to their death on the rocks with her mysterious songs and beguiling beauty.

I concurred that this was indeed a hazard of the job, as my own concentration was momentarily distracted by a group of young female backpackers, and I cycled into a bench.

With no large towns, no obvious signs of modern industry and an abundance of green forests and imposing stone architecture, I could see why this was a World Heritage area, and I found a pleasant campsite near Hattenheim, a village of cobble-stoned streets, shaded courtyards and pastel-coloured houses. By morning, ice had covered the tent and frozen my water bottle; the riverside tracks were muddy and icy, sending me slipping off in all directions except the direction I wanted to go. Even the pleasant proximity to the river was just not worth the hassle of these infuriating paths today, so I was cycling on the main road. However, there was no empathy from the average German motorist - within seconds of leaving the bike path someone would beep their car horn.

"Oi! *Radfahrer*! Get off the road!" they'd shout, gesturing toward the bike path until I followed their instruction. On the occasions where I was on the bike path and it subtly turned into a foot path, I would be equally admonished by the pedestrians instead.

All this bossing around was increasingly annoying, but I had to accept that this was Germany and rules are there to be followed; order must be maintained. Everyone knows that here, now I knew it, and amazingly even the dogs knew it; I could speed towards someone walking their dog, in prime ankle-chasing range, but with barely the slightest nod of the owner's head, the mutt would obediently sit down and wait patiently for me to pass. Oh, how I would reminisce about such canine discipline in the months to follow!

My emotions were like the undulations of the road - up and down. Atrociously lost coming out of Worms the next morning, I was working myself up to a foul mood until I found myself on some quiet farm lanes, and a measure of serenity returned. But then a puncture, and then *another* puncture led to much swearing and shaking of fists at the heavens. Soon afterwards, I was riding on a wonderful forest path and things were looking up again. All I had to do was head south-east towards Heidelberg, through the small town of Viernheim, and resist the extensively advertised highlights of bowling alley and bird park ("exotic birds like parrots and pheasants").

But by the Gods, what manner of mischievous forces operated in that area! After negotiating a handful of turns, I found myself back where I'd started thirty minutes earlier. I tried another road and the same thing happened again. And again! Every road led me back to Viernheim and its wretched parrots and pheasants. I had entered the Bermuda Triangle for bicycles and stared warily at the afternoon sky, resigned to the fact that I was probably about to be abducted by aliens.

After taking two hours to navigate through a town spanning barely a mile across, I decided to take the direct mountain road to Heidelberg rather than taking my chances with any other towns in this cursed area. It was steep and winding, snaking its way up into the hills through a thick canopy of green forest; I hadn't experienced a climb of this calibre since I had left Japan, and certainly never with a bike loaded as heavily as mine was now. The frustrations of the day wilted away as I stamped on the pedals, and the downhill was as breath-taking as the uphill had been arduous. I gave an un-British (and definitely un-German) whoop of joy as my odometer broke the thousand-kilometre barrier.

The downhill run spat me out near Heidelberg, an ancient university town. With its huge castle dominating the skyline and wonderful old houses lining the steep narrow cobble-stoned streets, it looked like it had been plucked from a book of fairy-tales. However the next morning's tiny set breakfast of toast, eggs and an odd kind of sausage was a disappointing departure from most of the guest-house breakfasts I had enjoyed up to now. I had got into the routine of gorging myself on a generous cooked breakfast followed by several helpings of muesli, fruit and anything else edible that fell within my reach at the breakfast table. I had an irrational fear of hunger between towns or in the middle of long climbs, so I could always be found stuffing my face at every opportunity. Despite riding a heavy bike up and down hills for eight hours a day, I realised, with some dismay, that I was actually putting on weight.

Luckily for the lycra-viewing public, my appetite would eventually return to normal and the body would get used to the routine of hard daily physical activity. In fact, I would eventually almost double my daily cycling distance, over much rougher roads, carrying more gear, and do it eating less than I would do in my normal sedate working life. But for the time being at least, it was obvious who ate all the pies.

$\sim$

THE COURSE OF THE NECKARTAL RIVER WAS A PICTURESQUE route of quiet paths and minor lanes. Mist hung heavy in the upper reaches of the valley as I found a road hugging the river, winding eastwards under the heavy boughs of a long line of ancient oaks, and followed it contentedly until it turned into a steep path winding high into the mountains. Legs rebelling against orders, face fixed in a death grimace and teeth almost cracking, I rounded the last hairpin turn as cuckoos seemingly taunted me in German-accented English.

Late afternoon, as I overtook an old man on an antique Raleigh ten-speed racer, he insisted that I follow him into Bad Wimpfen. He led me up his favourite short cut, a steep, narrow path with lots of stone steps, bounding up there with the bike on his shoulders then looking back down at me in mischievous amusement when I couldn't do the same. It was a wonderful looking town, the quirky name doing justice to the streets full of colourful half-timber houses and shops, bowed and leaning crookedly overhead. He recommended a hotel on the main square, surrounded by no less than three Gothic churches. The next day I woke up exhausted from the church bells, each of which sounded a full set of chimes on every hour and a single loud chime every fifteen bloody minutes.

I followed a bike path over rolling hills, patch-work fields, pastures and woods, all covered in a thin veneer of mist. Thanks to the rain, I had it to myself for the whole morning, but inevitably the cold and wet started getting more of my attention than the scenery, the path turned into busy road, and as I ate my waterlogged sandwich, shivering outside under the overhang of a local train station (rough dimly-lit bar, lunchtime alcoholics, and a bearded barmaid who extorted fifty cents from me to use the toilet), I was feeling pretty miserable. Later, the heavens opened like a flood, soaking me to the bone, and I splashed my way to the first farmhouse I saw. A filling meal and a couple of beers later, I was relaxing with the farmer's wife in the dining room, talking to her about my trip and the hardships I was expecting to face.

"Ah, eight months alone" she pondered aloud, "It is a long time, no?"

Yes, I agreed, it was a long time.

"For a woman, I think not big problem, a woman, she can be... *patient*" she continued, gazing out the window and pausing for effect. "But for a man? Mein Gott."

She looked me in the eyes, pityingly.

"For a man, it is a very long time, without..."

I mumbled something about the lovely meal and scuttled off to bed.

It was an uneasy night, pondering the months of monastic solitude ahead, and I headed out into the cloudy day earlier than usual, following the landlady's advice to take the scenic route north. It was good advice, as the path wound up and down through open countryside and forest, and joined the *Romantische Strasse*, a two-hundred-mile route through western Bavaria towards the Alps. Famous for its pretty towns and sleepy hideaway villages, this part of Germany is hugely popular with the Japanese and I noticed that even some of the road signs here were in Japanese.

The approach to Rothenburg took in the full Gothic majesty of its setting atop a sharp, steep bend in the Tauber River. Within its ancient city walls, the streets were steep, twisting and cobblestoned, the houses and buildings mediaeval, and the interiors decorated in old dark wood, softly lit and fashioned into cosy nooks and crannies. The approach of evening brought flickering candles and the orange-shadowed glow of wood-fires seen behind the lead-lined windows of houses and restaurants. I had long looked forward to a visit to the town's famous Christmas Museum, and the setting was more enchanting than I had ever imagined.

The entrance was buried deep in the front of an old stone building, with huge Christmas trees, twinkling with lights, just inside the open oaken doors. Presents were scattered underneath, wrapped with glossy red and gold paper, and finished with extravagant ribbons and bows. Oversized cuddly toys, delightful little Christmas elves and life-sized red-coated wooden toy soldiers lined the entrance to this magical grotto.

Excited children skipped ahead of their parents, wide-eyed with wonder as they crossed the threshold, and it only occurred to me then that a thirty-six-year-old bloke going in there alone would look so very sad. And a little dodgy. Miserably, I turned away from its innocent childhood charms, and made my way to the more appropriate Torture Museum instead.

~

IT WAS A PERFECT DAY AND IT IS IMPORTANT TO REMEMBER THAT there are such days, because as time and distance progress and the hardships increase, you need to know that there will always be the good times again, days to make it all worthwhile. I followed the Danube Canal all morning, cycling through picnic country, green and glossy rolling pastures sprinkled with dandelions. On the map at least, the Bavarian city of Regensburg looked like a navigational force to be reckoned with, but I threaded my way through the well-preserved mediaeval town centre effortlessly; with a hundred kilometres already done I was feeling great, and it seemed a shame not to make the most of the beautiful weather, so I decided that today I was going to do my first "century", one hundred miles (or 161 kilometres) of cycling.

A young guy on a mountain bike raced by me while I was taking a breather, looked over his shoulder at me quizzically for a moment and circled back, asking me something in German. My customary response of nodding politely, holding my thighs like a prize salmon and stating my destination elicited an introduction in English. His name was Lothar, and he was on his way home from work.

"Why not stay tonight with me and my family? I live up there" – he pointed distressingly upwards towards the mountains – "in the Upper Wald, a place called Sussenbach. You will have the use of your own guesthouse, as well."

After some thought (those were *mountains*) I thanked him for his offer but explained how I was determined to do the hundred miles today, and in the right direction. He wished me luck and carried on.

Ten seconds later, I thought what had I done? What was the whole point of this enterprise? If my intention was to get from one place to another as fast as possible, then I should have just taken a flight! I chased him down.

"Yes, of course the offer is still open!" he said, pleased that I'd managed to catch him up.

We turned onto a track of gravel, dirt and mud that threaded its way through deep forest, with slippery roots, fallen branches and deep muddy puddles to contend with. Tall, thick trees towered over us as we followed a crystal-clear stream that sparkled in the late afternoon sun, flowing down from green fields with breath-taking luminosity.

"Ah, it's not bad," said Lothar, with uncharacteristic German modesty, "for a commute, anyway. You should see the places I ride on the weekend."

Sussenbach itself was a small, neat village of farming households, immaculately painted in pastel shades and standing a good three or four stories high. Many displayed huge murals, reaching fully from the ground to the apex of the roof. All were of a strong religious nature, and I saw paintings of the virgin mother, the last supper, and the crucifixion on various homes. This had pretty much been a constant theme over the last few days; predominantly Catholic, Bavaria is serious about its worship, and the first thing I would see at the entrance to any village was a map showing the location of local churches, and the times of the services.

This meant there was also an unnerving propensity to erect large crucifixes everywhere; a disconcertingly life-sized one of Jesus on the Cross had been looking down at me sorrowfully as I ate my bread and cheese roll by the Danube earlier that day.

Later, over dinner with Lothar and his family, the conversation made me question once more what I had actually taken on.

"He's been planning a bike trip to the Alps with his friends - and I thought that was tough enough", said his wife. "But he doesn't have to worry about language, visas, where to stay, making every decision by himself...".

Lothar grinned.

"Nine days in the mountains has suddenly become a lot easier!" he added.

In the morning we left together, and he showed me the way back to the main road, his hand resting on my lower back as he gave me a gentle push up the final hill before we said our goodbyes. Lothar had to turn around for work, and me - well, I had to turn right for Japan.

∾

I CROSSED INTO AUSTRIA AND ENJOYED A PLEASANT RIDE ALONG the river into Passau. The number of grand riverside residences increased the closer I got, the houses bright with whitewash; I imagined teams of elves appearing magically every night after people had gone to bed, and surreptitiously scrubbing away at the streets before morning arrived.

Pleasure boats lined the Danube, packed with people. Relaxing in a cobble-stoned public square lazily watching the tourist throng pass by, I caught sight of the occasional touring cyclist continuing along the riverbank and wondered if I should not be making some effort to speak to them. But I was nervous. The thought of striking up a conversation with some possibly hard-core, world-travelled cyclist was rather intimidating; I feared the resulting conversation would soon reveal that I had been sleeping in comfortable lodgings, eating agreeable meals and covering rather modest daily distances.

A cyclist entered from the other side of the square, pausing to get some bearings. A quick glimpse - a woman, and not unattractive. Maybe I should be more sociable after all. The crowds briefly parted, and I could get a proper look. Her bike was solid-looking, black, obviously well-used and well-equipped with panniers (also black) and camping gear. She wore camouflage trousers, her biceps bulged from under a black cut-off T-shirt, and both forearms were heavily tattooed. Her black hair was pulled back tight with a red bandana and she looked very, very tough. I kept to my side of the square until she'd moved on, hoping she wouldn't notice me. Bloody hell, I thought, I'm not ready for this. I turned my attention to the map and guidebook, pondering my destination for the day, hopefully a town not too far away, with a nice hotel and a decent selection of pleasant eateries.

IN AUSTRIA, THE SCENERY HAD BECOME ALPINE, WITH STEEP pastures hugging the Danube and small clusters of white wooden houses perched in the upper reaches of the valley. Everything looked sharper, and the air felt fresh and crisp in my lungs. A wide cycle path followed the course of the river, occasionally diverting me through picture-postcard villages, vineyards and cool shaded forest.

On the first night I found a quiet spot in a remote corner of the campsite, unwilling to advertise my slapstick tent erecting manoeuvres to the other campers. It had been a long day, and I was too tired and too saddle-sore to get on my bike and look for a restaurant, so I pulled out the camp stove and for the first time on this trip set about cooking the only meal I knew: pasta, tuna and Bolognese sauce. I crouched there under the clear night sky simmering canned tuna, listening to the low roar of the burner and the croaking of a thousand frogs in the next field – maybe this was the humble beginning of the adventure cyclist I aimed to be.

Next morning, I got lost on the way back to the river, but I was not the only one; I ran into a couple of other cyclists in the same predicament. Harry and Roleka were from Holland – *You ain't much if you ain't Dutch* proclaimed their matching T-shirts – and they were on a short camping trip from Passau to Vienna. They invited me to tag along.

The weather was scorching hot and, as clouds of dandelions swirled in the air about us, a breeze would sometimes glide in from across the Danube to cool us down. More predictable cooling strategies, however, were rigidly employed by Harry.

"Beer time!" he'd shout, and we would stop at the next riverside beer garden or vine-straddled restaurant courtyard, to quench our mid-morning/lunchtime/late-afternoon thirst.

Harry and Roleka were ardent outdoor enthusiasts, and gave me useful camping tips as we cycled to Vienna.

"Watch out for ticks" warned Roleka. "They get on your skin from trees and bushes and burrow into your skin. If you're unlucky, you can be infected with Lyme disease, which is very bad". Paralysis, blindness, excruciating pain, madness... these were only some of the symptoms, she told me. "And now is high season for them".

Harry explained how to remove the little buggers - with a pair of tweezers clamped around their head, careful not to leave the infectious body behind.

"Pulled one out of Roleka, just the other night" he told me, proud of himself.

We parted ways at Vienna after an enjoyable few days of cycling. Life was good. In three weeks, I had cycled almost two thousand kilometres from London to Vienna. I had completed the Western Europe part of my plan.

~

THERE WERE A FEW CHORES TO TAKE CARE OF WHILST IN VIENNA, the priority being a visit to the Turkmenistan consulate. Turkmenistan was still so very far away, but it was the key to my whole trip - an impoverished, paranoid and largely closed desert nation that was my gateway into Central Asia. Governed with the iron fist of a certifiably mad ex-Soviet dictator, four-fifths of the country was covered by the inhospitable Karakum Desert - and I was planning to cross this wilderness in the middle of summer. I wasn't too sure which would cause me more distress - being turned down for the visa, or indeed, being accepted.

This visa being famously difficult to obtain, I had invested months working towards it, and with the help of a "fix it" man in Kazakhstan I had already been through most of the red tape. The ambassador was in good spirits – he had just been transferred here from Belarus and couldn't quite believe his luck – and after inspecting my documentation and querying my intentions while in his country, he stamped my passport.

The Tajikistan embassy was next. It was not essential to pass through Tajikistan, and not particularly desirable given its shattered economy, unpaved high-altitude mountain roads and rumours of Islamist rebel training camps. However, I wanted to keep my options open (what if the alternatives were even worse?), and I had heard from my Man in Kazakhstan that I could get a visa here without the formalities of a letter of introduction. It took me quite some time to find the embassy, a single room in an unmarked building, a table, two chairs, and a lot of furtive whispering. After writing a short fawning letter expressing my warm feelings toward the country and, more importantly, paying 100 Euros in cash, I got the stamp in my passport. I wouldn't have to worry about acquiring any more Central Asian visas until Istanbul.

I didn't spend much time exploring Vienna. It was dark, gloomy and raining, and my mind was already on the next country. I was desperate to get some miles under my belt, before it all went wrong.

CHAPTER 3

BUDAPEST REVISITED

A naked man stood to the side of the path and saluted me as I rode by.

Cycling past joggers, people walking their dogs and the occasional middle-aged naturalist, I was heading to Slovakia through an impressively spacious urban park that straddled the Danube, tapering off to a long straight embankment heading east. It was raining, and it seemed that with every mile I got closer to the border, the clouds turned a little darker on this lonely little path. The wind picked up, whistling around me, and just as the rain turned briefly into hailstones, I saw a drab sign indicating that I had crossed into Slovakia, and found shelter behind a vandalised toilet until the hail had stopped.

My guidebook on Europe had affectionately compared Austria's capital city to an "eccentric old lady". Following the river into Slovakia's capital, my first thought was that if Vienna was an eccentric old lady, then Bratislava could be her alcoholic husband, kicked out and sleeping rough.

Like the unfortunate-looking citizens shuffling morosely along the pavement, I hunched my shoulders against the drizzle and cycled through the grey city centre, precariously following a careful line in the gutter, tall jagged kerbstone on one side and slippery tramlines on the other. I found a room out in the bleak city suburbs - it was a dreary old apartment block, and the reception was staffed by a cheerless, heavyset, middle-aged woman with peroxide-dyed blonde hair, trussed up in a see-through, black lacy dress that sent shivers down my spine. She made me wait until she had finished the page of her magazine, and then with a sneering reluctance snatched away my passport, and in its place, viciously slammed the key on the counter while giving me a caustic glare.

It was a fleeting one-night stop in Slovakia and an easy way to tick off country number five. I followed the Danube Canal south east; it was very wide and continued on straight for many miles, the scenery constant and hardly a soul to be seen. I stopped to eat my sandwich at a derelict restaurant on the bald crest of a hill, the rusted corrugated iron roofing flapping back and forth violently in the wind, squealing insanely with every gust. When I felt the first light touch of rain in the air it was time to call it a day, and turn south into Hungary.

This was my first proper border crossing and, as I approached the control post across a bridge over the Danube, it struck me that I really *was* traversing Europe under my own steam. With some trepidation, I pulled up to the guard hut and was a little surprised that there was no electrified fencing or machine-gun nests; the border guard who met me was laid back and friendly, laughing and joking with everyone. I stayed the night in Gyor, resplendent with Baroque buildings and a buzz about the place that was in sharp contrast to Bratislava. I had been getting a little nervous about starting the Eastern European leg of this trip, figuring that parts of this region would be less tourist friendly and definitely less bicycle friendly. On top of the usual worries about language, food and accommodation, my fears were compounded further by thoughts of run-down infrastructure, rampaging drivers, criminal gangs and hostile locals.

Funnily enough, over the next few weeks all this paranoia would indeed be warranted, but for now at least, I could enjoy the calming streets and alleyways of Gyor.

~

FOLLOWING THE DANUBE, IT TOOK ME TWO EASY CYCLING DAYS to reach Budapest. The back roads were very quiet, with little more than the occasional horse and cart keeping me company, but the main roads were a different story - little or no hard shoulder, fast reckless drivers and huge potholes. I had to be conservative about viewing the scenery around me because there were so many other things to keep my eye on.

For the first time, I properly adjusted the mirror I had half-heartedly fixed to the handlebars before leaving home - more than anything else, this would become a fundamental tool in my survival. The roads would only get worse, the vehicles bigger and the drivers more reckless. With such a heavy bike you need complete concentration just to steer safely through potholes, debris, oncoming traffic, curious locals, or rabid dogs - there just isn't time to look back over your shoulder to check what the maniac behind you is doing. And the further east you travel the less choice of roads you have until invariably, there is only one very long road between your start point and your end point, and that is the road *everybody* uses.

At least for now there were choices, and I could avoid the direct highway to Budapest. The countryside was very green with a mixture of undulating meadows and patchwork fields, and apart from the relative scarcity of towns and villages it looked very similar to the English countryside. The threat of rain had finally abated, the skies were blue and there was nobody on the road; it was a gorgeous afternoon and the hillsides were cloaked in vineyards, while the River Danube served as a picture postcard backdrop in the distance.

Esztergom was visible long before I reached it - known as the Rome of Hungary, huge castle walls perched high on a steep hill which dominated the whole town, and high above them loomed the Basilica. The streets, steep and cobble-stoned, were not bicycle friendly but in the late afternoon light it was wonderful to push my bike around them, surprised at just how peaceful and void of people they were. This was because everybody was at Tesco. When I first saw the sign, I spent an hour fervently tracking it down. The aisles were packed, the coffee shop was packed, the pavement outside the front of the store was packed and the car park was also packed. The whole plot was a frenzy of people and it soon became depressingly clear that Tesco was now the place to hang out in this town. It was mayhem and I retreated back to the old town, past the castle walls and down to a riverside campground.

Cold heavy rain continued throughout the night, and I woke to find hundreds of creepy-crawlies covering my tent. I could see their magnified eight-legged silhouettes on the wall of my flysheet and was terrified that these little buggers were the dreaded tick, teeming with Lyme disease and looking for their next victim. What was it that Harry and Roleka had told me? "If you're camping during the spring", they had said, "just be sure not to camp under trees, or near any foliage". I had pitched my tent under a tree and next to a large, leafy bush. Paralysed with fear, I lay whimpering in my tent for most of the morning.

Pleasant leafy suburbs ushered me into Budapest; I found a room on the top floor of a crumbling, majestic five-story building, sharing a flat with the aged landlady and a couple of backpackers. It had been more than fourteen years since I had last visited Budapest, part of a mad dash one-month budget rail trip around Europe. It was 1991, just two years after Hungary had broken away from the yoke of the Soviet Union, and the country was still in transition; their first free elections had been held the year before and people were still getting used to the workings of a new market economy. There was a palpable energy in the air, and one could sense the optimism radiating from people, embracing the unknown that lay ahead. That energy had infected me also, and those few days spent here all those years ago had left such a lasting impression that I was almost afraid to come back, in case the reality could no longer live up to my memories.

I walked all over the city, crossing again and again the bridges spanning the Danube, while the lions guarding the Chain Bridge, frozen in granite, eyed me vigilantly with regal arrogance every time I passed them by. The Parliament building imposed itself onto every view of the Danube, its height matched only by the magnificent Saint Stephan's Basilica, a cathedral that manages to hide itself in the very heart of the city, only to ambush you with grandeur as you step out from a side street and it catches your gaze. There is so much physically imposing architecture in Budapest, much of it in quite a dire state of deterioration from years of neglect; but even the decay, the dirt and graffiti cannot hide the beauty of these old buildings, and the city has a poise unmatched by the pretentiousness of its downstream cousin Vienna. I treated my legs to the

Turkish baths in the Gellert Hotel and wiled away the afternoon in the thermal waters, staring up at the ornately decorated dome ceiling, hypnotised by the babble of different languages.

Budapest had been my first choice when applying for a job overseas, all those years ago. Although I had never received a reply, it had ignited an interest in travel and set in motion the steps that would lead to me nervously boarding a flight for Tokyo, images of severe-looking businessmen and dangerous fidgety food at the front of my mind. And in that first whirlwind month in Japan, I could never have imagined that a decade later I would be visiting this city once more, on a bicycle bound for the Orient, cycling my way back to Japan.

Saint Stephan's Basilica

I HAD BEEN ON THE ROAD FOR A MONTH. BREAKING AWAY FROM the Danube, an old friend by now, I was to head south across the *Puszta* - the Hungarian Plains - and on to Serbia. It took two wretched hours to travel just ten miles out of Budapest; the traffic was cruel, the drivers mercenary and I did a barely competent job of dodging potholes, avoiding errantly placed concrete blocks and not being killed. On the city limits I saw hitchhikers strung out at regular intervals along the side of the highway; they were all attractive young ladies, almost exclusively dressed in fluorescent miniskirts and tight tops, carrying nothing in the way of luggage but tiny handbags. How peculiar.

The land lost its colour, and the trees tired and gave way to clumps of hardy looking shrubs. By the side of the road a huge black dog was chomping enthusiastically on a deer which had just been killed by a car - at least I hoped it was a car, I thought, as I gingerly cycled past.

An overnight stop in the provincial capital Kecskemet marked the first in a series of alternative milestones of the trip – my first haircut. This, along with a count of debilitating illnesses, hundred-mile cycling days, life-endangering encounters and, very optimistically, romantic conquests, was a method I had dreamt up to measure my progress in terms other than just distance.

Households petered out, leaving me on a long road through farmland, now very green with the recent downpours, and I stopped the bike to enjoy the silence. But the silence turned into the rumbling of thunder, and presently the hiss of rain. With darkening clouds, cold rain pouring down so hard it hurt, and then a solitary sentry box manned by a couple of armed and pasty-looking teenagers on the muddy river embankment, I found myself at the Serbian border. The spottier of the soldiers pointed his finger at me, and then quickly jerked it towards the road, and the main border controls a hundred yards further on.

The rain was appalling. I handed my passport to the guard, a machine gun caressing bear of a man of about six foot five and paler than even the young sentries. He barked a couple of mean-sounding Balkan words at me, which might have been "stay here" or "sit" or possibly "beg" and took it off to a cabin to be examined. A few minutes later, with the cars and trucks slowly building up behind me, he came out with an even bigger and meaner-looking man, his sergeant I assumed, and pointed at me through the driving rain. The big man surveyed the drizzle, yelled over to me, waited, waved a fist, waited, and then started turning a fierce red. I realised that this meant I was to make my way over to his office at my earliest convenience.

Waving my passport at me, he opened it and pointed to one of the pages, eyes bulging with disbelief as he then gestured towards my bike.

"Tajikistan?" he asked, pointing at a visa-stamp in my passport. I checked the page and nodded, and he shook his head.

"You. Go. To..." he paused, checked his rage, and failed. "TAJIKISTAN?"

He seemed personally insulted and with words that I can only guess were some colourful Serb expletives, flicked my passport back to me, looked me hard in the eyes and made a Russian roulette gesture to his temple: click. Exasperated, he spun around and marched back into his hut, slamming the door.

Well, looking on the bright side of things, it seemed that there were worse places than Serbia to visit.

CHAPTER 4
A BALKAN RHAPSODY

Serbia offered an immediate contrast; highly agricultural, a preponderance of horses and carts on the road, and considerably run-down, I would feel more conspicuous here than I had felt anywhere else. This was not, I felt, a country to cycle through for leisure.

Yet the initially unwelcoming and crumbling suburbs of the border town of Subotica hid a well-restored central plaza, civic buildings of scrubbed red brick, elegantly decorated plaster facades lining the main town square and well-kept churches in quiet alleyways; the Serbs took obvious pride in the appearance of their town centres.

The evening brought everybody out to the plaza, parents buying their kids a five minute turn on radio-controlled toy cars, couples or small groups sipping coffee or beer in the many terrace cafes and bars, and apart from temperatures that had me wearing my thermal jacket, there was a laid-back, continental atmosphere - not what I had expected of the Balkans at all. The barbarous wars of the nineties, Serbia's prominent role in them, and the subsequent international reaction had left a compelling image in my mind which was hard to shake. Slobodan Milosevic, currently jailed in The Hague on trial for crimes against humanity, was the jingoistic president who had brought on many of the problems of this country, and I couldn't help but secretly play "spot the Milosevic look-alike" with the people walking past me (there were actually quite a few).

Unlike the women, dressed to impress on even this chilly mid-week evening, the menfolk didn't show much imagination in their attire, and I noted only two tribes: the shell suit tribe, mainly younger guys, and the black leather jacket tribe, for the older men. Half looked like teenage delinquents, and the other half, nightclub bouncers. And one or two looked pretty damned scary. Nobody was willing to approach me spontaneously, but when I took the initiative to say *Dobra Dan* (good day) I was sometimes successful in eliciting a smile or a few amicable words in response.

If the ordered and well-tended town centres were those of Europe, the villages were closer to the dusty settlements of South-east Asia; random shopfronts opened onto the road with a jumble of goods inside and out, a mix of noise, colour and chaos. Many of the businesses were car and motorbike workshops, which made a lot of sense - these people do like to drive fast - and top of the assorted beaten-up heaps of metal on the road was the much-maligned Yugo, flagship of the old Yugoslav automotive industry, and inspiration for a whole generation of jokes (Why did the higher-end models have a rear window defroster? To keep your hands warm when you pushed...).

BELGRADE WAS STILL A COUPLE OF DAYS' RIDE SOUTH AND I HAD done 70 kilometres straight before stopping for lunch in a village off the main road. The potholed main street of Vrbas was practically deserted, and most of the long line of old stone houses lining it were shuttered tight against the midday sun, like some movie-set for a Balkan-themed spaghetti western. I welcomed the chance to sit down to my bread and cheese, for once without the stares of strangers, and I seated myself on the step of a derelict house, old chair-legs and other bits of furniture poking out from the rubble of brick and roof-tiles littering the ground floor rooms.

A young guy strolled briskly by, saw the bike, and then saw me. Momentarily surprised, but then with the barely hidden signs of a mischievous grin he walked up to me.

"Be careful of the old people round here", he said in surprisingly decent English, and like a cartoon character with eyes darting left and right, looked carefully around and leaned in closer, lowering his voice.

"They are crazy, completely crazy. And they all smoke the marijuana."

He watched for my reaction, a slow smile beginning to form on his face. One venerable old man hobbled slowly past us on a walking stick, and he pointed straight at him.

"Especially that one", he said. "Very dangerous!" and at last, I laughed out loud.

Zlatko introduced himself; he was the local butcher and, incredibly, the only experience he had of English up until now was studying it in high school, over twelve years ago. He banged on the shuttered window of a neighbouring house, shouted a few urgent Serb words and soon a matronly lady raised the shutters and appeared at the windowsill holding a cool mug of beer for each of us, looking with particular amusement at me; she roared with laughter as I slugged the beer back and timidly asked if there was any more.

They invited me indoors (she was Zlatko's mother) and led me through the dark pantry where I collided with the carcass of a pig, hung up for curing, and out into a bright dusty courtyard, the ground bleached white under the harsh sun. Chickens pecked their random geometric patterns and on the far side of the yard there was a compound for the pigs, a large vegetable patch and stacked cages for rabbits. Ducks appeared, having just escaped from their wire-mesh walls, and I was amazed at how this menagerie was hidden so well from the main street. A pot of strong Serbian coffee was produced, and I was introduced to the rest of the family; Zlatko's wife, his three-year-old daughter and his brother, who had just rounded up the ducks yet again.

After coffee we started on the beer, taking us through the afternoon. The conversation touched on many things, Zlatko translating for his family when needed, or sometimes just showing me photos and playing with his daughter. He was a small guy – actually the whole family was quite slight, which I somehow hadn't expected in this country – but his energy and laughter filled up the entire household and gave him a chance to show off his wide-boy version of

English to everyone, often at the expense of his harassed father-in-law, working in the nearby vegetable patch.

"Hey baldy old man! Baldy old coot!" he teased him, "Where your hair gone?".

However, he could turn very serious when the topic of Serbia's recent past came up. This region, Vojvodina, he told me, trying to simplify its complicated history for my benefit, had always considered itself as having a separate identity from Serbia. It had been an autonomous state until its powers were abolished by Milosevic in 1989, and there was no love lost between Vojvodina and the government in Belgrade. Most Yugoslavs around here - the Serbs, Croats, Bosnians, Muslims, Roma gypsies – lived in relative peace. Everyone just got on with each other.

"Well, except for the Montenegrins", he corrected. "Never trust a Montenegrin."

The conversation inevitably moved on to the war; as with most Serb men now above a certain age, he had been drafted into the army and spent a year fighting in Kosovo. A dark shadow moved across his face and his easy-going demeanour disappeared at once.

"Those fucking Milosevic people", he spat, explaining that Milosevic had created an elite private army by releasing some of the worst criminals from the country's prisons.

"They were all rapists and murderers. My own squad-leader, he was a monster, a fucking psychopath. Rumour was, he was imprisoned before the war for murdering his own parents. From what I saw, I could believe it was true."

Zlatko turned unnervingly emotional, and I felt tense as he recalled painful memories and started to relate some of the darker episodes for me. His stories of the horrors he experienced were unrepeatable. He sighed loudly, visibly distressed at the memories he had failed to lay to rest.

"How can men do that?" he asked me, "How?"

I found it unsettling to know that I was riding through a country where the majority of young men have been in a war, and some have witnessed or even participated in atrocities of some kind. How do you deal with that? What kind of scar does that leave on a country's psyche? Zlatko, in trying to exorcise some of his demons, had brought home to me the terrible truth of horrors that up until now, I had only heard about from newspapers and television.

He leaned over to top up my glass, his wife laid out some more plates of food on the table and the conversation moved on to other things. I couldn't even begin to unravel the complexities of this country's recent history.

Zlatko and family

I REACHED THE REGIONAL CAPITAL OF NOVI SAD VIA MANY MILES of confusing farm lanes and rural villages. Locals glowered at me, and my greetings were met with silence and blank suspicious stares. The people here were poor, and I felt uncomfortable being seen on my well-equipped bike, red panniers still clean and shiny like some obnoxious advertisement of wealth.

Aiming for the many church spires that appeared above the Novi Sad skyline, and following the increasingly reckless traffic, I navigated into the historical centre fairly easily and again found a striking contrast between the austerity of the surrounding country-side and the apparent prosperity of the city. The entire centre had been pedestrianised - less from ascetics, more from self-preserva-tion, I thought, as there was a sudden terrible dull metal thump behind me, and I spotted one young lady flying over the bonnet of the car that had rammed her bike.

From the look of its spacious public squares and carefully restored townhouses, it was hard to imagine that this city had been hit hard by the NATO bombardment during the Kosovo war only six years earlier – all three of the bridges crossing the Danube had been destroyed at that time. Today it was packed with people. I didn't know if they were locals or tourists, but I didn't hear a single English voice in the crowd, and it was just about impossible to find a hotel. I wheeled my heavy bike around the streets for two hours (more staring) and met multiple dead-ends after asking directions from many different shopkeepers and stall-owners. I honestly began to think there was a conspiracy against me and ultimately, I found lodgings by myself, through a simple process of elimination; if you knock on enough doors, eventually one is bound to be a hotel.

I AM SUFFERING A THEOLOGICAL DILEMMA: I MIGHT NOT BELIEVE in Hell, but I believe there is a road that leads there. It is the stretch of highway between Novi Sad and Belgrade. Testosterone-fuelled drivers pummel rusty metal boxes through lanes of complete mayhem. Crippled buses and overloaded trucks lock together in deadly combat for road supremacy. Torrid fumes of oil, diesel and malevolence are left heavy in the air. Fleeting snapshots of faces, twisted with rage, behind cracked and smeared windscreens scream past at grotesque speed. I had just woken up in the lead of a Roman chariot race, reins wrapped around bloodied forearms, galloping into the final furlong and all the other charioteers out to get me at any cost. I had to keep up with the violent melee about me, pedal hard like my life depended on it - well, it did! - with ne'er a moment to glance behind, and barely chance enough to keep my eyes on the chaos ahead.

Forced off the road by a tractor reversing its way obliviously up the outside lane, I stood by the roadside, heart pounding, and watched the maelstrom speed past me. I could not *believe* that I had been in the middle of that carnage. The volume was turned up loud and a thousand games of chicken were being played out at once in front of my disbelieving eyes. Double-overtaking, *triple*-overtaking, drivers blind to the scattered detritus of broken automotive parts, oil slicks and potholes the size of bomb craters that seemed to make up most of this road, while cars duelled with each other for position and rendered U-turns across three lanes of traffic. I saw a car ram sideways into the vehicle he was overtaking and accelerate away past the rows of impotent red traffic lights. I saw this happen three times. Sweet Jesus, the worst part was building up the bloody nerve to get back into it.

"Watch out, Steve", I whispered shakily to myself. The more you ride the more invincible you feel, and the more willingly you take risks. I needed shocks like this to remind me of my rightful place in the road's food chain - at the bottom but with any luck, just above roadkill. I was only glad that I didn't notice the date until after I'd arrived intact in Belgrade: it was Friday the thirteenth.

THE SERBIAN URBAN MAGIC TRICK HAD AGAIN TRANSFORMED THE traffic clogged streets and grime covered architecture of Belgrade into a bright pedestrian shopping area, granite buildings scrubbed clean, and crowds of well-heeled shoppers that gave the impression of a Saturday afternoon in any affluent English town.

Unexpectedly in this country of automotive machismo, there was an underground cycling scene. One middle-aged man approached me to talk of his own bicycle touring in the countryside around Belgrade, another of his subversive ride around Serbia protesting the war in Kosovo. A taxi driver gave me the number of a bicycle-mad journalist friend; "you *must* call" he insisted (I did, but a woman on the other end of the line kept shouting at me and putting the phone down every time I tried). Yet another cyclist led me down to an open riverfront bar and bought me a beer. He had been a tour guide before the war and spoke superb English; he was morose as he bemoaned the sorry state of the Serb economy.

"Only the rich get richer," he complained. "It's very hard for ordinary citizens here, barely able to make ends meet, but those with connections in the government - they got rich from the war, smuggling provisions during the sanctions."

In Belgrade I met up briefly with the Danube once more, as it wound its way around the perimeter of the city centre, the banks lined with wooden barges in various states of disrepair. The ones not abandoned or rotted away were used to house restaurants, bars and nightclubs, and almost all were connected to the shore by rickety, makeshift wooden walkways, nailed together at precarious angles over the surface of the water. I chose one of the less rusty boats to enquire about lodgings for the night; it was ten euros for a cabin said the boat-keeper, and he ushered me down into the main bar area, pointing out colour photographs of ladies in various stages of undress on the wall.

"And there is strip show on weekends - free for guests!" he added merrily, nudging me in the ribs. "Much better than youth hostel, no?"

Belgrade is a cosmopolitan city, defined by its multitude of cafes, restaurants and chic shops, and I wondered how a sizeable propor-tion of the population seemed to have the money to enjoy all of this. On my final night I got lost on the way back to the river and found myself in the castle park. The sprawling grounds were enclosed by immense ancient stone walls and decorated with ancient cannon and Second World War howitzers alike; it was ten o'clock at night and the whole place was lit up, buzzing with hundreds of people strolling through the grounds, buying ice cream and drinks from the dozens of makeshift stalls. Giggling children ran circles around their parents whilst young couples caroused in the shadows, a discreet distance from the brightly lit pathways. From the battlements I saw the river curving away from the castle promontory and the bridge I needed to cross, if I was to make it back to my hotel barge in time for the last show.

FOR ONCE I DIDN'T GET LOST NAVIGATING OUT OF THE CITY; I couldn't really, as I had three lanes of ill-disciplined traffic on my left and a couple of busy tram lines screeching terribly on my right, keeping me in my place. The countryside was reclaiming skeletons of extinct industry; the shells of factory buildings had weeds breaking through concrete-floored yards, and rusting machinery was adorned with robes of dandelions. Only one huge complex stood out as a going concern, well pruned hedges leading up to its polished gates and the busy hum of engines, chains and muted shouts from within. I was surprised at the sign overhead which showed the company name: US Steel.

Pozarevac was a grey industrial town hanging from the main trunk road, and I checked into the one hotel that hadn't been boarded up. The two receptionists, Clara and Mikel, spoke good English – it had been their favourite subject in school – and begged me to come down later to talk with them for practise. We gate-crashed a wedding celebration underway in the banquet hall, hundreds of guests sweeping around the dancefloor, and occasional lively spurts of what I guessed was a kind of Balkan Chicken Dance. All the children were curious about this stranger and waited patiently in line, earnestly trying to say a few words in English with the help of Clara. One little five-year old girl sat very prim and correct in her white bridesmaid dress, hands crossed over her lap. She smiled a wonderful smile.

"My name is Alexandra", she said delightfully, gracefully giving me her hand to shake. "How are you?"

"Fine, thank you", I replied obediently, in this most well-oiled of English teaching phrases. "And you?"

She listened attentively, her face lost in concentration for a moment, shyly raised her eyes and beamed another broad confident smile at me.

"My name is Alexandra. How are you?"

It had been a good day and the small but increasingly dense black ball of loneliness in the pit of my stomach had been somewhat lightened. A cheerful *dobra dan* aimed at some surprised-looking Serb as I cycled past would sometimes elicit a similar greeting in response, and even the odd word of encouragement. And occasion-ally, when being overtaken by a car, instead of rubbish being thrown out the window at me, a waving hand or clenched fist might appear instead.

The hotel room was a bonus. It had a television with English speaking satellite channels and I even enjoyed a little politics, as the British firebrand MP George Galloway berated the US senate during their enquiry into the Iraq oil-for-aid scandal of the time. It was a thrilling address, but I had learnt to keep politics very much to myself in Serbia, as people were extremely bitter when it came to the US and the UK. If I mentioned that I was British, the reaction was uncomfortably frosty, and I might be harangued about the NATO bombings. As I was travelling on an Irish passport (Irish on my mother's side), it turned out much easier to say I was Irish. Everybody loves the Irish.

Before bed, I watched an episode of Top Gear, setting myself up for nightmares throughout the night – this was not the country to watch TV programs about idiots driving cars stupidly fast.

GRANITE CLIFFS LINED A NEAR-DESERTED ROAD TAKING ME EAST over several climbs and ending in a wide green plateau. In the dusty one-street village of Rabrovo, a talkative middle-aged woman bought me ice-cream and we sat outside in the street under the late morning sun. Her father had been a craftsman, she told me, famous throughout Serbia for his traditional handmade clogs; she disappeared into her house and proudly brought out a dog-eared photograph album, showing me a picture of him shaking hands with Slobodan Milosevic. Curious neighbours looked on and she basked in the role of village ambassador, while her son took me inside to show me bookshelves of Serbian literature and with a broad smile insisted that I choose one as a gift (for the next month, I carried a heavy volume of Serbian poetry in my left pannier).

Farmland views reminded me of England, and then when the empty road snaked its way upwards through low mountain peaks and vivid, untamed forest, it reminded me of Japan. But with one turn of the road this wholesome scene changed in an instant. Only now I became aware of the birdsong that had accompanied me all day, because it abruptly ceased. The air became suddenly still, and I was on a wide straight road leading upwards. The rusting hulks of cars littered the roadside as far as the eye could see, as if these vehicles had driven themselves here to die. I passed by an abandoned mining works, narrowly avoiding a bright red viscous liquid oozing down one side of the road, and then riding through a blue-green reflective film that covered the rest. Next to the road was a drop into an enormous quarry, a mile in diameter, its unnaturally hewn slopes the colour of a three-day old bruise. On the far edge of this chasm was the town of Majdenpek, founded to support the region's copper-ore mining and smelting industry, once the largest strip-mining operation in Europe, now all but lifeless.

Silence lay over the town like a shroud and only a few people were on the streets, most showing a tired indifference to my presence. The town was laid out in a practical grid pattern but there were no cars, and the traffic lights at every junction no longer worked. I passed row upon row of deserted buildings, all boarded-up - the faded signs told me they had once been shops and restaurants - and there was an absence of trees, grass or any kind of foliage, adding further to the strange notion that my eyesight had reverted to seeing everything in sepia.

Hotel Kasina, a dimly lit, grey behemoth of a structure, reverberated with the click of sprockets as I wheeled the bike through the door. The long empty lobby was being eaten slowly by hungry shadows from the walls and the ceiling above; they had already devoured a crumpled leather sofa in the darkness to the left, its cushions emaciated of any shape or softness. The outline of an old and broken man sitting on its edge, hunched and still, might have equally been a pile of ragged old clothes. Behind the front desk and not yet absorbed into the malignant gloom, was a young receptionist. Initially flustered at the appearance of a highly irregular guest (or quite possibly any guest) she made an incredible, visible, effort to recall English words and phrases unspoken for a long time. She checked me in, making a show of looking for a vacant room.

"Would you like to... dine... in the restaurant... tonight?" she asked haltingly, pointing back towards an anonymous door by the hotel entrance.

It swung open for a moment, revealing a snapshot of the small square room with stained linoleum flooring, two bare white light-bulbs suspended on a jagged wire, and a simple plastic table, not quite horizontal, behind the brown haze of cigarette smoke. Two tattooed, shaven-headed and phenomenally tough looking characters were stopped in mid-conversation, staring at me.

"No, thank you," I said.

I found a cafeteria outside, a bare concrete room, from where I watched the town while waiting for my hamburger. The whole place was quiet, all sound seemingly stifled as if in a state of mourning. Grimy fluorescent tubes flickered and hummed on and off like a hacking cough above me, and I watched the hard faces of a few middle-aged men in the dusk outside, as they paced slowly up and down the same street in groups of twos and threes. To me it seemed like they were waiting for something to happen, as if they just could not believe that life had ended up like this. A skinny mongrel sat in the middle of the empty road and leisurely licked his balls, looking across at me forlornly.

AN OPPRESSIVELY HOT DAY BORE DOWN, AND I ENCOUNTERED THE hardest climbing on the trip so far. These were real mountains now, no longer scruffy shrub-covered crags of granite by the side of the road, but steep and laboured approaches to proper passes, and it was decidedly less populous, just a few abandoned-looking hamlets and isolated farmhouses. Large dangerous dogs roamed these properties, firmly locked away behind steel gates and high fences, or restrained on a long leash chained to something solid. They had been trained from birth to hate cyclists and whenever I passed one it would reflexively leap up, murder in its black eyes, and run parallel to the road, barking and howling at me. It was nerve-racking, but the dog would inevitably reach the end of its leash and be jerked to an angry, painful halt, or reach the boundary of its owner's property and mercifully be stopped fast in his tracks by a secure fence or wall.

All except one.

The biggest shock was that I saw him before I heard him. Reflected in my mirror was a broad muscular shape in the middle of the road, pelting furiously towards me, saliva dripping from his black, fang-rimmed mouth. The shock pumped a shot of adrenalin through my legs and I peddled like a madman, but the bugger was gaining ground. I could see his bloodshot eyeballs and remembered the stickers they used to put on car wing-mirrors: *Objects are closer than they appear*. He was in my peripheral vision, and a moment later I felt a distinctive burst of hot air at my ankle - why, oh why, hadn't I got that sodding rabies jab! - and then as I waited for the inevitable... nothing. He slipped away silently behind me, as suddenly as he had appeared. By a stroke of incredible luck - or the conclusion of a callous act of premeditated local entertainment - the dog had been called off by his gruff master, watching from the neighbouring field. If the measure of a long-distance cyclist was their experience with wild and vicious canines, then today I had popped my cherry.

Today's goal was to cross over into Bulgaria; the loneliness and the despair of the Balkan countryside was starting to break my spirit. Dilapidated factories, lifeless towns, and surly men with nothing better to do than gather around decrepit little kiosks all day, drinking bottles of cheap beer. I needed a break from this misery as soon as possible, otherwise I really feared that I would get on the nearest bus, train or mule out of here and hurry back home.

Zajecar was the last town before the border with Bulgaria; it was late afternoon and there were street musicians and small fairground rides for the kids. I needed to harness this positive energy, to recharge myself before moving on... and because I had also spotted a bar, "The Rivendell", that advertised itself as an Irish pub, I promptly booked into a hotel. That evening I went there for a drink and asked for a pint of Guinness. The barman said he'd never heard of it.

CHAPTER 5

SOMETHING ABOUT SOPHIA

It's my first night in Bulgaria and I'm having a hell of a time trying to order something to eat. I'm the sole customer in a rough roadside cafeteria in the countryside, a Little Chef meets Mad Max, and I've arranged to stay in a wooden cabin in the back yard. The menu is in Cyrillic script and of course not a lick of English is spoken. A dodgy looking character in his early thirties walks in and ignoring the dozen empty tables, comes and sits at mine, orders a beer, and engages me in some chirpy miming. Smiling a little too hard, he breaks the ice by pulling out some photographs of his favourite "discotheque" and points out pictures of his female friends to me - with the help of pen and paper he informs me proudly of how much each one costs. I ignore him.

Leading into a long, elaborate story of a broken car and an urgent parcel to deliver, he inevitably ends by trying to extract money from me and I politely refuse. He doesn't give up, and soon starts hinting that he has other, less feminine friends nearby. I briefly admire him – using only the art of mime and gesture to make veiled threats is never easy – and then I surprise myself by holding his stare and telling him firmly to fuck off. I must have toughened up over the last few weeks, because I do it again and throw his photographs back at him across the table. He scuttles away from his chair, pauses with a pleading look and points back to his beer. "Well can't you at least get me this?" his expression suggests.

Bulgaria looked in worse economic decline than even Serbia, and many half-finished apartment blocks, walls open to the elements like giant dollhouses, accommodated desperate families, their daily activities open for all to see. Shifty looking teenagers lurked in the shadows and one of them half-heartedly threw a rock at me as I cycled past; it looked like the wealth of the touristic south was having a hard time finding its way up here. Although I had certainly felt conspicuous, I had never felt this uneasy in Serbia.

Yet ironically, the border crossing had been the most welcoming I had yet experienced. High up in the mountains and surrounded by fields of poppies, the guards were relaxed and friendly and one was particularly jolly, cracking jokes as people filed through. He bent double with laughter, incredulous when I told him where I was heading, shouting over to his colleagues in the guardhouse who chuckled along.

"You speak Japanese?" he asked curiously, and I admitted that I could speak some. "Teach me, then!" he said. "What is 'good morning'?"

"*O-ha-yo-go-zai-ma-su*", I told him.

He paused, gathered his thoughts, and tentatively repeated it a couple of times back at me, looking for approval. Pleased with his new phrase, he crossed over the road to attend to some people on foot coming from the other side, greeting the confused Eastern Europeans with a confident "*Ohayo gozaimasu!*". After stamping their travel papers, he came back to continue his lesson. Next was "How are you?".

"*O-gen-ki-de-su-ka*", he repeated, pacing up and down like a nervous schoolboy before a language exam, repeating his new words very carefully to himself.

"*Ogenki desu ka?*" he asked the next batch of travellers as he waved them through. He got the signal from the guardhouse that my paperwork was in order and handed me back my passport.

"*Domo arigato!*" he said, thanking me in Japanese.

"Do you get many Japanese tourists here?" I asked curiously, as I mounted my bike.

"Japanese... *here?*" he replied cheerily. "Oh no, never!"

～

Bulgaria had brought me through another time-zone – I was now six hours behind Japan. The roads were bad and the towns unmemorable. In one village I found a small shop that sold only meat and bread, so I asked for a sandwich. I can't imagine many other culinary combinations with just these two ingredients, but even as I mimed the process of putting pieces of meat between two slices of bread, the shopkeeper looked blankly back at me. He carefully followed my directions, slicing the bread and placing the meat inside, improvising a huge basic sandwich. He was still looking at the final result in quiet wonder as I paid.

The road was an evenly spaced series of exponential slopes, each one lasting about five kilometres. These were the foothills of the Vitosha Mountains towering ahead of me, the mountain ridge rearing up suddenly like a moss-covered shark's fin, grey granite karst pinnacles and green foliage reaching impressively up into the heavens. At the crest of one of the tougher climbs, a woman in a mini-skirt and stilettos suddenly appeared at the side of the road and grabbed at my handlebars, tugging my arm and gesturing towards the bushes.

"Not now, love", I told her. "Got to save my energy for the next bloody hill!"

I lodged in Vratska, about a hundred kilometres from the capital Sophia, a town with a quiet demeanour and steep cobbled lanes; it was resoundingly civilised, and an extensive choice of cosmopolitan restaurants complemented a small number of quaint tourist shops. In the evening I found a cosy cellar restaurant with an English menu. The first dish I asked for, a spicy goulash, was met with a curt shake of the head by the waitress. I tried to order an alternative, chicken in a rich gravy sauce, but she shook her head again. By the time this had happened four times in a row, I was convinced that she was trying to get me off the premises and was now mocking me with a patronising smile. I was close to screaming at her and the whole bloody restaurant, but when a final random angry jab with a shaking finger at the item labelled duck stew elicited a nod, I waved her away, drained.

I ate four dinners that evening, starting with a tasty traditional Goulash, and finishing with a substantial breast of chicken in a thick rich broth. The duck stew never arrived of course - I had discovered that in Bulgaria, a nod of the head means *no*, and a shake of the head means a very firm *yes*.

FURIOUS PELLETS OF RAIN SMASHED INTO ME LIKE A PORTENTOUS warning in Morse code: s t a y i n s i d e s t a y i n s i d e. The rain was freezing and filled the potholes quickly, and I braced myself for a crash every time I hit a large puddle. In an effort to get off the busy main road and a soaking of mud and spray whenever something passed, I had taken a few wrong turns and somehow found myself in the central lane of a busy motorway. I meandered over to the hard shoulder, peddling desperately, and unwillingly followed the highway upwards. The mountains and the drizzle had sucked most of the light from the afternoon, and my vision was concentrated on the line of red taillights converging to the horizon ahead of me, and the diffused beams of yellow headlights on the bike's raindrop-speckled rear-view mirror.

The hard shoulder disappeared and with a little mild swearing, I sidled up close to the guard rail, keeping a keen eye on the mirror in case something might be heading straight for me. About half an hour later the fog descended, and visibility was reduced to near-zero. At the sign of every bright light or vehicular noise that seemed to be in my lane, I would stop the bike and press up tightly against the guard rail in terror. But when I saw the long dark tunnels up ahead of me, now that's when I started crying.

There was an overgrown track just before the tunnel entrance, and I pushed and pulled my bike until it joined a narrow road littered with rocks and branches, which I tentatively cycled along for a couple of miles – some forest workers confirmed that this was the old road to Sophia. It was winding and steep, and although it was getting dark and the mist was closing in, I knew there was no alternative.

I got a puncture. Then another one. And then a deafening Bang! The rear tyre had finally given up, a large tear in the sidewall. I replaced the tyre and the inner tube again, keeping a wary eye on the darkening skies, and swore in disbelief as it just wouldn't inflate.

The next one, my last spare tube, wouldn't inflate either, and disbelievingly I considered that I might have to look for an emergency camp site for the night, weighing up the pros and cons of being flattened by an Eastern European truck driver versus eaten alive by wolves. I was wet-through from drizzle and mist, and my hands were numb with cold, covered with mud and slightly bloodied. As I ruminated over the fact that falling rocks would probably finish me off before anything else, the workmen I had met earlier appeared; concerned that I still hadn't been sighted passing their depot all these hours later, they had kindly come back to search for me.

It made for an inglorious arrival in Sophia as they hurried to unload my belongings from the back of their truck and on to the crowded pavement before the lights changed, leaving me standing in the middle of a crowd of rubberneckers and a jumbled circle of bike, damp bags and ruined tyres.

Sophia, the capital of Bulgaria, was not quite the Eastern European beauty that the name had me believe. That night I followed my map, walking for miles in search of something to eat, but found only near-deserted ill-lit streets and stray dogs growling at me unseen from the darkness of alleyways and abandoned playgrounds. Once or twice I was startled at what I imagined to be the urgent whisper of hushed voices, whilst the subway entrances were chained up, the stairs that led down to them chest deep in festering refuse, rustling with the industry of rats.

The next morning, I realised that I had mixed up north and south and had spent hours walking directly away from the city centre towards the outskirts which, interestingly enough, was explicitly warned against in my guidebook. This time - in the proper direction - the city centre proved itself quite compact, with streets of granite civic buildings, few overt tourist sights and a system of trams adding to an air of refinement. If you ignored the overriding presence of leather-jacketed Bulgarian Mafia types, you could almost say that it was a laid-back city.

All the money exchanges were locked from the inside, and some unshaven, broken-nosed bruiser with too many oversized gold rings would usually be leaning back on a stool, balancing himself with one patent leather shoe up against the reinforced glass. You knock on the glass while he temporarily puts aside his tabloid, levels his stool and warily lets you in to change your cash at the counter, locking the door again behind you until the transaction is done. They also seemed to have a monopoly on the hotels - there are always two or three of these goons lounging around reception, in their uniform of black leather jacket, shiny black trousers and black T-shirt, chatting up the dolly bird receptionist while their BMW or Mercedes Benz remained double-parked and unmolested outside. They never open the door or say hello; their sole job description seems to be chain-smoking cigarettes and intimidating guests.

It took a whole frustrating morning to find my way out of Sophia. I performed multiple U-turns, crisscrossing the same annoying streets again and again before a policeman directed me and my bike onto the motorway, despite my own protestations that it was illegal. By afternoon I had moved to a minor road in a poor state of repair but perfectly quiet, the rock-strewn surface winding exhaustingly through the mountains, roughly parallel to the motorway that could be glimpsed occasionally through the trees, a mile or so away down on the plains. At the brow of one hill, I was alarmed to see the figure of a lone man in the centre of the road; facing the other way, he was apparently unaware of the cyclist about to pass him on the outside.

I looked at him as I came alongside. He was covered in blood, streams of it running down his pale face and onto his white shirt, and he had both hands pressed tightly against a wound to his neck, bubbling blood. He stared calmly back at me, and I stopped, almost falling off the bike in shock. I made a confused move towards him in an offer to help, but he dismissed me with a wave from one of his hands, causing a little more blood to seep from under the one still gripping his neck. While I was still frozen, trying to register this appalling scene, a Lada appeared from nowhere and squealed to a stop in front of me. The injured man got in the far-side door, and the little car turned around and roared off down the hill. On the other side of the road I noticed the overturned car in the ditch, almost completely crushed, the rear axle stuck up in the air, one wheel still rotating very slowly. It squeaked with every turn and was the only noise I heard in the eerie silence.

PLODIV IS ONE OF THE OLDEST CITIES IN EUROPE WITH A HISTORY dating back to the age of Troy, and when I rode into it the following morning the contrast was immediate; while many towns here seemed to be simply surviving life, this place was living it. Locals and tourists wandered the wide shopping precincts and explored the old town's quaint tree-lined and cobble-stoned lanes. Museums and galleries hid in quiet stonewalled cul-de-sacs, and a winding climb led to a Roman amphitheatre, offering a pleasant setting for a solitary beer. As the bike was in my hotel room, I could melt anonymously into the background, and spent a couple of hours in a park, reading and occasionally engaged in conversation by strangers, not as a cyclist or even as a tourist, but simply as another person. My embarrassed lack of comprehension was enough for them to realise I was not local, and they would smile politely, or maybe try some greeting in German or English.

"Beautiful weather today."

"My goodness, have you ever seen so many people!"

Observing everyday life around me relieved some of the homesickness. An elderly gentleman asked politely if he could share the same bench and ushered his equally grey lady friend to the space next to me, the look of teenage infatuation in their eyes.

I returned to the hotel and switched on the television, flicking to the Gold Channel in expectation of a few classic British television treats like The Good Life or even Benny Hill. I was astounded to find instead The Best of British Porn. You can imagine my disappointment.

THE SKY WAS A CLEAR BLUE, THE SUN BLISTERINGLY HOT, AND THE fields of un-ripened corn looked like a green velvet cloak unfurled over the countryside. There was precious little shade, but the road was in good condition and the traffic not-quite-so-murderous most of the time. I almost tumbled from my bike with fright when a long piece of rope discarded near the verge animated into life, quickly slithered out of the way of my front wheel and sprang upwards to attack me. The snake hit my front pannier instead, leaving a smear of venom on the plastic.

As I got closer to the border, I had to further fine-tune my road-survival skills to concentrate on the traffic coming towards me as well as from behind, and reckless overtaking forced me off the road and into the dirt several times over the course of the afternoon. Collapsed over the top tube of my bike and lounging under the first bit of shade I had come across for twenty miles, I was invited to join a large group of people out for a picnic by the roadside. After some strong protestations, I managed to substitute most of the vodka shots forced upon me for coca cola, while we continued through a barrage of toasts. My hosts were all members of the same extended family and proceeded to get increasingly drunk. When a heated table-thumping argument in rapid Bulgarian between two brothers escalated into a fist fight, I quietly made my exit.

In Bulgaria you can get a beer or espresso anywhere at any time, but not a simple sandwich. For what would hopefully be the last time, I stocked up with a day's worth of hamburgers and rode in the direction of Turkey. The prospect of crossing another border lifted my spirits, a combination of excitement and a little fear. Entering another country overland proved I was making real progress but crossing into Turkey was more than just another box to tick off.

This was farewell to the Christian West and the beginning of the Islamic East - and I was nervous. In Europe I had found my rhythm, a certain comfort level in my interactions with strangers, and a pattern of practicalities when it came to food and accommodation. Into Turkey and beyond, I had no grounding, no experience, no real idea of what to expect and I would have to learn everything again from scratch.

It was almost June, and I had cycled close to 4,000 kilometres in a little over six weeks. The flesh was probably strong enough by now; I was just a little worried about the will.

CHAPTER 6
CARRY ON UP THE BOSPHORUS

"We love you Liverpool, we do!"

This was not a chant that I had typically expected to hear on approaching the Bulgaria-Turkey frontier. The car overtook me with waves and a good-natured beep of the horn, red football colours flapping from its rear windows. The Champions League final between AC Milan and Liverpool was to be hosted tonight in Istanbul and the border post was engulfed by English supporters, driving rental cars picked up in Bulgaria due to there being no available flights left for Istanbul. All lanes at Immigration were open to cope with the onslaught of football fans, and a sea of Liverpool flags and pasty Brits in red T-shirts surged across all of them. It lightened my spirits to suddenly see something familiar.

This was turning into a good day. Only an hour before I had met Silvain, a French cyclist three weeks into his own world trip, also heading in the direction of the Orient. Of Algerian descent, with his olive skin and black hair, you could almost mistake him for a Turk; but whereas I would soon conform to the more conservative dress ideals here, by swapping shorts for long trousers and T-shirt for a long-sleeved top, Silvain preferred to drape his *Olympique de Marseille* football jersey over the bike's rear-rack and ride in nothing but a pair of tight-fitting Lycra cycling shorts. He was also very hairy, and the glances from sensitive locals did worry me.

Erdine was the first Turkish town we met, only a few miles from the borders of both Bulgaria and Greece. It was modern and prosperous, lively with shoppers and nothing like as chaotic as I had expected; even the roundabout in the town centre had been planted with well-tended flowerbeds and shrubs and I was a little disappointed not to find at least one donkey grazing on it. We rested by a mosque (Silvain, thankfully covered up at this point) and were shown how to fill up our water bottles from the communal drinking taps. Across the road from us was the magnificent 16th century Selimiye Mosque, the central dome guarded by four minarets built at equidistant points around its circumference, Ottoman spears piercing the blue sky above.

It was late afternoon and for the first time I heard the *adhan*, the Muslim call to prayer, from the town's minaret. For me this would become synonymous with Turkey, drifting over both the largest of towns and the smallest of villages as I made my way east towards Iran, and would invariably remind me just how far I was from home.

Arriving in Erdine, Turkey

WE TOOK A HILLY ROUTE TO ISTANBUL, MINOR ROADS THROUGH A surprisingly luminescent sea of green farmland. This was the first time I had cycled with someone since Austria, and I was worried that I wouldn't have the strength to keep up or display the requisite amount of toughness. But at least I had gained a modicum of respect on the hill climbs – my new cycling mate asked if I had ever raced.

If I had chanced upon my adventure stripes by a freak spurt of speed, it was Silvain who really earned them by the way he decided his lodgings for the night; find the abandoned wreck of a building, wait until nightfall, then secretly sneak in under the cover of darkness.

"As good as any hotel", he told me, cheerfully.

This evening we were to view a couple of prime properties; a half-constructed two storey summer house (unfortunately no roof) and a small apartment block (too exposed on top of a hill), before falling for a row of dilapidated period brick and concrete farm outhouses.

"It is important not to draw attention to ourselves", lectured Silvain, so we cycled on several more miles past the town of Babaeski, slowing down as we came close to our chosen site, waiting for the moment when there were no cars on the road.

"Now!" he ordered, and we quickly pushed our bikes through a gap in the wall.

We looked around the grounds of our evening's accommodation; there still remained the concrete foundations and rotting frame of a very long shed, and half hidden under the long grass were a shocking number of bones. Judging from the size of the skulls, they were most likely cattle (the alternatives really didn't bear thinking about) and we guessed it had been a slaughterhouse. Silvain efficiently located the least soiled room in a small broken complex of adjoining buildings, and we wheeled our bikes in. After clearing a space amongst the damp refuse and the rat droppings, it looked almost cosy, and apart from a few unusual dreams ("The cows! The cows!...") I slept well.

～

WE RAN INTO A FRENCH COUPLE ON THE ROAD, CYCLING towards Edirne. They were deeply tanned, their clothes worn and faded on their thin frames and their bicycles had definitely seen better days; each had a couple of tyres tied to the rear-rack, bouncing up and down as they rode, and loosely packed camping equipment stuck out at all angles. They had spent fourteen months cycling around Europe and Western Turkey and were now on their way home. The last six months had been spent in Turkey alone, and they told us that they had one simple rule: accept every offer of drink, food or a roof for the night. This week they had averaged five kilometres a day, they said. I exchanged a quick glance with Silvain – these people had lost it.

However, as my own distance increased, the sluggish pace of this couple became less and less of a mystery. Generally, when you park your overloaded bicycle on a street corner or outside a shop, people will be curious. Some may pay a token compliment or offer a few words of encouragement, and a few may even stop and chat. But in Turkey, *everyone* who catches sight of you will yell at you to stop.

"Hallo! Hallo! My friend!" they will holler, and regardless of whether you slow down or not, will fire a salvo of enthusiastic questions.

At first, their friendliness and easy gregariousness is a pleasant change in tempo from what you may be accustomed to in Europe but, if you're cornered, you will be kept there much longer than you think is possible. Swiftly presented with a hot glass of çay (Turkish tea), any premature effort to leave will produce a look of extreme hurt on the face of your host and a growing throb of guilt in yourself; there is already a second cup of tea waiting for you as you finish your first, and a third one waiting for you as you get up to leave - in the end, it was far better just to smile widely, wave back and cycle on. Stopping the bike to eat, drink or check the map was best carried out as furtively as possible, in the middle of a field, preferably halfway up a tree.

TRAFFIC WAS GETTING INCREASINGLY HEAVY AND I BRIEFLY LOST Silvain while waiting at a crossroads for the traffic-lights to change. Bewilderingly, this had turned into several cups of tea outside a grocery store. I was sat down at a makeshift table in the shade of the shop's awnings and the light-footed elderly shopkeeper fussed around in the back, content to leave me to my thoughts. I distract-edly watched the speeding trucks and motorcycles throw up dust from the tarmac in front of me, as the lights remained red. Customers, from young children to old ladies, smiled and wished me good day, "*merhaba*", as they made their purchases. Later that after-noon, I ran into Silvain in the resort town of Silivri, as we both walked through the ornate doors of the same hotel at the same time. The place looked rather expensive and we exchanged sheepish glances with each other over our choice.

The final stretch into Istanbul was phenomenal; six to eight tightly packed lanes of fast-moving traffic, roads splitting off and abruptly rising into the sky or veering off in a Turkish crescent to fall gently back to ground level. Cars, buses and trucks wove in and out of each other with measured chaos, like some cosmic executive toy. It was terrifying and surreal, and the danger and excitement were intoxicating; when we at last escaped this lunacy for the coast road we were both laughing uncontrollably, the last two hours of trauma released in a flood of high-pitched giggling.

We cycled into central Istanbul along the promenade skirting the Bosporus, the straits separating west from east Istanbul, and caught our first glimpse of Asia across the water. It was an incred-ible feeling – *we had cycled to the edge of another continent!* – and we deliberately took our time, haggling with bread sellers and posing for photographs like any other tourists, our overloaded bicycles and the Bosporus Bridge as the backdrop. A blur of people and traffic saw us enter the warren of streets that border the grounds of the Blue Mosque and check in to one of the many cheap youth-hostels in the area. I felt a little intimidated by the sudden surge of tourists and backpackers, and only reluctantly agreed to a dormitory once I'd exhausted the possibility of finding a cheap single or twin room.

Rolling our bikes wearily through the lobby invited questions and looks of curiosity, even admiration. Initially self-conscious with all this unwarranted attention, in the short time it took to unload the bags I had begun to rather revel in my self-imagined role of international man of mystery, and even hammed it up a bit, limping stoically into the adjoining restaurant. Hey!! I have cycled from London to Istanbul!

~

"HALLO SIR, HALLO! PLEASE, STOP FOR A MOMENT, JUST GIVE ME A chance to rip you off!"

The souvenir seller had commendably, if perhaps unconvention-ally, summed up the attitude of almost anyone who sells anything in this city: bargain, cajole and cheat as much money as you can from your customer. Trawling through quiet backwaters on a bicycle exempted me from the worst of the price gouging, but at any place listed in the guidebook I was fair game. Prices were particularly fluid here, and you would have to work quite hard before you'd arrive at a reasonable price, usually half. I expected this buying a T-shirt or a pair of sandals, but not for almost every bleeding bottle of water.

Being a tourist again wasn't all bad, and I realised how much I had missed the company of other travellers, lounging around a comfortable hostel, and eating proper meals in good restaurants. I relished joining those late night "my travel story is bigger than yours" ramblings from the bunk beds, especially now that I was rather generously endowed.

Silvain had led the sightseeing charge around Istanbul the day after we arrived, and I staggered behind his youthful footsteps. We took the weight off our cheeks and put it on our poor feet instead, covering the entire city on foot. It was the obligatory tourist agenda, starting with Istanbul's centrepiece, the Blue Mosque; already spectacular during the day, at night its huge nested domes and fairy-tale turrets were flooded in a magical brilliant white. Mosques, museums and bazaars held us briefly in their spell as we pushed through the downtown riverside activity of the Bosporus and made our way up to Beyoglu and Taksim. Nineteenth century European architecture, quiet bookstores, upmarket restaurants and even a couple of venerable churches presented a picture of prosperity.

We continued on our feet past the Dolmabahçe Palace and on to the Olympic Stadium. Liverpool had beaten AC Milan here three days earlier and there were still odd groups of English fans looking worse for wear in the same replica football kit in which they'd arrived. We wandered deeper into residential areas where kids played in the road and deftly dodged the madcap local drivers. Away from tourist Istanbul we were free of pugnacious street traders and aggressive sales pitches, whereas outside Sirkeci station earlier that morning I had to physical disentangle my legs from a shoe-shine man, who was thoroughly determined to polish my flip-flops.

Silvain decamped the next day, onward to Ankara in his self-proclaimed quest to "visit a discotheque in every capital city". He had left me with bruised feet and a returned sense of foreboding; I was back on my own again and had to turn myself to the serious task of preparing for the next leg of this enterprise: eastern Turkey through to northern Iran and Azerbaijan. Until today, these regions had assumed a rather vague and romantic image in my mind, a kind of scenic travail along the Silk Road. But as I caught up with email at an Internet cafe, I also lingered with paranoid attention on the British Foreign Office website and its long list of travel warnings. I checked the "dangers and annoyances" section at the back of my guidebook and took a closer look at my new maps and the vast, seemingly barren space between villages.

I was already entertaining serious doubts that I could continue. The fear of dusty unknown towns on isolated, lawless roads put me in a cold sweat and my comfortable stay in Istanbul got extended day by day. I brooded over a question that would surface again and again; if I had an excuse to quit, would I take it?

LIKE THE SIZE AND EXTRAVAGANCE OF A VISA STAMP, YOU CAN assume that the bureaucracy involved in getting it is inversely proportional to the appeal of the government concerned. With the help of my Man in Kazakhstan, I had painstakingly researched the best cities in which to maximise my chance of getting a visa for any one country and had subsequently arranged letters of introduction for both Iran and Uzbekistan to be delivered to their respective consulates in Istanbul.

The Iranian consulate was utter chaos, starting with the line of people outside and continuing with a swirling mass of people inside; three times I queued at a counter labelled "Visas" and three times I was dismissed by the clerk behind it and told to join the queue next door until, round-robin style, I ended up at the front of the first queue for a third time running. The staff, with a defeated sigh, accepted my passport and application form, made a lot of sweeping moves and noise with some stamping equipment and handed me a receipt, in lieu of my passport.

"Come back in three weeks", he said, smiling at me. "Next!"

It took a couple of seconds for this to sink in, and I only just had the presence of mind to refuse to budge from the counter and insist that he check my documentation again; he found the letter and revised it to three days. On the way out, I chatted to an Irish couple standing in the queue, and here for the third time.

"He told us to come back on Monday to pick up our passports", said the guy morosely. "But he didn't say *which* Monday."

The Uzbekistan consulate was located deep in a distant leafy suburb, only one street away from the Bosporus, and I could see East Istanbul over the other side of the water. It was closed, but the sympathetic guard made a few calls and summoned an official to deal with me. It was only two weeks since the Andijan massacre, which caused international outrage when the Uzbek national guard fired into a crowd of protesters, killing possibly thousands. I guessed that visa applications had dropped off since then, and they were happy to have any applicant.

Istanbul was in all probability the last place to obtain anything of quality until the eastern reaches of China, four or five months hence, and I felt under pressure to supplement my equipment wisely. Before leaving home, I had purchased everything I would need to see me through to Japan - spare bike parts, maps (bilingual where possible, to point at towns I couldn't pronounce) and guidebooks.

The process was to email a wish-list to my sister-in-law and an estimated arrival date at a major city, so that she could dispatch a parcel to that city's general post office. I was using the universal *poste restante* mailing system, where you can address a package to a main post office, practically anywhere in the world. Timing was paramount; send it not so late that I might have moved on before its arrival, but not so early that it would be disposed of before I got there. It was somewhat of an acquired skill, from labelling the address of the post office (often no information available other than just the name of the city), and then actually finding it once you finally arrived in town.

I picked up the first such package from Istanbul's central post office, and as well as practical items (spare tubes and a part for my cooking stove), I also received a couple of long-awaited novels. Light reading was essential – when you're stuck in some fleapit hotel or lonely, wild campsite, the escapism that such books offer is a godsend. In turn, I sent a parcel home containing backups of photographs, old guidebooks and maps that had served their purpose, and a lemon-coloured cycling top for which I had endured obnoxious comments in half-a-dozen different languages so far.

Following up rumours of a "bicycle street" in the Sirkeci district, I found a well-hidden but surprisingly well-stocked bicycle shop in an unassuming little alley. Foreign faces and loaded touring bikes occasionally surfaced through the homogeneous crowd, and I started chatting with a German couple.

"We were hoping to get through Uzbekistan late last year", said Anna, "but when it started snowing, we had to take shelter in a village teahouse. And there we stayed until Spring". Her boyfriend, Frank, spoke up:

"Of course, there's not much else to do in such a place", he said, rubbing the noticeable bump under Anna's cycling top, "so our journey is finished for now."

❧

AFTER A WEEK IN ISTANBUL, THE FACES OF THE TRAVELLERS around me had changed, I had visited all of the palaces, mosques and bazaars I could ever wish to see, and my little tricks of procrastination were starting to sour even the sweet caffeine buzz of my leisurely morning coffee. It was time to move on. I had been thinking hard about what to do next and needed to plan several countries in advance. My biggest headache was the Turkmen visa, the conditions of which had been fixed many months ago. I would need to get a ferry across the Caspian Sea to arrive in Turkmenbashi - the westernmost port of Turkmenistan - on *exactly* the 29th June.

"Not a day earlier, nor a day later!" the Turkmen consulate had told me back in Vienna.

This was less than four weeks away and an estimated 2,800 kilometres by road, heading east across Turkey, through northern Iran and following the Caspian coast into Azerbaijan. Even barring mechanical glitches, sickness, difficulties at border crossings and any other number of things that could go wrong, there just wasn't enough time...

I was going to have to cheat.

The Sultan Ahmed Mosque at night

CHAPTER 7

ANATOLIAN HIGHS AND LOWS

"**E** *rzincan! Erzincan!*"

I was shaken awake from my frozen slumber curled up tightly on the back seat of a bitterly cold bus, and the driver was standing above me, shouting the name of my stop and pointing to the darkness outside. Through smeared windows I could just make out what looked like someone foraging about in the cargo hold below, and my bike and luggage were laid out on the road, already grey with a light dusting of snow.

"Come on, come on!" he seemed to yell again, and propelled by the hollering of the bus driver I hurried down the aisle and out of the door, into a freezing sleet that jolted me awake. It was completely dark – *where the bloody hell was I?* – the bus doors eased shut, the transmission cranked noisily into gear and it accelerated off, leaving me standing by the side of the road in utter confusion. Wearily, I wheeled the bike up a short hill to the bus station. It was a little before 3am and I was shivering.

Whenever questioned about the dangers of bicycle travel, I would always readily argue in response that travelling by bike avoided most of the main tourist crime centres, that you were actually less vulnerable on the open road, and far more likely to meet violence or robbery at a train or bus station. And now here I was about to sleep in one. As with most bus stations, this one was ill-lit and depressing, a few weak lightbulbs suspended randomly from the dark rafters above masking several shady characters lingering on the periphery. Somewhere I could hear miscellaneous bangs, echoing voices and the scraping of heavy items being moved across the floor. I pulled out the sleeping bag, locked the bike to my leg and tried to get some sleep, hoping my leg would still be there in the morning.

~

SETTING OFF INTO AN UNFAMILIAR COLD AND GREY MORNING, I recalled that a great advantage to travelling long distances by bike is that you have time to acclimatise to new surroundings, new people and changing cultural norms. You are able to adjust your reaction to new experiences in increments; changes in language, food and customs happen subtly, over days or even weeks, regardless of a physical country border, and it is less of a shock to your system than it might be through more conventional, accelerated modes of modern travel. On this occasion, however, in eliminating most of western Turkey by bus, I had missed the chance to "settle in" and would ride with some apprehension for the first few days.

There was little traffic on the road, just a few trucks and buses, and it followed a wide valley floor, the low hills nearby an unexpected vivid green thanks to recent rainfalls, while snow-capped mountains could be seen through the clouds in the distance. The valley narrowed into steep slopes of black scree, and only four hours and one very cold downpour later, did it open into wider plains and finally a small restaurant. I knew then that the difficulty stakes had been pushed up a notch.

While I waited in the restaurant for another sustained bout of heavy rain to finish, three men pored over my map, arguing amongst themselves over the best route to the Iranian border. The owner traced his fingers over the place names as he repeated them slowly under his breath; he admonished me over some tears in the paper and shouted something to the cook, who came running out with a roll of Sellotape. Both of them moved around the table, carefully repairing the fraying folds of the map, urging me to take more care of it.

A long steady climb brought me in the late afternoon to Tercan, where I could see yet more mountains laid out ahead of me. It was a small dusty town, just a few modest streets, in what was otherwise an isolated mountain pass, and home to a small but charming 12th century *caravanserai* - a traveller's inn. The town centre was a handful of two-storey stone buildings, rutted roads running between them, and lined with an assortment of tea shops, simple restaurants and a number of small open-fronted stores, cardboard boxes of their wares on display outside on the pavement. They all sold exactly the same things: basic household items, general provisions, and an identical choice of fruit and vegetables.

Immersed in the aroma of a myriad of spices as I browsed for supplies, I took a quiet corner seat in a restaurant and asked for a kebab. This was a world apart from the towns I had passed in the west of Turkey and marked the first time I had seen so many men dressed in Islamic style baggy trousers and long *kurta* shirts, many wearing skullcaps and toying with prayer-beads. Friends greeted each other with a dignified "*Salam alekum*" and a firm clasp of hands, but I noticed very few women on the street. There were no other foreigners here and the eyes of a hundred men followed my every move, every step under scrutiny, a mixture of bemusement, curiosity and a little suspicion in their stares.

I sat down at a sprawling roadside tea stand. The tea was served in small glasses and a couple of older gentlemen at the next table showed me how to drink it: place a generous lump of sugar between your teeth and sip the piping hot tea, straining it through the sugar. It seemed that half the town's male population was at this tea shop, and with mounting alarm I realised that I might not get a beer until Azerbaijan. I was overcharged for accommodation, a tiny tiled room with a narrow prickly mattress and a window too small to be of any use for light or ventilation. The manager, I suspect, was in collusion with the local policeman, whom I'd found behind the hotel reception more often than at his police station next door, but I didn't mind. They were friendly and encouraging and wished me luck as I left in the early daylight, the sun already glowing fiercely.

There was a very hot and dusty climb, the road gripped tight between a narrow canyon and a weaving violent river, its steep craggy walls a vivid orange cut sharp with deep shadows. The sky was a deep azure, and as I slowly pedalled my way upwards, I heard faint calls and spotted silhouettes of shepherds, their charges of sinewy sheep and goats perched precariously on near-vertical slopes hundreds of feet above me.

A couple of road-workers, smeared with dried dirt, came over and struck up a rudimentary conversation, fascinated by my mode of transport. I was transfixed by the appearance of the younger lad; with his ginger hair, blue eyes and freckles, my immediate thought was that it seemed far more likely to find him stacking shelves in an Edinburgh Sainsbury's supermarket than digging trenches under a blistering Anatolian sun.

I felt a weird pang of loneliness when he called over to me in foreign language (so he wasn't Scottish after all!) and it took me a few moments to accept that our conversation was halting at a few basic Turkish words and gestures. He said he was seventeen years old, which was close to what I'd guessed. His colleague came up and greeted me with a smile and a gentle "*Salaam*". This man was older, more typically Turkish-looking and somewhere in his mid-forties I reckoned. I couldn't believe it when he said he was twenty-five. I tried hard to hide my surprise, lying about my own age by knocking off five years to save his feelings. They live a tough life around here.

TURKEY IS THE ONLY COUNTRY WITH A HIGHER PER CAPITA consumption of tea than the United Kingdom, and it's not surprising, given the enthusiasm with which the locals try to get me to pull over and stop, even running after me for an excuse to brew up a pot of *çay*.

In one small town today, a couple of excited teenagers led me out of the midday sun and into a cafeteria of sorts, to meet their friends. It was a restaurant that doubled as a pool hall and I was sat down at a table while they hurried off to get me a cup of tea. Everyone interrupted their conversations and games of pool to come over to me, two dozen young men competing with each other to shake my hand. They sat and stood in a close semicircle around my table, faces looking almost identical in the dim light of the pool hall, hustling each other for position, smiling and staring closely at me.

The murmuring dissipated into silence and the tea arrived.

Unusually, it was served with milk and in a cup and saucer; they had made a special effort to make a proper "English" cup of tea for me, and were frozen like statues, wide smiles fixed and watching me intently as I sipped at it. The world stopped and I could hear the seconds tick by on my watch. Grinning inanely back at them I nodded my head appreciatively - *yes, this was indeed a remarkable cup of tea* - and there was a collective sigh from the room as the tension broke and we all relaxed.

THERE WERE NO MAJOR PASSES ON THE WAY TO ERZURUM CITY, just a steady, gentle climb through green hills, levelling out onto a wide and arid plain flanked by mountains still capped in snow. The tents of nomads had claimed some of the greener slopes, marked by an expanding circle of balding pasture due to their herds, whilst the Turkish military had claimed others with their extraordinary graffiti; a hundred-metre-tall insignia of the Turkish flag and a "Long live Turkey!" slogan carved into the hillside. This was a show of power by the authorities, and a reminder for me that I was in Turkish Kurdistan, more contentiously known as Turkish-occupied Kurdistan. The military presence would become more obvious the further east I travelled.

Erzurum is the largest city in this part of Turkey, and was once a key crossroads for caravans of travellers on the Silk Road, with routes splitting off towards Istanbul, north to Trabzon on the Black Sea coast and the route that I was to take, southeast past Mount Ararat, the mythical resting place of Noah's Ark. For me, Erzurum counted as the start of the Silk Road and my plan to take the northern route, with a few variations, would entail over five thousand miles of cycling through to Xi'an in Central China, the terminus of this collection of ancient trade routes.

It is in a striking location. The citadel, overgrown and deserted, stands guard on a hill in the middle of the old town, and by scaling the rickety old clock tower that lies within, you have a grandiose 360 degree view of the surroundings; old narrow lanes radiating outwards lined with dilapidated stone buildings, some modest timber and brick houses, and a few ugly municipal offices like pock marks across the panorama. In the distance was an almost unbroken ring of snow-capped mountains.

Turkish military bases became conspicuous throughout the climb from the city, and after the first half-dozen I stopped counting. The road flattened out and patches of recent tarmac were half melted by the sun, slowing me down like quicksand and priming my tyres like glue. Whenever I veered back into verge, the wheels became heavier and thicker, a spiky gravel-encrusted mess of rubber and tar. Every passing bus and truck left me spluttering in clouds of swirling dust devils and I wouldn't spot a pothole in the road until the saddle had suddenly burrowed itself halfway up my backside.

The bike was holding up very well in these jarring conditions - no odd noises, no creaks, no rattles - in contrast to its rider, weary with the abuse of the road, compounded by the sun searing down from above. From my map, I had hoped that the town of Horasan would be a much-needed chance to rest up and escape the worst of the afternoon heat. It was a dirt-poor place, parcelled up into a few squares of brown and yellow, a one-horse town without the horse. I passed swiftly from one end to the other, aiming for the sole patch of green I could see, a tiny grove of olive trees in the front yard of a small police station, and I rested for a long time in their shade while a policeman disappeared inside to fill up my water bottles.

It was late afternoon and a beautiful time of the day, perfect to start climbing the dusty road that wound away into the foothills of the next mountain range. I knew from the map that there wasn't much beyond this point other than a long valley up to a 2,400-metre tall mountain pass. It led me through spectacular hill country, green pastures speckled with yellow buttercups and hilltops revealing bright white chalk cliffs; small villages, a few basic houses at most, lined the road in the lea of the hills.

If I had examined the map a little more closely, I would have noticed *two* high passes, only one of which I had now completed in the lengthening shadows of dusk. What the map could not warn me of, however, were the packs of mangy young kids, yelling "Hallo Hallo!" at me, slapping my thighs with sticks as I cycled past, and trying to thieve things off the back of my bike. Even through narrow gorges, steep rocky walls squeezing me between cliff-faces and blanketing me in near darkness, I would hear that dreaded "Hallo Hallo!" again, echoing down from yet another young boy in rags with his herd of goats, perched on some perilous outcrop of rock far above. Worried that he might look for his next entertainment by dropping boulders on me, I would shout "Hallo Hallo!" with all the remaining enthusiasm I could muster, and we would continue repeatedly in this jolly manner until the next turn in the road, when I'd likely come across a pack of feral dogs.

Originally, I had thought it would be easy to just pull off the road and camp somewhere around nightfall, but the thought of being mauled by rabid mongrels while a small army of eight-year-old brigands ransacked my tent did not appeal, so I slogged on as the light disappeared, clueless about my options. It was dark now, and I carefully picked my way along the pot-holed surface of the main road, finding a turn-off for the town of Elskirt.

For the first ten seconds nobody noticed me as I turned into a long dirt street, the dim florescent lighting from a few shops and houses sparing little for the pavement outside; but a young boy, head down, concentrating determinedly on turning the pedals of his own bike as he wobbled from side to side, looked up just as I passed – and then I truly understood the expression "jaw dropping". It took a few moments for him to regain his composure, and, more confident on these dark potholed streets than I, he sped ahead, legs just a blur around the pedals, announcing my arrival to the town with excited cries.

"Turist! Turist!"

Another boy riding his bike appeared from the shadows of a side street and pulled up parallel to me.

"Turist!" he hollered, grinning at me.

Another one joined, and then another. Within minutes I had become the star of a convoy, flanked by two dozen scruffy boys riding their rickety bicycles alongside me, singing "Turist!" at the top of their lungs while bemused townsfolk looked on. By the time I got to the main crossroads I had attracted quite a following, and now a police car appeared, blue flashing lights rotating on the roof as it pulled ahead of me. A policeman leaned out of the car window and signalled me to follow him, and I was off again. They sped up, leading me through shadowy streets towards the outskirts of town and one by one my old escort tailed off, the occasional hoot of "Turist!" still faintly discernible in the darkness behind.

We stopped on the forecourt of a shabby looking petrol stand and restaurant, with a huge parking area for trucks. The police car parked up and the police went to talk to someone sitting at the back of the forecourt, occasionally looking my way. They called me over and I was relieved that one of the policemen could speak some English.

"You stay here tonight", he told me and pointed to the figure sitting in the shadows. "Please pay him."

My host for the evening got up from his seat and when I saw his face, for no other reason than the way he caught my eye, he somehow struck me as utterly evil. It was the strangest feeling, but I sensed this slightly built, weathered-looking man emanate wickedness, and I was immediately glad for the company of the local constabulary, who I suspect were there to warn this guy away from any mischief.

I carried my bike and gear up to a dormitory above the restaurant. My room was barely functional, a narrow cot sagging deeply in the middle and covered in a tussled and stained blanket; the door didn't lock so I rigged up something with my cable and bike-lock. When I visited the shared bathroom, the single toilet was overflowing, and with a subdued appetite I re-joined the group downstairs. The two policemen were still there, and a couple of the workers from the restaurant joined us on an outside table as we ordered a chicken casserole from the kitchen.

The meal was eaten in silence but for the English-speaking policeman, who made great efforts to talk with me, and we discussed his family and his job while the other one looked quite sullen throughout. As for the owner, he just stared at me, and that stare told me he would likely have a knife to my throat in a second if it wasn't for these fellows. When eventually it came time for the police to leave, the chatty one shook my hand and gripped it tight for an instant.

"Lock your door", he told me.

His quiet colleague raised a sympathetic smile as he got into the car, though I didn't half jump when he accidentally dropped his machine gun to the ground with a loud clatter. Even the owner flinched at that.

Military-scale graffiti

I WOKE UP FEELING LIKE I HAD BEEN PUNCHED AND KICKED ALL over; my body was sore from head to toe and a dull throbbing headache was gathering in intensity. In a brief moment of panic, I groped behind me - "My kidneys! My kidneys!" - rubbing my hands across my lower back, relieved to find that my internal organs seemed to have escaped relocation.

Utterly exhausted, the thought of moving from my bed left me with a sense of lethargy I hadn't experienced for a long time. I had cycled 150 kilometres yesterday, not excessive in itself, but with the rough conditions of the road and then the unexpected and prolonged climbing at the end, it seemed to have taken an obvious toll on my body. The physical signs included a railway-crossing of tender welts rising like miniature loaves of purple bread across my scrotum, and I whimpered with every movement.

The sensible thing to do was to return to bed and not move from it for a couple of days, but there was no way another night here was on the cards. I girded my loins, so to speak, and got on to the road for another day of punishment, saluting farewell to the police who had just arrived to see me off and to make sure that I had not been murdered. My already shaky spirits faltered completely when I stopped to review the map – oh dear God, today's route looked exactly the same as yesterday's. I gritted my teeth against the agony of leather saddle grating against flayed flesh, every bump and patch of gravel bringing tears to my eyes, and I set my jaw squarely against a crippling headwind in what was becoming a truly horrible day.

Time slowed. Every turn of the pedals became a struggle and I paid no attention to the landscape I was cycling through. A solitary roadside truck stop appeared from the middle of nowhere, a basic shelter from the sun and wind, and I lingered there long after I had finished eating, loathe to continue. I was shattered and felt so alone. I wanted to lock myself away in a comfortable hotel room, safe from the elements, away from prying eyes, and I wanted it to have a colour TV with movies, any movies, so long as they were in English and had a happy ending.

And that was one of the hardest things about this kind of journey. You can't just turn it off when you most need to, you can't just hide away, sit back and take a timeout. No matter how miserable you feel, you just have to keep going, hoping to goodness things will get better – and knowing that if you do nothing, then they likely will not.

PASSING THE TURN-OFF TO THE VILLAGE OF TASLICAY AND halting a mile down the road, I was very much out of sorts and I felt my willpower snap like a dead, dry twig. Faded scrubland surrounded me on all sides except for a surreal six-metre-high mural; a painted panorama of blue sky over a turbulent green ocean, white foaming surf swirling and breaking against a beach. I could almost taste salt in the air, feel the cool spray on my face, watch the waves rush up and envelop my feet... until I saw broken bottles scattered on the ground and an orange flap of rusted corrugated iron hanging from the roof, creaking nosily in the wind.

I was in a sorry-looking state, body crumpled over the handlebars, utterly spent. My pitiful appearance had stirred up some interest from the building next door and a rugged-looking, fair-haired guy appeared. With a genuine smile on his face and a reassuringly close resemblance to Kurt Russell, I was immediately put at ease, and he handed me a bottle of coke.

"*Salaam*", he said, placing his hand over his heart, and his two teenage sons behind him shyly did the same. Amicably, he initiated a stream of questions; they were of course, in Turkish, and once he realised that any communication with me was going to take a long time, I was ushered into his restaurant.

The interior of the place looked at odds with the rather weathered appearance of the outside. White plastered walls complemented sturdy dark wooden beams and furnishings, and a main wooden pillar reached to the apex of the high ceiling while a wrought iron staircase led up to a red-carpeted platform overlooking the rest of the restaurant. Arin explained that he and his two sons had come here three years ago from Trabzon, on the Black Sea coast, to build and run this place. I could see that it had been crafted with flourish and a great deal of love, but it looked out of place in this tough landscape and I suspected guests were few and far between. It was Arin and his sons who had painted the mural next door, to remind themselves of home.

They let me set up camp in the garden at the rear of the restaurant, and again I was in awe of the craftsmanship they had put into it, a veritable Garden of Eden away from the arid and dusty road, landscaped with tiered lawns, flowerbeds and a small brook. There was a pond which provided fish for the kitchen, and a couple of ornate statues proudly spouting water into it. The late afternoon sun threw rays of sparkling orange light over the water, and I lay down, exhausted, the trickling of the water easing me into a light sleep.

"Mr Steve! Mr Steve!"

The two sons, Edith and Youan, were calling my name and a few seconds later tentatively poked their faces around the flap of the tent door. It was dinner time, and I was the special guest. In the restaurant they had laid on a feast of different dishes, with a huge fish stew as the centrepiece. The cook joined us (after all, there were no other customers) and we all ploughed into it. Luckily the consumption of food and the chain-smoking of cigarettes between courses kept us pretty busy, and we had no need to get into too many difficulties with language – I had mastered the usual topics of family, places and football teams by now. In any case, after Arin had ransacked a couple of shelves, found the tape he was looking for and turned on the stereo system, the speakers were soon blasting out a frenetic mix of fiddle, guitar and some other instruments that I couldn't place.

All four of them were up now, in the middle of the restaurant floor, their bodies facing one way, legs kicking the other, dancing "Trabzon style" to this loud, frantic music. Inevitably I was also invited up, and now there were five blokes dancing the Hokey-Cokey to an empty Anatolian restaurant.

WHAT STARTED AS A FEW RUSHED VISITS TO THE TOILET, SOON turned into violent stomach cramps, and then from 3 o'clock in the morning I was throwing up with reckless abandon. It was a diabolical state I now found myself in, and when I wasn't crumpled over the toilet – an unfortunate hole-in-the-ground affair – I was collapsed in the tent trying to get some semblance of sleep.

By dawn I had run out of toilet paper and old newspapers and had picked an innocent mulberry tree half bare of its leaves. Delirious, I lay panting in my tent as the sun rose higher and rays of sunlight started steaming the contents, myself included. I was semiconscious at best, acutely dehydrated, very nauseous and now starting to sizzle. No water left in my water bottles and too weak to look for clean water elsewhere, I looked unhappily over at the fishpond and knew that it was time to debut my water filter.

It must have been late morning when Edith and Youan came running down to my tent, excited to invite me up to the restaurant again for brunch. It was certainly a relief to be out of the sun and into the cool interior of the restaurant, and I did appreciate the endless cups of çay, but the sight of all these plates of food put me in a cold sweat, and I was barely able to pick at a little plain rice and bread.

I was facing a dilemma – it would be rude to everyone if I didn't at least try the dishes presented, but just the thought alone had me almost retching. Worried that Arin might think last night's feast was the cause of my sickness, I got out my travel dictionary and maps and managed to explain that I had been already feeling unwell for a couple of days, and the distance I had cycled had only made things worse. We all agreed that it was probably the water.

As likely the first foreign traveller to have stopped at this restaurant, I felt a peculiar sense of responsibility. Despite my rising fever and nausea, paralysed intestines and a pounding headache, I felt it would be wrong to retire to my tent - so I tried to focus past the misery, plastering a mad smile across my face through the worst of the stomach spasms. Stuck as I was, too sick to move on, too diplomatic to disappear into my tent, this was a watershed moment for me – over the course of an afternoon and evening alone with my hosts, I started to understand this mysterious art of communication, a skill that would only improve as I travelled further.

This incredible human facility to exchange ideas, stories and emotions without a common language is something that dumbfounds me to this day. I must have been juggling dictionaries, drawing pictures in the roadside dirt and performing slapstick pantomime all the way from Istanbul to Shanghai, but for the life of me I don't remember it as such - I recall these conversations as clearly as if they were spoken in plain English.

"WHY DOES EUROPE RESIST TURKEY JOINING THE EU?" ASKED Arin, "Don't you think we have just as much right to membership?"

"Why did the UK and US really attack Iraq? Do you know just how many children have died there so far?"

"Why does Tony Blair hate us *mussulman* (Muslims) so much?"

Questions were fired at me, less accusatory than genuine desperate enquiry, as if I could provide some kind of answer to the issues burning deep inside so many people of this region. My guidebook to Turkey caused a great deal of interest and allowed me a short respite while Arin and his sons flicked through the pages, reading the Turkish place-names listed next to the English ones and smiling in recognition of photographs of some tourist spots. But it was apparent that they had visited none of these places and they seemed as far away to them as England or Japan.

"Children leave school here at eleven years old", explained Arin, "and then they start work". Life certainly wasn't easy here, far away from cosmopolitan Istanbul.

By evening I was feeling even worse. The cook had prepared a feast, a spicy fish stew that was a dish from his hometown and which I suspect had been prepared especially for me – he looked heartbroken when I couldn't touch it. Just looking at the thing, a couple of beady fisheyes staring right back at me, put me in a cold sweat again and for the first time they realised just how poorly I really was.

"Can you walk two kilometres?" asked Arin, concerned. "There is a small hospital on the edge of town." He led me there in the pitch darkness, arm around my shoulders, supporting me along the unlit road.

"You are lucky", he added, "it's the only one for miles around."

It was a basic concrete single storey building, with dull paint peeling from the bare walls, and muffled noises of coughing, spitting and other sounds of human distress that echoed from the dark corridors. I really didn't care too much at this point and felt only slightly guilty as Arin ushered me to the front of the queue to see the doctor. They greeted each other like old friends, clasped hands, and chatted animatedly, occasionally looking over in my direction. While I had been sitting there dazed and hollow-cheeked, my symptoms had apparently been discussed and after another couple of warm handshakes between them, I received two enormous injections in the bum, one in each cheek, and an extremely long prescription.

We hitched a lift back to the restaurant from a cheerful bloke built like a grizzly bear and nursing an axe wound to the head. I was already feeling better.

~

MY APPETITE WAS NOT YET BACK, AND I WAS STILL TOO WEAK TO cycle, but I really wanted to get to a town with a hotel room and a bed to rest up properly. After taking photos of each other posing

against the huge Black Sea mural, and warm handshakes from everyone, I mounted the bike - a little unsteadily - and freewheeled
downhill into the village.

At the bus station, three cheerful young guys kept me entertained in the three hours wait before the next bus. They were
enthralled by my map of Turkey and I was glad that it was now
looking much better after its recent facelift with sticky tape. They
joked and gently ribbed each other over a photograph I took of
them. I had no idea who might be Turkish or Kurdish, but what I
had noticed since arriving in this part of the country was the gentle
amicability of the people here, the lack of a hidden mercantile
agenda and the easy resort to laughter. Trying to squeeze my bike
and belongings into the baggage compartment caused great mirth
amongst the bus driver and his passengers; in Istanbul this would
have provoked nothing but angry swearing.

It was fifty kilometres to Dogbayazit, the last town before Iran,
and I watched the parched land passing by outside the bus. I was so
very glad that I was in here and not out there. The bus passengers
competed with each other in their efforts to approach me, each one
asking my permission before starting a conversation.

"I am studying tourism in Ankara", said the young man in the
seat in front of me. He was heading back to Dogbayazit to visit his
family.

"This region is so poor, and we really need to attract more
foreign visitors like you", he continued. "Tourism is our future!"

An older man sitting across the aisle asked me many questions
about my trip and was interested in my thoughts on Turkey. He
offered to show me the way to a hotel I had found in my guidebook, and patiently waited for me while I reassembled my bike on
arrival.

"I was in prison once", he told me, out of earshot of the other
passengers now disembarking. "I was fourteen years old and they
jailed me for ten years, for so-called political activities."

"This government represses our people and destroys our
culture", he continued, "yet all we wish is the right to educate our
children in our own language, to have Kurdish newspapers, radio
and television stations."

There was a heavy police and military presence and he pointed out an inconspicuous two storey building, the police station where he said his family were first tortured.

"They made my brother and I walk barefoot over glass", he explained quite calmly, "and then much worse."

He led me to the guesthouse entrance across the road, wished me good luck, and with the now familiar endearing sweep of hand across heart, he said good-bye.

Arin and Edith in front of their Black Sea mural, Eastern Turkey

DOGBAYAZIT IS A DOWNTRODDEN AND DUSTY FRONTIER TOWN, lacking comfort and conveniences, and situated in the middle of a harsh high altitude plain. Physically and politically oppressive and crawling with nervous soldiers, it nevertheless could be my favourite town in Turkey. I didn't expect to come across so friendly and engaging a community, especially one so remote as it is, hanging onto a far eastern outcrop of territory.

"The reason so many of us can speak English", explained Amul, a fifteen-year-old schoolboy, "is so we can..." - he paused briefly, searching for the right word - "*appeal* to people like you, to tell our story when you leave."

I had been waiting for a bus to Ishak Pasha Palace for almost three hours and Amul, a Kurd, was the umpteenth person to have approached me while I sat at the makeshift bus stop. I had likely missed it a dozen times, but I was so taken with these people, practically queuing up to chat with me, that I wouldn't have noticed. A middle-aged shopkeeper from across the street kept bringing me refills of tea and seemed happy to listen, smiling contentedly as other people asked me questions, showing annoyance whenever a customer went into his shop and he had to run back across the street to attend to them.

"You have seen there are many police and military here. Why can the UK not help us?" asked one lady.

"Until Kurdish rights are protected Turkey should never be allowed to become part of the EU", stated another astute eighteen-year-old student, encouraging a nod of heads and murmuring of agreement.

The passionate discourse continued. I didn't know how to deal with so many admirers and as each successive person charmed my attention away from the last, I felt guilty with my serial infidelity. It was almost a relief when the bus finally came, and I could spend a few quiet moments up in the hills of Ishak Pasha, an Ottoman palace which could have been plucked straight from the Arabian Nights. I gazed down upon the town in the plains below; it would be the last of such pensive moments for a while, as the evening would prove to be as animated as the afternoon and I would leave Dogbayazit with a long list of names and addresses and photographs of the region given to me by some local school teachers.

The Kurdish are the largest minority in Turkey, and I didn't even scratch the surface of their grievances against the government, their lack of representation and the violence and injustices they had clearly suffered as a people. I couldn't understand the complex history of the region or the nuances of its present-day politics. But there was at least one immutable fact; my hosts in this country, both Turks and Kurds, had overwhelmed me by the graciousness of their hospitality, and I was leaving this country frustrated that I just had no more time to give.

CHAPTER 8

WELCOME TO MY COUNTRY!

I was on the wide, smooth asphalt road to the Iranian border, practically free of other vehicles, just a dead-straight dusty line east heading into the heat haze for the next 35 kilometres. No villages, no houses, no restaurants, just a single implied colossal statement: there is only ONE destination on this road. To the south, cliffs and pinnacles of jagged rock were the only break in the monotony of this parched plateau; to the north loomed the dormant volcano of Mt Ararat, at almost 5,200 metres high the tallest mountain in Turkey, its lower slopes cradling this road I was on, deep rivulets of snow capping its peak like white veins on a frozen abscess.

This mountain has been subject to numerous expeditions trying to locate the mythical Noah's Ark, based on a Book of Genesis verse that states it came to rest "in the mountains of Ararat". Since the first century there have been records of priests, rabbis and imams talking of it, and even Marco Polo mentioned the rumours of its existence during his travels in the 13th century. Compelled by various eye-witness accounts – a World War II US serviceman also reported finding it, split in two by glaciers, in 1943 – there have been a multitude of explorers involved, from 19th century Oxford professors through to a modern day American ex-astronaut.

However, there was a rival; a large, vaguely boat-shaped rock formation in a place called Durupinar, thirty miles south. Some proponents of the whole Noah's Ark mystery claim this is actually the fossilised remains of the Ark, and fortunately this one was not stuck on the ice bound summit of an extinct volcano but much more conveniently located near a main road, clearly sign-posted, and part of any budget half-day tour package from Dogbayazit. It was good to see some local entrepreneurship in action.

Although I was still feeling a little weak and queasy, the fact that I would be cycling over the border into Iran within a couple of hours left me surprisingly energised rather than terrified. Back home, this is the point where I would resoundingly be labelled a nutter. *Iran...* now that was a headline. Not a place known for its Mediterranean beaches and cheap package holidays.

The political dialogue between Iran and the West had grown increasingly belligerent over the last year, from the International Atomic Energy Authority's constant browbeating over their nuclear program through to regular reports of American covert operations inside the country. Iran was pissed off and frustratingly impotent. That was why I had been unable to obtain an Iranian visa with my British passport ("Political problem, sir.") and turned to my Irish one instead; and that was also likely why I didn't meet any other Westerners heading this way.

Yet it seemed the next perfectly logical step, a graded escalation in the challenge I had set myself; not a full descent into madness, but just a couple of notches closer.

~

THERE WERE TWO LINES OF STATIONARY TRUCKS AT THE BORDER, engines turned off and the drivers standing to the side of the road smoking, feeding off the heat of their cigarettes, eyeing me with bemusement as I approached. Money sharks swiftly appeared from between the lines of vehicles, attracted by the smell of Western currency, gliding around me, testing for weakness.

"Sir! You won't be able to change any money after the border", they claimed. "Sir! They will search you and take your dollars and your euros", they warned.

I let them change my Turkish *lira* and a little sterling into

Iranian *rials* – yes, give them a little blood! – but managed to reach Customs otherwise unscathed.

Immigration went faster and smoother than any time I've arrived in Heathrow. The guards were well turned out, pristinely uniformed and both men and (head-scarfed) women were smiling, polite, and patient as I wheeled my leviathan of a bicycle through the doors. I was the only visitor who hadn't arrived by car or truck, and going through these gates I got the feeling that they didn't deal with many people arriving otherwise; they got confused a couple of times when leading me through the various checks, but did a sterling job of lifting and struggling to fit my bike, fully loaded, through their X-ray equipment. The official, with a disappointingly cursory examination of my passport, stamped the visa and handed it back to me, smiling.

"Welcome to Iran!" he said.

Yellow prairie was encircled within a rim of faraway mountain peaks and my first thought was this: harsh, very harsh. And not for the first time I wondered if I'd completely lost the ability to see the colour green. I spent considerable time hesitating in the shade of the immigration building, checking maps, setting the clock forward (a full one and a half hours), reviewing a few Persian words and delaying, delaying, delaying. I knew I had only 30 kilometres to Maku and most of it downhill, as I descended from the Anatolian plateau, but when I looked out over that rather barren view before me, familiar worries came back to beleaguer me. What, where and how do I eat? Where do I find water? And how on earth am I supposed to read these road-signs written in undecipherable Persian script? I also had to remember to keep completely covered up; my hairy legs were unappealing at the best of times, but here they could actually get me into trouble. Deservedly so, some may say.

Barely a mile beyond the border crossing, I was pulled over by a police car. Two policemen got out and as requested, I showed them my passport and told them I had started out from the UK.

"So – who do you support?" asked the older, higher-ranking officer, quite solemnly.

I was expecting some harassment, but this caught me completely unawares; was he asking about my views on Northern Ireland? Israel? Or perhaps Iran's nuclear energy program, which was always in the news as of late. Or was it Iraq, still very much an enemy in the eyes of many Iranians.

"Yes, tell us who you support?" urged the younger officer this time, a little more excitedly than his superior, impatient for an answer. I was even more confused - what were they after? Were they looking for me to incriminate myself? I was starting to get worried, but before I could think of anything in response this delicate dilemma was solved for me.

"I support Manchester United!" beamed the young officer, pleased to get it off his chest. His boss shook his head, tut-tutting as he would to an errant child.

"These young people", he said to me, "they take only the easy choices. Myself, I have always supported Liverpool."

I told him I couldn't agree more.

THE PAYKAN IS THE NATIONAL CAR OF IRAN, THE DESIGN BASED on the British Hillman Hunter of the sixties and unchanged in over 30 years of production. Dozens of them trickled past me as I headed towards Maku, beeping their horns in encouragement. Mountains lapped the road with an orange foam of parched earth, and it was quite a thrill to know that I was now cycling through Iran, alone, unsupported, and with really no idea of what to expect.

The intense curiosity of the Kurds had given way to the gentle inquisitiveness of the Persians; polite interruptions and invitations, many *many* handshakes, and a resounding "*Welcome to Iran!*" from a hundred or more people. The road followed a narrow gorge flanked by the escarpment on one side, and a long unbroken row of single-story houses and shops on the other; thick fingers of shadow advanced across the canyon floor, breaking the glow of the late afternoon sun into orange shards of light.

I found a cheap guesthouse in Maku, thanks to forthright advice from the friendly staff at a more expensive hotel, and I was given a room that was basically a makeshift space on top of the landing. The place was certainly cheap, only a few *rials,* but it was dark and gloomy with middle-aged, moustachioed men relaxing in the shadows, and they eyed me with some suspicion. It was an intimidating atmosphere, in contrast to the welcome I'd experienced on the street, and I felt that I was intruding a little too deeply.

~

"I HATE THESE BLOODY CLERICS - THEY ARE RUINING THIS country!"

I was in a grocer's shop buying some water, and the owner was complaining to me about the frustrations of ordinary folk in present day Iran.

"These *ayatollahs*, they don't understand the real world, they don't let the young people have fun, they don't let *anyone* have fun", he said, fuming. "They isolate Iran from the world and make life for us more and more damned difficult!" he roared, punching my change into my palm.

He didn't look like a reactionary; middle-aged, balding, and a slightly severe-looking appearance that would have you actually believe the polar opposite. He spoke English well and explained that he had worked for many years at the nearby border post. His tirade against the religious hierarchy that ran the country was much like I'd expect to hear from any shopkeeper in England about their own government, though I suspected the repercussions could be a little more serious here. His other customers looked on in bemusement and I realised that nobody could understand what he was saying, and this was an ideal opportunity for him to vent his dismay.

Two university students entered the shop and after a few quick words with the shopkeeper approached me.

"Hello sir, may we have the pleasure of talking with you?" one of them asked. "My name is Kamal, and this is my friend Hasan."

In what would prove typical of my relations in Iran, I felt I had been efficiently passed on to the next curious Iranian waiting in line, and my new friends took me for ice-cream. Strolling along the street and making sure we were out of earshot of anyone else, they provided an eloquent condemnation of the regime, almost rehearsed as they swapped turns with the speaking role, all the while looking around with theatrical apprehension, making it absolutely clear to anyone who might be interested that we were engaged in some subversive discussion. I was paying little attention until Hasan voiced a rather dramatic conclusion.

"...and we will take to arms if needed!" he declared passionately, triggering enthusiastic nods and agreement from Kamal as we finished our ice-cream.

Despite the fervour of these two young would-be radicals, Iran felt less oppressive to me than much of eastern Turkey. Women were certainly covered up, but they seemed to be more visibly engaged in day to day activities (almost half of the customs police were female), and people in general, at least towards a westerner like me, were open and approachable.

I had dinner at the more expensive hotel, searching for a temporary respite from the geniality of strangers. I was the only guest in a restaurant of thirty tables and had a private army of waiters, alert to my every move. On leaving, I fell into conversation with a hotel guest who had just entered the lobby. He was in his mid-thirties, smartly groomed and dressed rather a little too cosmopolitan for this town. He spoke excellent English and told me he was from Tehran.

"I work for the government, as a nuclear physicist", he volunteered quite cheerily. "Just here on business for a few days."

We talked for a few minutes and he invited me to dine with him, but I declined, having only just finished my own meal. Afterwards I wondered if I had passed up an opportunity for some international espionage.

∾

"*Should I stay or should I go?*"

It was the sound of The Clash in my head, and the dilemma that faced me almost every single morning. Today, it was the choice between the crushing austerity and bare discomfort of this guesthouse I was staying in, or the vast unknown of a completely new, raw and no doubt inhospitable country outside. It was always an unenviable choice, and bar the occasional delay of a day or two, the answer was of course always the same. I had to go.

Great stacks of round bread and honey at a road-side stall (oh the stares!) fortified me for a long day in which I would be torturing myself with words like *lush*, *green*, and even *moist*. Rock formations initially offered some variation to the monotonous scenery, but the road soon returned to a stark and arid landscape, cutting through flat yellow-orange plains, with the wispy vista of mountains in the far distance offering the only hint of something different. It was exactly what I had imagined Iran to look like.

In my initial planning I had made an extensive search for maps which had resulted in nothing more detailed than a scale of 1:2,500,000 - in other words, one centimetre to every 25 kilometres. I had worried how on earth would I be able to navigate Iran with a topological scale that could fit greater London onto my thumbnail, but now I was actually here, the shocking fact was that indeed I could! In one stretch of a hundred kilometres there were no towns and only one place to get food and water – some bread and cheese, and a sweet semi-fizzy pop that was some Iranian imitation of Fanta. It was a one room mud-brick shop in the middle of the desert, furnished with a couple of wide wooden planks under a tattered tarpaulin which at least provided some respite from the searing sun. A weathered old man served me, while half a dozen young boys sat in relative silence, eyeing me in semi-reverence.

A few hundred yards away from the road stood a settlement, designed more like a fortress, with decrepit brown brick walls encasing the village in a rectangle, and a gate at the centre of one wall. No building seemed over a single storey in height, and the walls were daubed in colourful graffiti of some kind. Throughout the day I saw several villages like this, set back a little from the road, self-contained walled settlements with little sign of what went on within.

The road rose slowly, not steep but enough of an incline for gravity to take its toll on a 50-kilogram loaded bike and a rider still somewhat weakened by illness. A rider who was wearing long trousers and long shirts in 40-plus degree temperatures in an effort not to offend local sensibilities. Descending the other side of the pass the scenery was unchanged, bare grey hills of rock and sand-stone rolling down to meet the road, pockmarked by tiny brittle green shrubs. However, it wasn't completely unbroken; at one point, a strip of land skirting the road burst into a brief parade of greenery, with long grass, thick bushes and tightly packed trees, all drawing their life from a thin silvery stream. Within the space of a hundred yards it had all vanished, as if I had imagined the whole thing.

By late afternoon my map indicated I should be approaching a village, and a few simple houses started appearing in the arid plains. They were built of large mud bricks, two stories in height, with no apparent doors or windows on the ground floor. The only entrance was seemingly via the roof, by a wooden ladder that could be dropped down and pulled back up again. My first thought: that's not very convenient. My second: maybe there was a damned good reason for it. I speeded up with a worried eye on the lengthening shadows around me.

Thirsty riding, Iran

THE FIRST REAL SIGN OF LIFE WAS A TRUCK STOP A FEW MILES further on, where my map indicated the village of Ev Oglu should have been. There was a large dusty forecourt with a number of eighteen-wheeler trucks parked up, and a basic automotive workshop off to the side - it looked like any dilapidated gas station you might see in some American road movie, a few rusty signs creaking in the wind and even a couple of tumbleweeds dancing across the road. A simple single-storey wooden building behind the petrol pumps housed a canteen but also a prayer room, its carpet adding an incongruous touch of luxury, and a strip of flimsy corrugated iron lined the eaves of the building to provide a little shade. With a couple of tables and a few random chairs and stools thrown around in the dust, it had all the makings of some apocalyptical terrace cafe.

The owner was originally from Turkey and most of his customers were Turkish long-distance truck drivers, with a few Iranians thrown into the mix. They were a tough but friendly bunch – you have to be, doing a job like that – and we ate dinner together in the heat outside. I gulped down coke after coke, failing to quench a raging thirst, sweating profusely just sitting still, now that the breeze had died down. We talked a lot, yet again long conversations without a language in common. They were all heading to or returning from Central Asia, some as far as the Chinese border, still another three or four thousand miles away. The Turkish seem to have a monopoly on dangerous and unpleasant truck journeys of the world (these are the guys that risk their lives delivering goods into Iraq and Afghanistan amongst other places).

Everyone talked about the hazards of the central Asian route, and one grizzled old fellow spent great energy describing his recommended route through Iran, Azerbaijan and Turkmenistan, drawing the entire 2,000 miles on the back of the napkin and handing it to me, confident that this should see me through to Uzbekistan. Here they all joined in, concern on their faces, warning me of the risky crossing over the River Oxus. It was an old army bridge, they said, a dozen floating box sections linked together, and depending on the current these plates could jump up or down by a metre or more. Difficult enough to drive a thirty-ton truck across, never mind a bicycle.

Later that evening two Czech motorcyclists stopped to refuel. They were happy to be on their way home after two months of touring around the region and complained bitterly about their experience.

"The mountains and the deserts are beautiful but no matter where we go the police are fucking bandits, always looking for *baksheesh* – at every checkpoint they hassle us until we pay."

"I'd think twice about going there, if I was you", said his companion.

They stopped only as long as it took to fill up on gas, impatient to get as far away from here as they could.

With little enthusiasm I unrolled my sleeping mat in a dusty corner of the forecourt, expecting a long night of biting insects and restless vermin, but the truck drivers had worked something out with the owner, and they suggested that I move into the prayer room for the night. It was very comfortable, and I felt far safer, but I still didn't get much sleep; the sounds of hammering, drilling and shouting, as well as a noisy generator carried on through to early morning.

From the window of the prayer room I could see the blue sparks of heavy welding equipment from the workshop next door, and one or two of the drivers standing around supervising the operation taking place on their rigs. They were removing the original petrol tank and replacing it with a much larger one. In the morning, I noticed that they had also performed an expert job in repainting the tanks so that from the exterior you would have never known they'd been changed. The only clue to the whole procedure was the row of old petrol tanks, lying in the dust around the back.

When you consider the cheap cost of petrol in Iran compared to that of Turkey it made sense to carry a little more, but to go through the trouble of finding an isolated gas station to make the repairs covertly at night, and then repaint everything so it looked exactly the same seemed a little odd. Maybe there was a living to be made in smuggling cheap fuel back to Turkey, or maybe they were planning to smuggle more than just bootleg gasoline. I didn't know and didn't really care; all I knew for certain was that as I cycled out to join the main road, it was going to be a very hot day.

THE SUN HUMMED LIKE THE FAN OF AN ELECTRIC OVEN; IT WAS now mid-June and I would be spending the best part of the summer cycling through a number of desert nations. When planning this journey, I had thought hard over the timing of my departure, trying to make the seasons work in my favour, but there really was no perfect plan. If I had delayed my departure a couple more months, it might be quite bearable cycling through some of the hotter countries like Turkmenistan and Uzbekistan, but I would have been risking heavy snow in the more mountainous areas of Kyrgyzstan and Tajikistan, and possibly be cut off from China until the spring thaw.

Alternatively, I could have left England earlier in the year, but there would have been a miserable European winter confronting me right from day one - I was aware that in the first month of the journey I would be at my most vulnerable and weeks of freezing rain, sleet, gloomy skies and gloomier people might have pushed me to divert to the nearest airport, dump my bike and buy a one-way ticket to Thailand.

As it was, fantasies of cold rain and cloud-covered skies were all I could think about as I struggled through another blistering 100 kilometres - 4 centimetres - of my Iran map. Even here, in dry featureless steppe, I could find people. Sometimes I would stop to dig out something to eat from my panniers, and in those few minutes of preoccupation I might turn to find some smiling bloke had appeared by the side of the road, shepherding a dozen goats. Where the heck had he come from? It was a bleak parched waste-land out there, and suddenly there was an intently curious local, fascinated at finding someone on a bicycle in the middle of no-man's land, patiently asking me questions in a language I didn't understand.

The children were far less passive. On the approach into most small villages there would be a few of them kicking a ball around on some patch of dirt. Once I'd been spotted, the initial shouts of surprise would soon turn into a terrible infant battle cry and they would start running towards me, converging on me like a breaking wave as the news of my arrival quickly spread. Usually I'd have seen them first and would have built up enough speed and momentum to stay out of reach of my young opponents. Other times I wouldn't be so lucky, and I might have to run the gauntlet of half a dozen pairs of grimy hands snatching at the bags secured to the back of my bike as I powered past.

Before long the villages thinned out, and the harassment from these young hooligans gave way to the more familiar torment of a long climb in a migraine-inducing Middle Eastern sun. It was the longest climb so far, and just as featureless as the rest. The summit was disappointing. By my reckoning I should have been able to see Tabriz in the distance, but a heavy heat haze had sandblasted the landscape in front of me, and thick smog would hide the city itself until I'd descended to the plains and was already riding through its outskirts. Sprawling petrochemical works and cement factories started appearing around me, and the traffic was starting to get thick. Occasional roadside canteens and rows of shops now peppered a wall of heavy industry.

It was so very hot, and the fumes of the cars and trucks only added to this oppressive heat. I stopped to fill up on water from a gushing drinking fountain - it tasted of petrol and the liquid burnt my lips. Along one five-mile stretch, I saw dogs lying dead at the side of the road, legs extended and pointing skywards, stiff with rigor mortis, as if a creative but canine-hating landscape gardener had been given full artistic license to decorate the roadside.

Buildings increased, as did the number of storeys, from one to two to four, but when a gap offered itself through the smog, I saw there was still a considerable way to go. Stuck alone in the far north-western corner of Iran, Tabriz is the fourth largest city in Iran with nearly one and a half million people living here, and probably all of them, at this very moment, were on the same road as me.

The traffic was truly insane, with trucks, cars and motorbikes passing me on both sides and switching suddenly between lanes like a real-life, high-speed, deadly game of Tetris, and it seemed that throughout all of this, *everyone* was shouting and waving at me. It would become the definitive phrase of Iran, the English sentence that everybody knew, synonymous with the unfettered friendliness of its people:

"Welcome to my country!"

Holy moly though, it was impossible to wave back, as I was far too concerned with staying alive on these roads. If there were traffic lights, I certainly didn't see them. At major intersections the drivers didn't stop, they just slowed down enough to somehow thread their way through the maelstrom to the other side, kind of like a round-about but without the roundabout. Everyone did this all at the same time, and the amazing thing was that it actually worked; all I had to do was aim my bike at the road I wanted, and somehow a path opened up through the cars and lorries. The key was not to deliberate or think too much, nor dwell on the mayhem unfolding around me. I felt like Indiana Jones taking my last perilous steps towards the Ark of the Covenant, as scythes and hammers swung ahead and behind, missing me by inches.

But most alarmingly of all, I was beginning to enjoy it.

More thirsty riding, Iran

CHAPTER 9
A TRIBUTE TO TABRIZ

Dusk descended as I threaded my way through increasingly busy thoroughfares, while cars and motorcycles tore wantonly around me. I stared at the colourful kaleidoscope of hand-written signs and modern neon lights, and the groups of people sitting lazily around open shopfronts on folding chairs in the muggy early evening. In a teahouse I saw people relaxing on thick Persian rugs sucking on *hookah* water-pipes, the long line of these exquisite devices looking like some ancient alchemist's apparatus.

It was impossible to get my bearings and identify something that looked like a hotel. I pulled over to ask a traffic policeman ("Welcome to Iran, sir!") and he called his colleague over who in turn called another colleague. All attention was focused on me, but language difficulties had completely slowed down my line of enquiry and I got the feeling from the odd word I heard ("Hilton", "Inter-Continental") that they were going to direct me to the regular, and extremely expensive, tourist facilities.

As the debate between the policemen was heating up, and the untended intersection behind me was looking increasingly like the aftermath of a Hollywood car chase, a man stepped into the fray and said a few words to the policemen before he was begrudgingly allowed to approach me.

"Can I help at all?" he said, smiling, "I fear you will be standing here all night if you leave things to these gentlemen."

I had stopped outside an English conversation school and the commotion had attracted the attention of a few of the teachers, who could be seen looking out of the window a few floors up.

"My name is Mr Ahmeni, and I am very pleased to meet you", he said, while the three traffic policemen looked on.

"Why don't you come upstairs to our teachers' room for a cup of tea?" he continued, and deftly brushed aside my weak protestations about the need to find a hotel, and my concern about leaving my bike alone.

"Don't worry, we'll help you find a hotel", he assured me, "and we can carry your bike upstairs as well", he said.

Two more smiling teachers appeared, and gamely pushed and pulled my fully loaded bicycle up the stairs. They were all extremely good-natured about it and if any Persian swear words did escape under their breath, I didn't hear them.

Other teachers joined us one by one and as we drank our tea, I picked out American, Australian and even cockney accents in the multitude of questions fired at me. All the teachers were Iranian, but each had his or her preferred "flavour" of the language.

"Please do accept our apologies for the poor level of our English", said Mrs Khadem solemnly, in a perfect Scottish burr, "especially my colleague Mr Asep", she said, turning to look at him and breaking into a smile.

"She's right, I wasn't smart enough to learn proper English", joked Mr Asep in a California drawl, "but at least I don't feel the need to wear a ridiculous bow tie every day like Mr Jawal does over there!"

The good-natured teasing and banter of the staff room reminded me a little of my own brief experience as an English teacher in Tokyo many years before, albeit far better behaved.

Time was pressing and Mr Ahmeni, as the senior teacher there, had the right (not obligation!) to offer his hospitality, and invited me to stay at his home. We wandered for an hour through a disorientating maze of alleyways and quiet streets, arriving at a three-storey building that housed his apartment. He had warned his wife already about their unexpected guest, but I suspect he probably took me on the long route home to give her time to prepare, for when we arrived, she had already laid out an impressive spread on the low table in the lounge. There were all kinds of dishes, served up tapas style; stuffed vine leaves, brittle *shirmal* bread, *kofta* meatballs, aubergines soaked in olive oil... we all relaxed on plush Persian rugs while their energetic two-year-old son kept trying to stick forks in my arm.

This province of Iran is confusingly known as Azerbaijan, meaning "country to the north" and like its northern neighbour (the actual country of Azerbaijan) has its origins in Turkic culture. The first language spoken here is Azeri rather than the predominant Persian (or *Farsi*) spoken elsewhere in Iran, and I spotted a fierce regional pride amongst the Iranian Azeris, including Mr Ahmeni. It seemed nobody had much time for Tehran.

One thing was certain though; I had picked an auspicious time to visit. Tomorrow was the first round of the Iranian presidential elections, and as we watched the various candidates parade on television, I pointed out one who was dressed rather like an absent-minded professor in a plain shirt and a scruffy jacket with elbow patches.

"He seems like a decent bloke", I said, taken in by his rather harmless, academic appearance.

"*That* man is the worst of the lot!" rebuked Mr Ahmeni. "He is Ahmadinejad."

Mr Ahmeni, along with most of his colleagues and friends, was to vote for Mostafa Moeen, the reformist candidate, most liberal of the bunch and the great hope of the young and educated. Already barred once by the Grand Council - until overwhelming student protests overturned the decision – his chances didn't look good, and he would be consequently knocked out of the first round, with his supporters making accusations of vote-rigging. The final round of elections to be held one week later would of course propel the infamous Ahmadinejad to victory.

THE NEXT MORNING A COUPLE OF FRIENDS OF THE AHMENIS HAD come to pick me up, taking over the hospitality duties for the day. Mahdi was a slightly chubby, studious looking man in his mid-thirties, and had brought his car to help us get around. He had money, having worked in the oil industry in Saudi Arabia for several years, and also spoke very good English. He was accompanied by his cousin Mohammed, painfully shy, very serious, and quite possibly the thinnest man I have ever seen. We all left together, as Mr Ahmeni wanted to stop in at the local mosque to cast his ballot on the way to his school. A couple of armed policemen were on guard outside, and he joined a small queue snaking its way around the corner.

"About the only time these places are busy", joked Mahdi.

First stop was Il Goli park, located in one of the young professional areas of Tabriz. "Not every woman wears a chador here", Mahdi had promised me conspiratorially, "and a rebellious few may be seen in nothing more than a flimsy headscarf!"

Now that got my attention. Alas, Mehdi was talking just about headwear.

The park itself was wonderfully green and expansive, most of the area taken up by a huge rectangular pond with an elaborate golden dome-topped pavilion in the middle, the summer palace of an Iranian royal dynasty many generations past. Nowadays it was easily reachable by any number of swan pedal boats, bobbing around a small pier.

There was an expansive system of landscaped pathways following the hills around the perimeter of the pond. This offered impressive views of the city, emphasising the very dramatic nature of Tabriz's location, hedged in by steep red mountains on every side (Tabriz itself is already over 1,300 metres above sea level). It was a nice way to spend a morning, walking the paths and chatting. Mehdi talked in great depth, often with a particular wry humour when the conversation turned to the state of affairs in present-day Iran, and Mohammed also started to open up (he spoke surprisingly good English).

"Most Iranians like the United States. We love their way of life, their culture. I have many American friends back in my old company and would love to visit them in the US someday", explained Medhi.

"This government is not representative of the Iranian people", he continued. "I hate them, and all of my friends hate them, but what can you do when most Iranians outside of the city are poor, have little education and are just trying to make a living. They don't have time for politics, they just do as they are told."

"So are the elections rigged?" I asked.

"Yes, in all likelihood, and I won't be surprised to see Ahmadinejad in power at the end of it." He paused and smiled.

"And then we'll all stop shaving, taking showers and wearing ties", he said, referring to the future president's rather scruffy demeanour.

"However", he stressed. "we do not need the US and Europe telling us what we already know and lecturing us on how to behave. When Western governments criticise us so freely it has the opposite effect to what they intend. It makes us want to stick together, to show we are a strong people – and the government knows very well how to manipulate this Iranian pride."

It was a lazy day of eating ice cream and sipping pomegranate juice. We talked on a multitude of topics and, like most Iranians, both Mehdi and Mohammed were so very eloquent and informed, whereas I felt out of my depth; an unmarried Brit, fast approaching middle-age, talking a year off work on a whim to do some travelling.

Some topics, however, were a little less cerebral. Mohammed told me to look carefully at the small groups of people patrolling around the pond, usually two or three young men or women, never mixed.

"Notice anything unusual?" he asked, a grin half-forming on his face for the first time since we'd met. I had no idea.

"Look again, more carefully."

I noticed a boy briefly pause and drop a small piece of paper on approaching a group of girls. Once he and his friends had walked past them, with no hint of acknowledgement, one of the girls picked up the piece of paper, swiftly and discreetly pocketing it. I was fascinated; this was dating, Iranian style. The piece of paper would have the email address of a possible suitor written on it.

"Even in Iran..." Mehdi started saying but fell into silence. There is, of course, an unspoken rule that blokes just don't talk about these things, no matter where in the world you're from. Even in Iran, he had wanted to say, you can't stop love.

∾

Mehdi and Mohammed in Il Gohi park

WE WENT FOR A DRIVE, PUNCTUATED BY SEVERAL STOPS: ICE cream (again), soft drinks (again) and a late lunch of *abgusht* lamb stew, a local speciality that both Mehdi and Mohammed insisted I had to try. They both argued heatedly over which was the best restaurant, and it was closed by the time they had finally agreed – we covered a huge chunk of the city as we looked for another place that would meet both their culinary criteria. We had quite an appetite when we arrived, and wolfed it down with freshly baked naan bread, too famished to pay any attention to the subtle flavourings.

The rest of the afternoon was spent at Mehdi's house and I was introduced to his parents and his sister, who was dressed casually in jeans and T-shirt. Up until now I hadn't seen a single woman with her hair uncovered. Occasionally (as indeed promised) I may have seen a "flimsy headscarf" but generally it seemed that women wore a chador, not necessarily the heavy black device that is typically (and mistakenly) attributed to Iran, but certainly something that covered them from the hairline through to below their knees (with a cheeky flash of jeans or brand shoes underneath); even Mrs Ahmeni in their own home had worn a long head scarf. I didn't know where to look.

We settled down for more eating and Mehdi's mother brought out some homemade *dolma*, for which she was well known in the neighbourhood. I tried out a few Azeri words (*"dadli dadli!"*) to tell her how delicious they were - she was overjoyed, happily rattling off a flood of Azeri words in return. Then she went to the kitchen and returned with a crate of the things to take back with me.

"Shall we watch some television?" Mehdi asked. "We have BBC, you know."

We went into his bedroom (still unmarried, he lived at home) and he switched on the TV to BBC World catching the tail end of Top Gear (the only programme they seemed to show).

"The satellite dish is in the alleyway behind the house, but we are not actually allowed satellite TV. Officially, this law is to protect us against foreign decadence... but really it's to stop us accessing the *Farsi* speaking channels, run by Iranians abroad", Mehdi explained. "They are much more dangerous."

"However," he continued, fussing around with the remote control, "they are not particularly interesting, so I prefer Sky." And with that, he switched the channel over to a repeat of Superman II which we all settled down to watch. Whenever there was a mild love scene - Clark Kent and Lois Lane kissing, for example – the 35-year-old Mehdi would hurriedly lower the volume and rush over to the door in a fluster, remote-control in his hand, ready to switch the channel at the first sign of his mother entering the room and catching him watching it.

~

Overdosed on hospitality, I had extracted myself from my hosts and was exploring Tabriz solo. It didn't take long to see that this was a city to bring out the best in even the most retiring and timid of travellers. People are interested in *you*, the visitor; they want to know what you really *think*, what is your *opinion*. I was stopped by countless people on the street asking me what I thought about the recent election result and the likely consequences for relations with the West.

The first time I was approached by a young woman in the street I was terrified. Panic! A lone foreign male taking to a head-scarfed local girl, without any chaperone; they'll surely have my goolies for this! Decades of stories about "mad mullahs" in the tabloid press triggered an unwarranted knee-jerk reaction, but by the end of the afternoon and after many more such encounters, I had relaxed, enjoying the occasional interruption and short volley of questions, followed by the woman hurrying back to her group of girlfriends, as they excitedly gathered round to interrogate her on the conversation.

I was fortunate to come across the Covered Bazaar, almost by chance. One of the oldest bazaars of the Middle East, it was a well-known Silk Road commercial hub at even the time of Marco Polo's adventures. In my search for a compass, a guide working at the tiny tourist office led me down an unassuming narrow flight of steps, along a quiet flagstone corridor and turned the corner into a spectacular hidden world, a brightly lit, colourful gallery of thriving shops and small businesses.

This honeycomb of decorated caverns, domed halls and courtyards added up to over twenty miles of covered walkways jammed with shops selling anything you could need. This all-encompassing maze was loosely organised into "villages" according to the goods on sale: gold and silver, jewellery, carpets, clothes, spices... the stone floors were worn smooth from generations of traders and patrons alike, and to me the exits were as elusive as the entrance. Beams of sunlight filtered through circular portholes high up in the intricate vaulted roof, and the occasional glimmer of daylight, bouncing across walls and floors, teased me into thinking that I had found a way out - but it was almost always a closed courtyard, open to the elements and closed to the world outside. There were no exits but only more entrances, leading into yet another piece of the labyrinth.

At least I was not to be assailed by a bloodthirsty army of street vendors, chasing me down and blocking my escape like in Istanbul. There was a dignity to the shopkeepers here, and several invitations to sit down with them for tea. They were not really expecting me to buy anything (what would I do with two kilograms of liquorice?) and most couldn't speak much English in any case. They would plant me down on a chair with a cup of tea in my hand and then, satisfied I was comfortable, wander off to conduct their business; and when I'd get up to leave, they would acknowledge my departure with a wave.

One of the courtyards held an ancient-looking stone water fountain, where the traders queued up to fill buckets of water (no doubt to keep making me tea), and other men were hanging up sheets of leather hide. One sat down next to me on the stone bench I was resting on (flummoxed again, searching for a way out), and as was typical with Iranians, politely asked permission to talk with me first. His name was Davoud, an energetic 19-year-old who came from a long line of shoemakers and, astonishingly, spoke excellent English.

"I learn from the classics; Mark Twain and Charles Dickens", he explained, "and I practise my listening through English speaking radio stations. I am also learning French and Spanish right now, but my real passion is mathematics and philosophy."

He was extremely curious about everything. We talked about the UK, Japan, and moved on to the topic of books, and I promised to send on some of my own, once I had finished with them. We talked a little of my cycling trip (I was stalling to avoid any talk of mathematics or philosophy) and he added that he also enjoyed being physical active.

"I get up before 5 am every morning for exercise; running, weight-training and boxing", he told me. "It is important to exercise the body as well as the mind."

"Have you ever thought about going to University?" I asked, a little gingerly, unsure of the entrance criteria in terms of money or social position. He brushed it aside.

"Not at all. Why would I need to go to University?" he replied, a touch defensively. "I have a job I enjoy and the freedom to study what I wish! I just love learning."

Loading up the bike and tackling Tabriz traffic filled me with dread (The Clash was again playing inside my head) and sure enough the traffic out of the city was delightfully terrifying. I was heading east towards the Caspian Sea, only 300 kilometres away but the first 40 kilometres of that was a fiercely hot climb to get over a ridge of mountains. Perceptively, if only slightly, the temperature dropped a notch and the occasional feeble flourish of green could be spotted in the sandblasted landscape. With few signs of habitation and even fewer signs of actual people, only the 5,000-metre-high snow-capped Mount Sabalan to the south-east was there to keep me company, and I was beginning to miss the gangs of thigh-slapping, stone-throwing children.

So, what is the ideal personality for this type of endeavour? Is it the extrovert, energised by interactions with other people, easily able to make immediate friends but struggling to enjoy meal after meal alone? Or the introvert, content in his or her own company but worn down by the need to be sociable with a never-ending succession of strangers? The obvious answer might be that the outgoing type wins every time; after all, there really is no better way to be the centre of attention than riding a bicycle halfway around the world!

However, loneliness *will* get you, whether it creeps up slowly over a long desert crossing, or suddenly, in the middle of a noisy market in an utterly alien city. It is my guess that when it does, the quieter guy is that touch more resilient, able to take refuge in his own thoughts. His gregarious counterpart has probably cracked and is already on a bus or train out of there, forming animated stories of his adventure, ready to tell the first person who will listen to him about his travels.

THERE WAS AN ABSENCE OF ANY SHADE UNDER THIS SCALDING sun, and I started to employ another couple of the extra 2-litre plastic water bladders I had brought with me, tied to the top of my front panniers. I arrived in the small town of Sarab, literally in the middle of nowhere, and marked by a crooked row of flimsy three-storey buildings on my left and the open expanse of pitted desert to my right, like the tired movie set of some low budget Western. A man offered to lead me to a "Tourist Inn", part of a chain of government-run hotels built in the seventies, now well past its prime and aimed at foreign visitors to bring in a little western currency. I wondered: what on earth would tourists be doing in this place? At $15 a night it was too expensive, so I found a cheaper option back on the road into town. It was one of those buildings I'd passed, decrepit and dirty, a dosshouse for 40,000 *rials* (about $4) a night.

I shared a room with a young teenage lad and his uncle who had both travelled here from a neighbouring province. The uncle was here for a medical check-up and treatment for injuries received during the Iran-Iraq war. He came here every year, he said, but this time his nephew was helping him. Speaking English for the last couple of days had spoiled me, and I found the return to the art of non-verbal communication arduous. In the end the uncle made it easier for all of us and unbuttoned his shirt, showing me an array of coarse evil scars from his fifteen-year-old shrapnel wounds.

In the morning, the hotel manager tried to make me pay for the room a second time as I checked out, mysteriously unable to locate the assistant manager who I had paid a few minutes earlier, leaving me fuming and swearing at him. A few minutes down the road, I stopped for a breakfast of cheese and honey. In any half-decent restaurant in Tabriz this would usually come to 10,000 *rials*, or just under a dollar, but in this dirty, dilapidated cafe in a dusty, forsaken backwater of a town, the unshaven and particularly unhygienic-looking owner wanted to charge me 50,000! He looked anxious as I exploded in a torrent of rage, shouting profanities and banging the tables. Caught off guard, he immediately halved the price, but from that point, composure regained (and me exhausted) he wouldn't budge, arms crossed, and shaking his head while the motley crew of gap-toothed regulars looked on in amusement.

Why was I so angry for the sake of a measly couple of dollars? I should just cough up the extra change, avoid the stress and happily be on my way. But for the sake of me I just couldn't do it. The further I travelled, the more stubborn I would become over every minor scam, and the more risks I would expose myself to. If I didn't die a premature death through illness, robbery or accident, there were plenty of other possibilities I was creating for myself. Only long after I had arrived in Japan did I stop to consider the real, and unnecessary, danger I might have been dropping myself into. Bloody hell, just how many times did I tell some local scam artist from some far-flung country to go and screw himself? What the hell was wrong with me?

Back on the bike, I recalled that the only honest people I had met were the war veteran, his nephew, and a schoolboy who had cycled next to me for a while when I had first ridden into town.

"Sarab is bad town, Sarab is bad town!" he had cheerfully called out to me from his bicycle.

That evening I stayed in Ardebil, an ancient Silk Road barrack town and nowadays a carpet-making centre. The evening air had a barely perceptible chill to it, reminding me I was almost at the shores of the Caspian Sea, whilst the city itself was small enough for me to enjoy a night-time stroll around the compact centre. The shops were softly illuminated, their fronts open to the street and the richly woven carpets sowing reds, oranges and yellows into the night outside. Stalls and restaurants sold kebabs with a wide range of meats and vegetables on the menu, and the small wooden skewers they used reminded me of the *yakitori* I used to eat in Tokyo. I sat by myself in a small eatery, half a dozen skewers of meat in front of me and attracting the stares of a few locals, while I leaned back against the wall and tried not to reminisce about Japan.

IT WAS MY LAST FULL DAY IN IRAN AND THE CLIMATE AND scenery had changed as suddenly as it had dramatically, as I headed closer to Astara, on the border with Azerbaijan. The air was heavy, the humidity especially trying after the arid semi-desert I had been riding through for the last couple of weeks, and the skies were now curtained in dark clouds. The bald orange-grey peaks that had been assaulting my peripheral vision for so long now gave way to soft, downy green hills.

According to my map, the mountain pass I was now laboriously climbing would be the last one for a while – at least on this side of the Caspian – and it was famous for outstanding views down to the sea. However, my wretched efforts were rewarded by nothing more than a blanket of low-lying cloud which cut visibility down to a few yards. I hoped that the predominantly mad Iranian drivers would notice my rear flashing light in time to brake.

It took half an hour of careful descending before the last wisps of cloud had disappeared, and I could see that I was on a steeply winding road following a river valley, enveloped by lushly green wooded slopes. Yet again I was reminded of Japan, and in that moment a nagging feeling, a masked uneasiness I had just about been managing to restrain, crystallised in a shock of realisation, hitting me like a karate chop to the solar plexus... *what on earth was I doing here?*

This brief respite of pleasant woodland had made matters worse, sharply reminding me that this was not the rural hinterland of some Japanese mountain, but a transient glimpse of forest in an otherwise unbearably yellow, arid landscape. Why allow myself only a mere taste, when in Japan I would be able to feast over such indulgent panorama day after day? All the people would be polite and honest, speaking a language I could understand... lodgings would be clean and comfortable, campsites well-tended... drivers considerate and careful... there would be a proliferation of shops and convenience stores to keep me safely pampered... and beer machines, well, they would be pretty much everywhere.

Oh, how I longed to see something familiar and consummately Japanese! A red shrine glimpsed through forest leaves. Rectangles of flooded rice fields. The clay-tiled roof of an old Japanese inn. And if I got tired of it all, or if it got too hot or too cold or too wet, then I could just hop on a train and be home to a comfortable apartment within hours!

But that wasn't going to happen for at least another 10,000 kilometres.

THE TOWN OF ASTARA IS SHARED BETWEEN IRAN AND Azerbaijan, the border splitting it down the middle to the shore of the Caspian Sea, a frayed chaotic lattice of tiny restaurants, cheap hotels and an uncountable number of small shops selling a myriad of dusty products from lengths of silk and other fabrics, to clothes, bags, shoes, and a categorical rainbow of spices and sweets. This is the gateway to the Caucasus and a number of surly non-Persian traders could be seen amongst the crowds, as well as the occasional pale skinned Russian. Border influence showed itself in other ways as well, the women dressing far more casually in jeans and T-shirts, with generous fringes of dyed blond hair escaping from under head-scarves. The reception was staffed entirely by women, as were the multitude of shops - they seemed very much to have the upper hand when it came to commerce in this town.

However, I wasn't really interested in exploring, preferring instead to arrange lodgings as efficiently as I could, get dinner eaten as quickly as possible, and lock myself away in my room until it was time to leave the next morning. I was in a funk, a double hit of physical and mental exhaustion from the last few days and the uncertainty of the road ahead. Despite having made it through Iran with its infamous podium position in the "Axis of Evil" league table, I was more apprehensive about the next country.

Azerbaijan was the first in a whole string of nations I had barely heard of a year ago, the launching point for the Central Asian stage of my journey, and I had no real idea of what to expect. Turkmenistan, Uzbekistan, Tajikistan, Kyrgyzstan, Kazakhstan... I could barely pronounce the names of these countries and some I would never learn to spell properly. Yet in a little over a week, I would take a ferry from Baku across to the port of Turkmenbashi, step out onto the parched orange fringes of the Karakum Desert, mount my bike and cycle over two thousand miles through them. I was more than a little apprehensive - I was bloody terrified.

I cycled the half-mile to the border post looking about as conspicuous as you can get. A scene of complete mayhem awaited me, an army of Iranian money changers yelling at me from all sides, and dozens of seedy blokes squeezed up against the iron railings of an apparent immigration compound, arms thrust through the bars and flailing around, some gesturing me closer, others shooing me aggressively away, and all of them shouting things at me. There was a series of confusing passport controls and the last of the well-drilled and professionally conducted Iranian border officials disappeared, to be replaced by their Azeri counterparts. A squat mass of a man, in an obscenely huge old Soviet-issue peaked cap and soiled police uniform, sat slumped on a stool against the railings of a small bridge that marked the border between the two countries.

"Hey friend", he rasped from behind the cigarette hanging limply from his fleshy lips, pointing up at me and then rubbing his thumb and forefinger together.

"Give me present."

CHAPTER 10
LAST STOP BAKU - ALL CHANGE
FOR CENTRAL ASIA

A dozen radios and CD players merged into a single wavering stream of manic Azerbaijani pop, matched by the colourful hustle and bustle of a busy border town. It was similar to the Iranian side in many respects bar one; no chador and no headscarves. After weeks through Eastern Turkey and Iran suffering a dearth of the visible female form, I now abruptly discovered that the local women were not only attractive, but also entertained far less conservative fashion choices. If the Iranian women looked anything like the Azeris, I thought entirely inappropriately, then I now understood why their husbands and fathers wanted to keep them safely covered up.

Around town there were a few Caucasian faces and it was strangely comforting to see the Lada, that Soviet stalwart of jalopies, back in vogue. Cycling away from the immediate town centre the boulevards were wide and the houses uniformly ordered, Soviet style, but the scenery was a gorgeous lush green, scrubs and low trees bursting out onto the road, and with the abundant vegetation and stifling humidity this felt more like Southeast Asia. The sun was shining, the road was clear ahead, and I felt the heavy air of religious authority which had been with me since eastern Turkey disperse with every revolution of the pedals.

The Azeris felt obliged to compete with the Iranians on the hospitality stakes, with lots of shouted greetings from the side of the road and even an honest policeman who offered me a shot of his vodka (it was ten o'clock in the morning). It didn't look particularly prosperous, with many of the houses built simply of breeze blocks and corrugated tin roofs, but the owner of one small shop, which had a dozen bottles of cooking oil on the shelves and little else, sat me down and excitedly called across the road to his rather severe-looking mother, who really didn't know what on earth to make of me. They desperately wanted to show some hospitality, rummaging around in the bare storeroom until they presented me with a can of tuna and a large round loaf of bread, urging me to rest and eat.

Azerbaijan had lifted my spirits just as I badly needed it, a pattern that would be repeated countless times over the following months. In my lowest moments, when I was impossibly lonely, missing the security and predictability of home or second-guessing myself over the point of this whole enterprise, it was crucial to realise that the feeling would pass. You just have to ride it out; tomorrow really is another day.

Grand and austere Soviet architecture was starting to make an appearance. The otherwise nondescript town of Masalli had a huge public plaza surrounded by granite fountains and grim, larger than life statues of soldiers in heroic poses, bare chested, square jaws set defiantly forward with a Kalashnikov rifle gripped in one strong hand. These old Russian monuments always seemed to attract clouds, and a fierce looking one started moving in as I headed to the town's designated hotel, a behemoth of a building, eight stories tall and apparently empty but for me. At eight dollars a night it was expensive but today I deserved it. Not only had I entered a new time zone, bringing me another thirty minutes closer to Japan Standard Time, but I had also broken the 5,000-kilometre barrier, and already I was wondering where I would be when I hit the magical ten thousand. Kazakhstan? The Gobi Desert? Or back in Japan, working twelve-hour shifts in a cramped office cubicle?

∾

AZERBAIJAN WON ITS INDEPENDENCE FROM THE SOVIET UNION IN 1991, throwing off more than 70 years of Russian rule in an instant. Prior to the Russians it had been passed between various empires –

Mongol, Ottoman, and Persian – as well as going it alone as an independent Muslim *khanate*. As such, it had followed a not dissimilar trajectory to the Central Asian republics, so I was hoping a week or so here would be a gentle transition into the compounded challenges of "The Stans" which were to follow. A free trial, so to speak.

There was evidence of one parallel already, in the form of political nepotism and the making of Azerbaijan's own personality cult. An inordinate number of enormous billboards lined the highway depicting President Ihlam Aliyev standing proudly in front of the Azeri flag and looking into the middle distance, hand resting on the shoulder of his father Heydar Aliyev – the previous president – also standing proudly and also looking into the middle distance. The elder Aliyev was ex-KGB (most rulers in this part of the world are ex-KGB) and had engineered a feudal style power transfer in 2003 after a serious heart attack, so that his son could continue to run the country with an iron hand, keeping any dissent firmly in control.

Every mile or two I came also across billboards with nothing but large white text on a black background. I couldn't read the Cyrillic characters, but I could recognise the name of Aliyev marked at the bottom of each; these were words of wisdom attributed to the old president, advice given freely to the masses, and I found out later what they meant. "Respect your parents!". "Azeri is your mother tongue!". And my personal favourite, "Democracy is not an apple you can buy at the market!".

Apart from a fairly lucrative line in caviar farmed from the Caspian Sea, Azerbaijan derives the vast majority of its wealth from oil. However, there was little sign of those fat oil revenues being spent on infrastructure around here. I found it easier to cycle on the dirt verges than on the abysmal road surface, and my arms and shoulders ached from fighting a ferocious headwind and dodging scores of drivers bouncing with reckless abandon over the broken tarmac.

The entire place still felt like Southeast Asia, this despicable road forming the focal point for so much everyday life; Thai-like *tut-tut* single-stroke three-wheelers moving goods up and down the outer lanes, makeshift food and tea stalls lining the dusty highway, flocks of geese crisscrossing the thoroughfare with miraculous traffic awareness, and even random cows in the middle of it all, oblivious to the insane traffic trying to swerve around them.

The trees thinned out and then disappeared altogether, the air became dryer, the road flatter and passing vehicles threw up dense clouds of dust and dung in my face. On a busy stretch of highway I heard a vicious barking and growling above the noise of the traffic and the blood froze in my veins. A crazed dog on the other side of the road was attacking every car and truck that raced past him, trying to bite off their tyres or doors. This fearless monster looked like a pit bull terrier fed on a cocktail of steroids and amphetamines. Two lanes of traffic shielded me from its attention, and I stayed motionless on the bike, trying to not catch his eye, relying on momentum alone to freewheel out of range. *Don't move the legs Steve, for pity's sake, don't move the legs.*

Fast and dangerous drivers put me in a dark mood, and it was late into the afternoon before I eventually caved in to one of the many friendly offers of tea from a team of amicable road workers. Listening to them chatting quietly amongst themselves, I realised I quite liked this softly spoken Azeri dialect, and there was something about the lazily pronounced vowels and stretched out syllables that that sounded almost familiar. One of the men swapped a few words with his mate and smiled at me as he passed me a cup of tea, and for a moment, I was genuinely convinced that these were two blokes from Dudley trying to speak French.

As twilight approached, I found myself cycling through parched agricultural land, too exposed for me to comfortably camp and setting me off in the hunt for a hotel in the nearby town of Salyan. I found the usual Soviet-era multi-storey monstrosity, broken grime covered windows and a neglected overgrown lawn that centred around an enormous portrait of the older Aliyev. If the state of this place was any reflection on his presidency then God help the people here, I thought. Only the top floor had rooms in any kind of habitable state, and as I slowly climbed the stairs, heaving my bike up every step, the long unlit corridors of each floor threw up clutches of small angular shadows - when my eyes got used to the gloom, I saw that it was a sea of torn up and splintered floorboards. I wheeled the bike to my room, being careful to avoid the gaping holes in the floor that dropped into inky darkness below, and heard the echo of dripping water and muffled sighs. I wondered if this place was haunted and if these were the cries of ghosts suffering eternal torment, but it was just the janitor suffering a more earthbound reflection on his fortunes.

Friendly shopkeepers on the road, Azerbaijan

IT WAS ANOTHER DAY OF ABUSIVE ROADS AND AN UNRELENTING headwind, with a fierce dry heat that felt like a hairdryer pushed into my face. After a barren 130 kilometres (and 2,400 telegraph poles), the empty savanna transformed into a complex circuitry of industrial metal pipes, covering the desert like a giant net; the start of Baku's petrochemical plants. I felt a slight but cool breeze on my face and glimpsed a sliver of brilliant turquoise glinting under the cloudless sky. I had reached the Caspian Sea at last.

Azerbaijan's oil provides substantial economic benefits (for a few, at least) but the scars of progress are not easily hidden. The coastline is a dreadful display of the detritus of the oil industry with abandoned shipping containers, cranes, winches and large rusting pieces of unidentified metal sitting in a polluted, eerily quiet wasteland. Apart from the occasional truck entrance, the nearest sign of life was often no more than the mechanical derricks, a sandy coup of giant mechanical roosters picking resignedly at the same piece of land, again and again.

With an azure sky and the ocean as a backdrop, this stark scene was quite beautiful in a way, and as I followed the highway towards Baku, the long monotonous stretches of heavy industry were occasionally relieved by seaside resorts with manicured grounds and luscious white beaches. Judging by the line of tinted-windowed Hummers and BMWs queued up at the security gates, they weren't just open to just anyone, and I was turned away every time. Even so, the sight of deck chairs, beach parasols and families and couples swimming and sunning themselves nudged me happily back into a state of normality. Before long the road had moved closer to the sea, separated now by only a narrow spit of parkland, and I was in the Baku suburbs, the majestic state of decay of the older buildings oddly in tune with the more modern eyesores.

There were some beautiful women in this city, many to be found on the arm of some overweight, puffy-faced sugar daddy, often Caucasian and more likely than not an oil industry expat, living his US Dollar/Euro package to the full. It had been quite a while since I had been exposed to this much flesh and it was intimidating. I couldn't compete, and neither could my lodgings, the centrally located Hotel Azerbaijan, cheap and nasty, which was rapidly becoming my speciality.

"It's hard to imagine a scenario in which a stay at the Azerbaijan Hotel would ever be a good idea", I read in my guidebook, after checking in. I was staying in a musty room with a dodgy lock that had been forced too many times; it lay off a cavernous unlit corridor where people (men? women?) wearing far too many layers of clothing lurked in the shadows like drug dealing Wombles. On the mouldy wall above my tiny soiled bed was a faded poster of pristine alpine scenery, snow-capped mountains framing swathes of lush green forest and a small idyllic hamlet of Swiss lodges that looked as clean and wholesome as the Sound of Music cast. Opposite was an ill-fitting rotten wooden door which opened into a puzzling long and narrow room, full of refuse, impenetrably dark and not entirely noiseless.

Yet life was good. The sights and sounds of a modern city were a welcome and immediate reprieve from the barren tedium of the last few days, and a break from the assault of the wind and sun of the Azeri hinterland; it would also be my last opportunity to enjoy some cosmopolitan comforts for a while. After all, I was here for a reason; to board a ship to Turkmenistan, and the beginning of my Central Asian adventures.

~

LONG BEFORE THE MODERN RELIGION OF OIL, AZERBAIJAN HAD entertained a number of other faiths: Zoroastrianism started as far back as the 6th century BC, Christianity from the 4th century AD and then the steady emergence of Islam three hundred years later, going on to dominate the region by the second millennium. Its history was long, and Baku especially prospered as a major hub on the Silk Road, shipping oil, carpets, spices and, of course, silk through its harbour. Some of this rich legacy was still preserved in the walled old town of Icari Sahar, a mediaeval escape from the bling of the modern city.

In here, ancient lanes wound haphazardly past old mosques and cobbled courtyards, through small gardens of olive trees and trellises of flowers adorning the red mudbrick walls. The *Qiz Qalasi* - Maiden's Tower - was the oldest structure, dating from the 7th century, and perhaps the most iconic. A thickset structure, looking like an upturned bolt with its threads running around the top two-thirds, it provided a panoramic outlook over the Caspian Sea and the rest of Baku.

However, there were errands to run, and I had been feeling pressure to buy everything I might need while I still could, before I boarded that ferry to the Badlands of Central Asia. Guidebooks on the Stans were few and far between and detailed only sights and lodgings in the main cities, there rarely being any mention of the long stretches of scorched scrubland and desert in between. The only books that did offer more information were the history books I had read, recounting the initial forays into this region by British and Russian explorers during the 18th and 19th centuries, and those stories dwelled heavily on tales of armed brigands, and random desert ambushes by Turkoman slave traders. They were not what I would call a relaxing read.

Everything took a long time to get done in Baku. I had arranged to have some essentials sent to the FedEx office and spent a morning locating an address in the outskirts that I'd been given by FedEx, not easy when the signs are in Cyrillic, nobody speaks English and the police can't be trusted. Aside from bike spares and books, far more importantly it contained the latest instalment of maps, taking me through Central Asia and as far as Western China. Maps like this were priceless in this part of the world and impossible to buy locally. This was actually the second shipment - my first was meant to have been delivered to the central post office in Erzurum but nothing had turned up, so I had activated my Plan B, which was to get the same maps shipped by courier to the next major city on my route (I had bought duplicates of everything in advance, in case of this eventuality).

Another task was to find a place that would exchange my travellers' checks (difficult) and get the substantial wad of cash safely back to my hotel room (very difficult). I hid most of the funds in the bike itself - $800 stuffed up the saddle post and another $700 hidden in the stem. Other smaller amounts I stowed deep in my panniers and a little in my underwear (no fear of having that stash stolen). The old traveller's trick of a dummy wallet filled with a little cash and some out-of-date ID (business cards, Blockbuster membership, and so on) proved a useful decoy on more than one occasion, especially in the Baku subway system where the half-drunk, unshaven, bulbous-eyed cops (yes, they really did look like that!) were more difficult to avoid.

Two of them stopped me at the entrance to Sahil station, and the sergeant performed a cursory check of the contents of my backpack.

"Terrorism. Terrorism..." he repeated tiredly. And then with far more enthusiasm:

"Wallet! Wallet!"

He emptied its contents into his deputy's grubby cupped palms and fondled a couple of the banknotes with his fat sausage fingers, clearly disappointed that there was not enough here to get away with any tricks, and he indicated that I should go and treat them to a bottle of vodka instead. He did this by craning his head up a little and flicking his throat - this was Central Asian sign language for "I want a strong drink", and I would see it repeated hundreds of times between here and China (I would get pretty good at it myself).

I pretended not to understand. Even as he pointed at a bottle of the stuff on a nearby kiosk shelf, shouted "Vodka! Vodka!" and started flicking his throat again at a bruising intensity, I gave him a clueless look and shrugged my shoulders. Then when I started talking about bicycles (including my own well-rehearsed pedalling gesture) they finally gave up, exasperated, and let me go.

THERE WAS AN AIR OF MYSTERY ABOUT THE FERRY THAT RAN between Baku and Turkmenbashi. A phantom ship that everyone had heard of, but few had ever seen; no one seemed to know who ran it, or even if it still existed. I made my way down to the passenger port marked on my tourist map, finding nothing but a giant granite building, severe concrete columns and dozens of impracticably tall steps leading up to an ornate gothic facade covered in uneven scaffolding. The windows and doors were boarded up and rubbish littered the perimeter. I could tell it was Soviet – dark clouds were forming above – but I wasn't sure if it was in a state of renovation, or a state of disrepair.

A solitary man sat at the foot of the steps smoking, the only soul seemingly for miles around, and quite obviously waiting for me to approach him.

"Ferry?" he asked and nodded across to his taxi parked nearby.

The ticket office was a windowless prefab hut, fronted by a muddy forecourt and located down a confusing myriad of side streets. The odds and ends of rusting ship iron in the yard and a pot-holed track that led to the quay, were the only signs that it was somehow marine related. The old man sitting on the steps and enjoying a beer was at least wearing a sailors cap.

It took two hours and a half dozen cups of tea to explain to him that I wanted a ticket to Turkmenbashi, and he to explain the documentation and conditions, leaving a trail of scribbled drawings and numbers on scraps of paper by the end of it. We had come to an understanding, but the departure schedule was still a mystery.

"Every couple of days," he said, "give or take a day. Departing eight o'clock in the evening... give or take twelve hours. There's actually one departing tonight."

He paused, musing over his statement. "But then again, that might be tomorrow."

~

It was my longest break from the bike since Istanbul and I covered a lot of ground on foot, much of it spent tripping over potholes and the curiously tall kerbstones of Baku's unlit streets. My left knee had started aching, a blunt pain at first, but in the course of several excursions around the city it had grown more and more uncomfortable. I had dismissed it as inconsequential, nothing that a little rest wouldn't fix, but it was impossible to ignore any longer as the mounting discomfort first slowed me down, and then – suddenly and distressingly - stopped me in my tracks.

The hotel was just a few blocks down the street, but I could barely move. Every step felt like a bullet fired high up into my kneecap, the pain making me swear and gasp.

My ferry would leave in 24 hours, and in less than 48 hours from now I was to arrive in the port of Turkmenbashi, a tiny enclave sandwiched between the vast Caspian Sea and the emptiness of the Karakum Desert, the hottest desert in the world. Less than three days from now, I should be back on my bike and cycling through this very desert in the height of summer, under the forbidding cloak of one of the most secretive and paranoid nations in the world, devoid of modern medical facilities and equipped with just the barest of communications infrastructure. Yet right now I couldn't even walk the last hundred freaking yards to my hotel!

I hailed a taxi and asked him to take me to a doctor, faint with the worry of it all. The doctor knew a little English and with the use of my English-Russian dictionary I described the symptoms; with another taxi ride across town for X-rays, it was evening before I got back to him for an analysis of the results. He held the image up to the light.

"You have osteoarthritis", he said, pointing to the word in a medical dictionary and then pointing to the jagged edge of my knee shown on the X-ray plate, looking like the blade of a saw.

"This is an old person's disease", he said, smiling sympathetically. "Very unusual in a young person like you. There is no cure of course, but progress of the disease can be... slowed."

All kinds of things were going through my mind. Slowed? *Slowed?* How about *stopped?* How about some bloody pills which will fix everything, and I can be on my way? A flurry of dictionary activity followed, the doctor also displaying some considerable mime and gesture skills himself, in explaining his recommended treatment.

"I would strongly suggest a ten-day course of physiotherapy, acupuncture, massage and oil baths. This is the most effective treatment."

It was an unusual prescription and I was somewhat intrigued about the oil bath - but I didn't *have* ten days! I barely had *one* day, as I had to be on that bloody ferry tomorrow night otherwise my whole plan would collapse. The visa would be void, the painstaking arrangements through Turkmenistan on which I had spent so much time and energy would have been in vain, and any subsequent documentation invalid. It was a catastrophic turn of events.

The doctor thought about it for a couple of moments, considering my predicament. Impressing on me again that I should get treatment as soon as it was practicable, he did however have a Plan B: drugs. He wrote a prescription for regular oral painkillers as well as vials of a stronger drug, with syringes, "for the bad days". Then he called in a nurse to stab me in the bum with the first dose, to show me how it's done.

"Take this and show to any doctor", he said, writing down his diagnosis and passing me the piece of paper, along with the X-ray images, to take with me. He saw the bewildered look on my face as I tried to make sense of the lines of Cyrillic.

"Don't worry", he told me, smiling. "Every doctor can read Russian, even in Japan!"

Back in my hotel room I considered the situation under a growing cloud of anxiety. By my reckoning I still had over 10,000 kilometres to cycle, and most of that through some considerably challenging terrain and countries – some terrifying countries in fact – and I wasn't expecting any decent medical facilities until at least the tourist cities of eastern China, four or five months away. I had a debilitating medical condition that could presumably flare up at any time with little warning, and I might well be in the middle of the desert or stuck high on some mountain pass when it did, helpless and alone. I looked again at the damned X-ray photos scattered on the bed, close to tears.

How could I continue with this thing? Just how the hell could I go on?

The cloud of despair lifted, and I felt the slow tentative progress of a smile across my face, the muscles somewhat out of practice. This, I realised, was just what I had been looking for.

~

ALTHOUGH THERE ARE MANY LESSONS TO BE LEARNT IN attempting any kind of adventure, the most important one I learnt is this: accept that you have a split personality. Then, figure out which one you are inhabiting at any one time.

One of those people is the visionary, the one who thought of the whole idea in the first place, instilled in you the passion, fired up your imagination and urged you into doing something about it. The adventurous fellow who sees opportunity in adversity, who reads the British Consulate homepage warnings like a travel guide. However, when he's not around, you might be left in the company of his associate - the pessimist. Unwaveringly cautious, this guy sees nothing but a succession of steps (too few in truth) that lead to calamity. Watch out for that one. He's the bloke who interprets the daily drudgery of a tedious office existence as a comfort, a sanctuary from uncertainty, and his was now the voice jabbering excitedly at me, telling me this was my Get Out of Central Asia Free card.

He pointed out, quite reasonably, that I had been looking for an escape option, a face-saving about turn. That the fears lurking at the back of my mind since I started this endeavor were all too real. Of course, they might have been hidden during the easy riding and the pleasant and familiar surroundings of Europe, but as I found myself in tougher, altogether more exotic lands, I had been getting increasingly cold feet about the whole enterprise.

But now - at last! - I had legitimate reason to call the whole thing off. Look on the bright side, he whispered in conspiratorial tones, London to Baku is itself a mightily impressive journey.

I played the scenario out in my head in detail, how I would announce stoically to family and friends.

"*Yes, osteoarthritis of all things - an old person's disease apparently. Damned unlucky really, but the pain was just too crippling to continue.*"

People would sympathise. I'd show them the evidence of the X-ray photo buried in my panniers, and they would shake their head sadly, commiserate on my misfortune.

"*I'm just amazed you made it as far as...*", they would falter a little, having never heard of Azerbaijan, much less Baku, "*... as far as you did. You must be devastated - but who could blame you, with a knee looking like that.*"

With the story settled, I went to bed and slept soundly, comfortable in the knowledge that I didn't need to worry about Turkmenistan anymore, or any of the other dreadful countries following it, knowing that I could be back home in England in just a few days. This was a face-saving way to pack it all in, a completely plausible story that conveniently skipped over the true reasons behind my premature retirement – that it was just too bloody hard, and I was just too bloody lonely. When my head hit the pillow that night, I was convinced it was all over.

Yet when I awoke the next morning it was the most remarkable thing... something I still haven't figured out. I had reached rock bottom and had a face-saving reason – some might say imperative reason - to quit, but the weak-willed charlatan of the previous night had vanished, and the optimist was back in town, elbowing his way back into my psyche, stubborn and determined. Only by coming this close to giving up had I acquired the resolve to carry on, and I'd be damned if I was going to quit now!

It was my born-again moment.

"Harden the fuck up Steve", I had been repeating to myself countless times over the course of the last few thousand miles. And now at last, it seemed I had.

THE FERRY WAS TO LEAVE TONIGHT, AND NOT A MINUTE TOO

soon. Baku was a fascinating city, worthy of more than the superficial browsing I had lent it, but I was glad to be getting out of that damned hotel. I sat on the makeshift terrace of a restaurant by the ferry port and watched the sludgy sea lap up against the concrete walls of the promenade. Couples walked hand-in-hand along the seafront while I ruminated over the map of Central Asia laid out in front of me.

Two tough looking characters sat at the next table, both attired in chunky gold rings and heavy medallions. Seeing that I'd finished my meal, one of them smiled over at me and with a quick flick of the throat, invited me over to help polish off their bottle of vodka.

"Ahmed", he said, sweeping his arm across his chest as way of introduction, and gestured over at his companion, "Nabul". They were brothers.

I turned down their offer of vodka, having just taken a shot of painkiller in the bum, but the map proved a far more successful icebreaker, and I traced my fingers over the route I had taken, patting the panniers of my bike. As I listed the names of the countries and cities I had ridden through, the more animated both of my new friends became. Ahmed was impressed and mentioned something about hotels. I couldn't understand what he was saying, and he called a number on his mobile phone, rattled off some fast Azeri into the receiver for a minute and handed it to me.

"Hello, is this Mr Steve?" said a young woman's voice at the other end, business-like. It was his secretary, she said, acting as a translator for the both of us.

"Mr Ahmed has told me to inform you that he is the director of Tale Construction. It is one of the biggest construction companies in Azerbaijan, and he invites you to stay at his hotel."

I was lost for words, while she continued.

"It is five-star resort hotel, just outside Baku, and you will be the personal guest of Mr Ahmed. He likes your story very much."

Ahmed was grinning at me, nodding expectantly while his brother smiled. She was back on the line, asking if I would accept, while I silently cursed this ridiculous Turkmen visa for the second time in twenty-four hours and declined the offer. So much pain, so much frustration for one country - it had better be worth it.

The ferry finally slipped into the darkness of the Caspian around

10 pm, creaking horribly after the last consignment of steel pipes had been loaded. Boarding was quick – there were not many passengers going to Turkmenistan – and the heavy bike was tightly secured to some railings above deck. The young deckhand smirked at me after tying up my bike, flicking his throat a couple of times. Best to keep him on my side I figured, so I tossed him a dollar. Tomorrow, with my creaky knees, I would be stepping onto the parched soil of one of the world's most secretive countries, an empty desert nation run by a paranoid, self-worshipping megalomaniac.

And all things considered, I was rather looking forward to it.

"Democracy is not an apple you can buy at the market"

CHAPTER 11

ASHGABAT - A DICTATOR'S
DISNEYLAND

I was to meet my guide, Dimitri, after disembarking from the ferry and passing through Immigration. This was a condition of the Turkmenistan tourist visa: you had to hire the services of a government approved agent. Ostensibly he was there to get you through the country in relative safety, but he was also there to keep tabs on your whereabouts; the hidden microphones in tourist hotel rooms and restaurants and a healthy number of informers amongst the local population would take care of the rest. "In the event that you can find Internet access", said my guidebook, "rest assured that the authorities will be likely reading your email."

The man behind this paranoia was President Saparmurat Niyazov, originally an obedient Soviet Politburo favourite, groomed to take power after independence as a discreet puppet of the Russians. Yet on doing so, he rather surprised everyone when he denounced them and immediately gave himself the new name of President Turkmenbashi ("Saviour of the Turkmen people"), did away with the month of April (renaming it after his cherished mother instead) and while he was at it, renamed January after himself. And why not? In the tradition of all good dictators, he then started an extravagant program of monument building to honour his achievements, and on a more spiritual note cast himself as the conduit for messages from God, rewriting history in a colloquial collection of mad ramblings and dodgy theology in the form of the *Rukhnama*,

Book of the Soul. It was compulsory reading for all citizens and had been insidiously introduced into increasingly more aspects of their downtrodden lives, from sitting an exam on it to proceed into any form of higher education, through to making it part of even the driving test.

However, it came with some good news.

"I have interceded with God", Niyazov had announced to his people, "and he has told me this: if you read the *Rukhnama* three times you are guaranteed a place in heaven."

One of my fellow ferry passengers, an Azeri teenager with tight oiled hair and a gold chain around his neck was wearing a jumper in the 48-degree heat. He was on the way to Ashgabat "for business" and offered to take my photograph as we approached Turkmenbashi port.

"Smile!" he instructed, but there was nothing much to smile about. Beyond the cobalt blue of the ocean was a craggy brown-yellow escarpment housing a snatch of one and two storey apartment blocks wedged tight up against the Caspian Sea. Rusty tugs and floating cranes lined up higgledy-piggledy against the shore like sickly carp in some neglected pond, hoping to be fed. There was a little greenery, brittle looking ferns here and there, but beyond the lip of the low cliffs forming this enclave I knew there would be nothing more. This really was the end of the Earth.

"Marginally more suited to habitation than the moon", had reported one of the earlier guidebooks to the region. I now understood why.

It took two and a half hours to get through immigration, but they were polite and disciplined, and nobody demanded a bribe, which I appreciated after the unpredictability of Azerbaijan.

"You are Steve", said a stern looking fair-haired man, suddenly towering above me, his tone more of a challenge than a question. Glaring at me through his blue-grey eyes, he extended his hand in a steely handshake.

"*Zdravstvuyte*, and welcome to Turkmenistan", he said, rather unconvincingly. "I am your guide. You will call me Dima."

Dima was perhaps best described as a Slavic version of Crocodile Dundee. A larger than life character, survival expert and extremely knowledgeable about the region, he would turn out to be surprisingly candid about the country and even about the president - when he was far enough away from any public places.

It would take almost two weeks to cycle through this country, heading east to the capital Ashgabat and then due northeast via Mary, site of the ancient Silk Road city of Merv. I would eventually cross the Amu Darya river (the ancient River Oxus) and then into Uzbekistan. At 90 dollars a day for Dima's services it could turn out to be expensive, but with the help of my Man in Kazakhstan I had been lucky enough to get in contact with three Swiss cyclists who were planning to travel through Turkmenistan around the same time, and I planned my schedule accordingly. They were coming directly from Iran and we would meet in Ashgabat in three days' time. From there we would share the services of Dima as far as the border - this would cut costs substantially for me but perhaps more critically it would provide some much-needed companionship through this, the harshest country so far.

I LET DIMA PUT MY BIKE IN HIS CAR — HE CONVINCED ME THAT this wouldn't be cheating as I would be cycling back this same way in the morning — and we headed to the hotel 20 kilometres down the coast. He drove a standard saloon car, a Japanese model, and I was secretly disappointed that it wasn't a battle-worn jeep with hunting rifles and drying camel skins. I mentioned as much to Dima and he snorted in derision.

"Yes, I have also a four-wheel drive for deserts, but you will not be cycling over sand dunes. Our roads are good in Turkmenistan."

On the way to the hotel we stopped at a beach, bleached sand and luminous sea stretching unbroken for miles. It was deserted but for a few people casually skirting the shore, fully clothed. It couldn't be more than a couple of hours to sunset, but I could practically hear the heat bubbling away at my skin.

"You can swim", suggested Dima — it felt more like an order - and apparently in a holiday mood himself, he took off his shirt and planted himself on the sand. It's not every day you get a chance to swim in the Caspian Sea, so I also stripped down to my cycling shorts (usually hidden under long trousers) and ran headlong into the surf, enjoying the relative coolness of the lukewarm sea water.

A burly looking bloke made his way across the sand towards us and Dima greeted him enthusiastically. He was another guide, a friend of Dima's, and was leading two other travellers around the country for three weeks – they caught up with us a few minutes later, an American and a German guy in their late twenties. The American was walking hand in hand with a young local woman, very pretty, who spoke as little English as he spoke Turkmen. She giggled in nervous embarrassment.

"Hey, I'm Andrew", he said, and we talked a little about our travels. He was animated and friendly and talked enthusiastically about Turkmenistan; this was his fourth visit to the country. He nodded across to the other guy and continued.

"I met Thomas on my first trip here and since then we've been coming back pretty much every year, mostly travelling together."

Thomas looked across at me sulkily and mumbled a greeting, whilst Andrew cheerfully carried on.

"You see this girl", he said, flashing a brief grin at his giggly companion. "She's beautiful, right? I want to take her home to the US and marry her, but do you know what this country charges a foreigner to take a local girl out of Turkmenistan?"

I admitted I didn't.

"Fifty thousand dollars. A fifty grand marriage tax! How the heck can anyone afford that?" He paused, and then smiled at me like an insurance salesman. "And anyway, why bother when there are so many others like her available."

I asked where he was going next and at this point Thomas interrupted, seemingly keen to change the direction of the conversation.

"We head into the desert interior, then north to Khiva. This country has some incredible history. In the desert there are ancient cities that have barely been touched. Every time we discover something new."

I asked Dima later about archaeological tours into the desert, something he mentioned that he leads.

"Ah, they are just sex tourists", he said disinterestedly. "Maybe see a few ruins, take a few photographs, yes. But mainly come for cheap sex."

Tonight's lodgings were a "resort hotel", standing isolated between the shores of the Caspian and miles of featureless desert. A number of two-storey wooden apartments centred around a patch of scrubland, an open-air restaurant on some rickety decking and no other guests. In the restaurant, which felt more like a nightclub, half a dozen attractive young waitresses gathered around to take my order, as long as it was Caspian sturgeon. I dined to the sounds of Europop echoing off the walls of the chalets and apartments; they cranked it up to full volume as I went to bed and the door vibrated violently in its frame all night.

It was somewhat of a shock to rise barely a few hours later, Dima banging on my door and ears ringing to the tune of "I'm a Barbie Doll...". Bewilderingly I found myself on the road at 4 o'clock in the morning, barely awake and cycling into darkness ahead. These early morning starts would be crucial if I was to make any progress in this country. It was the height of summer in one of the hottest deserts in the world, and by 11 am it already would be far too dangerous to do anything other than sit under a fan and sweat passively until the evening arrived. The landscape was blanketed in dark velvet and the sky punctuated with the pinpricks of stars, while the distant flares of oil and gas platforms could be seen far off into the Caspian Sea.

"Take this road", Dima had told me, "and I will follow behind."

It was the road we had come along yesterday, and I cycled cautiously through the darkness. I felt strangely vulnerable and uncomfortable, and I realised that this was the first time I had had to completely rely on someone else for my journey. I glanced behind but there was no sign of Dima's car and instead a police car pulled up alongside me, two red-eyed officers looking over.

"Hello, hello! Where from?" the nearest one on the passenger side slurred, unshaven and looking the worse for wear.

He flicked his throat two or three times, directing an inane grin at me. The driver joined in as well, throwing the car into an erratic arc each time he leaned forward to get a better view of me.

"Vodka!" he shouted, tirelessly. "Drink vodka!"

This could get a little awkward, I thought, as they dismissed my attempts to decline their invitation, and after what seemed an eternity Dima arrived, driving up behind me and shouting something at them from his window. After a short exchange they beeped their horn and a little unsteadily, accelerated away. We continued on without incident through the town and its outskirts, and after a brief rise through some hairpin curves, we were into the desert proper. At the first checkpoint spotty teenagers in oversized and faded pea-brown uniforms brandished automatic weapons and questioned me first in Turkmen, and then in Russian, getting increasingly frustrated as I shrugged my shoulders at their questions. Again, Dima saved the day, pulling up ten minutes later in his car and furiously berating the young recruits. They submitted quickly, performed a cursory check of my passport and papers and politely ushered me through, glad to get rid of this foreign nuisance and his scary Russian escort. I was starting to enjoy Dima being around; he could be quite useful.

"See you eighty clicks down the road", he said. "I will wait there. Should be no more problems."

Dima got in his car and sped off, a cloud of fine dust left in his wake and I took stock of the situation, viewing the panorama of sand and rock around me. How many minutes, I wondered, would it take me to fry steak and eggs on that rock? How many kilowatts of electricity could you produce with a couple of solar panels? And how long would it be before I die, I thought, eyeing the five litres of water strapped to the back of my bike. I missed him already.

A long scorching climb to a high plateau marked the start of a long stretch of arid scrubland and desert leading eventually to Ashgabat, over 500 kilometres away. There was just no relief from this freaking heat; I saw trees and lakes in the distance, but these were just mirages from telegraph poles and the asphalt of the road in front of me. As the hours progressed, my handlebar bag seemed to turn into an iron brazier of hot coals, fierce heat stirred up with every imperfection of the road's surface and forced by the wind into my face, drying my eyes and making it difficult to take a breath without searing my lungs. The sun, burning a 15-million-degree hole in the cloudless sky, showered me with javelins of boiling plasma, piercing every pore of my skin, making my head pulse with razor-sharp pain. This was utterly insane - how the hell could anyone live in this?

It was ten thirty when I caught up with Dima. I had reached a truck stop, with a few restaurants and houses. Dima's car was parked up at the side of the road, air-conditioning at full tilt and he was dozing in the driver's seat. The heat was immense by now and I tapped furiously at the window knowing that an oasis of cold air was so close.

"Come in", he said, gesturing to the passenger door and I leapt in, relishing the kick of air-conditioned air as the door opened.

"You know this?" he asked, flicking his throat with his thumb and forefinger, smiling for the first time since we'd met. Reaching into the footwell of the passenger seat he pulled out a cooler box and opened it, revealing a bottle of vodka and two glasses.

"The good stuff, for completing your first day", he said, pouring a generous portion for each of us. "We celebrate!"

Typical views, Turkmenistan

RELUCTANTLY I PUT THE BIKE IN THE BACK OF DIMA'S CAR; WE had to be in Ashgabat the day after tomorrow to meet up with the Swiss, and it was painfully obvious there was no way I'd be able to cycle the whole way. We drove for over an hour and stopped at his friend's house a little off into the desert. We would stay here tonight. It was a single-storey, well-constructed mudbrick house with some outhouses and a courtyard, and we made ourselves at home in the marginally cooler interior. While Dima and his friend chatted, I tried to sit totally still and not suffocate from the heat, perspiring profusely just through the effort of breathing in the torrid, heavy air.

Meanwhile, my thirst was relentless and glass after glass of water didn't seem to help. Our host passed me a two-litre bottle of warm, milky looking water, urging me to drink.

"Camel's milk", said Dima, pouring himself a large glass. "Very refreshing."

One-part milk to two-parts water, fermented to produce a slight alcoholic buzz and some bubbles, camel's milk is ubiquitous in Turkmenistan, cheaper than bottled water and outside of the cities, easier to find. Maybe it was the delirium overtaking me, but I didn't think it was all that bad - which was fortunate, because I'd be drinking gallons of the stuff over the next couple of weeks.

This was no way to live, I kept thinking, while Dima explained how the standard of living in this country was very high for the region, and gas and electricity were free for Turkmen citizens. That free electricity would surely be put to better use providing some decent air conditioning I thought, manoeuvring myself more directly in front of the fan grinding away next to us. Dima continued to boast about the country's economy, now talking about the price of gasoline.

"One dollar for 60 litres of petrol, or 80 litres of diesel!" he declared, which I admitted was damned cheap, but considering the few cars I saw on the road I expected that very few could take advantage of it - and those that could would still have to suffer a some badly potholed surfaces, despite Dima's claims. At least they would have air conditioning I mused, unable to shake off the thought. And they wouldn't have to suffer the state-controlled television.

There are eight television channels in Turkmenistan, all carrying the same dismal Stalinist footage of shiny new agricultural hardware and usually culminating with a squadron of tightly choreographed bright red combine harvesters, pictures of overflowing sacks of grain and the spectacle of farmers paying homage to their president. Yet that's not to say that the television was entirely without amusement. The next programme paraded world leaders, one by one asking President Niyazov for his advice on world affairs. First, a clip of some dignitary walking up some steps, then the scene abruptly changing to that of Niyazov smiling and rising from behind the desk of his presidential office. A brief shot of him shaking hands with an anonymous forearm, and then sweep back to Niyazov giving some sage advice to camera. Finally, pan to scene of the dignitary nodding his head in agreement and smiling - usually wearing a different suit, in a different room and possibly three or four years younger/older.

The editing was amateurish and hastily put together and I thought surely people couldn't fall for this rubbish, but with international news as tightly controlled as it was, strictly curtailed personal freedoms and an incessant cult of personality built up around the president, maybe this kind of crude propaganda really worked? I began to admire the imagination of the whole undertaking; among the "visiting" dignitaries you could spot Tony Blair, Silvio Berlusconi and even George Bush.

DINNER WAS A SIMPLE DISH OF *PLOV* - A MIX OF RICE, VEGETABLES and chunks of mutton - and afterwards we bedded down in the courtyard, on mats of camel hair.

"No need for a tent", explained Dima, "the camel hair is a natural repellent to snakes and spiders."

That's funny, I thought. Until now I hadn't been worrying about snakes and spiders.

A slight breeze kept flies and mosquitos away but didn't fix my raging thirst; I slept lightly and drank another two litres of water through the night. By the time dawn came I had already put in twenty kilometres, enjoying the cool of the early morning air and the complete lack of traffic on a road skirting the Karakum Desert. The absence of cliffs or rocky outcrops meant that I could witness the full glory of dawn over the desert, before the heat was turned to gas mark 10 and I started counting the hours to when it would be over for the day.

During the course of the morning I entered a wide arid valley, the landscape making some feeble attempts at greenery with small hard-leafed shrubs scattered around like dried petals. High craggy hills lay parallel to the road, folding into a line of much larger mountains, behind a blue-brown haze in the distance. These were part of the Kopet Dag range that separates Turkmenistan from Iran to the south. Scattered here and there were small oasis villages, a dozen houses suckling at a few green trees.

People averted their gaze from me when I passed and avoided coming close to me whenever I stopped, the complete antithesis of countries like Turkey and Iran. Maybe they were worried about who might be watching; behind those portraits of the president lining the road, was there a pair of beady eyes following our every move? Only out in the open did I have any chance to talk to someone; a couple of young men riding a beaten-up old motorcycle and sidecar pulled alongside me and shyly asked where I was from, any possible paranoia overcome by their curiosity.

In fact, it was a welcome relief knowing that I didn't have to entertain a score of villagers every time I stopped. The reticence of the people here meant that I didn't need to struggle in conversations going around in circles and show a friendly outgoing countenance to everyone I met. There was no need to play the diplomat and that alone was a big weight lifted from my shoulders. I could appreciate where I was and what I was doing.

Bloody Hell! I was cycling through the guarded and mysterious desert nation of Turkmenistan, my twelfth country on this trip, and I hadn't seen the inside of an office for nigh on five months. There were camels watching me from the side of the road with benign amusement as a long stretch of cracked asphalt disappeared into the wavering distance. It was nearing fifty degrees centigrade in an utterly barren landscape, torturing me with no sign of shade nor shelter, and I was overwhelmingly thirsty, crazed with the thought of a cold drink. My legs were cramping violently and the humongous image of a god-dictator looked down at me suspiciously from a billboard on the side of the road. Life, I thought, really doesn't get much better than this!

～

New friends, Turkmenistan

ON THE LAST NIGHT BEFORE REACHING ASHGABAT I STAYED IN Dima's own home in the western outskirts of the city.

"I have a very comfortable living compared with most Turkmen", he said, showing me into his apartment on the second floor. It looked like any modern flat you might find in a smart London suburb and he introduced me to his young wife – blonde, Russian and attractive - and his cute three-year-old daughter.

"My salary is about $1,000 a month, ten times the average person's", he explained, almost challenging me to question his financial solvency, "and I get paid in dollars."

The local currency was the Turkmen *manat* and the official exchange rate was 5,000 *manat* to the dollar. However, the only way for ordinary citizens to obtain foreign currency was on the black market, and here the rate was a staggering 25,000 *manat* to the dollar. So, Dima could make his salary go much further.

"I used to be an athlete when I was younger, competing in decathlon competitions all over Russia and the world. I was once under-20 federal champion of the USSR and I still hold the record for decathlon in Turkmenistan." He said this deadpan, as if giving me directions to the next checkpoint.

"I planned to go to the Olympics and make a lot of money – Russia treated its athletes well in those days - but then came the breakup of the Soviet Union and there was suddenly no money for sports." He sighed.

"So, I had to start again, look for something else to do. With all the travelling I did as an athlete I had picked up some English, and of course I was well known in Turkmenistan, so I became a guide."

This probably explained his apparent influence with the authorities. I was being guided through Turkmenistan by the Russian Daley Thompson.

THIS WAS THE ROAD TO DISNEYLAND. A SWELTERING CENTRAL Asian Disneyland with a rather sinister middle-aged and power-crazy Mickey Mouse, but a fantasyland all the same. Another blistering day in the desert and a final meandering, draining climb took me within ten miles of Ashgabat, and it was here that the realm of the Magic Kingdom truly began. The road was spotless; smooth, unblemished asphalt, no dust, no oil stains, no litter. Teams of women wandered the carriageway, covered completely from head to foot bar a thin slit between a face scarf and hat. These ladies were the brigade of street sweepers employed to keep this road clinically clean, sweeping the roads, painting and repainting the verges, and tending to the wide row of trees and plants running between the two lanes. A green line of life in an otherwise arid and sparse wasteland.

Niyazov had diverted water from the already depleted Amu Darya river to provide irrigation for this project, and the extent of his vanity became only more apparent the closer I got. My route approached the city from the south, joining the main highway from the Iranian border and I was practically alone on this wide six-lane highway, my only company being huge pictures of a semi-benign dictator smiling down at me. I was cycling into Berzengi district, the pride of the president's city planning extravaganza, and a central reservation half the width of a football field was a lush green thanks to the system of water sprinklers spanning the entire area and the silent army of sweepers watering plants and picking up imaginary litter.

A high-rise hotel reared up on my right, cloaked in white marble and elaborately designed in a crescent stretching away from the highway. In the centre, a column of glass elevators rose up its twenty stories while a wide concourse led to the impressive portico entrance, lined by water fountains gushing water into giant-sized marble lilies. A vast empty parking lot sat to the side and all of this was surrounded by a narrow belt of greenery that stopped abruptly at the hotel perimeter. An extravagant resort hotel in the middle of the desert, completely empty, eerily silent.

There were dozens of these enormous structures, some with gigantic blue tiled domes, others set within acres of Corinthian marble columns, and still more in an alliance of four or five identical buildings. Each one was as silent and deserted as the first. I started taking some photographs, and an exhausted mechanical whine announced the arrival of a Lada, appearing from nowhere, looking out of place in this marble city of the future. Two diminutive men in brown suits hurriedly struggled out of their seats, waving their hands and shouting towards me.

"No photo! No photo!"

They wouldn't leave me alone until I had put my camera away.

My own hotel was much further along the Berzengi strip and a little less flamboyant. Here, waiting among the obligatory portraits and marble busts of the President, I was to meet my companions for the rest of the journey through this country. Alex, Pascal and Evo were three old school friends from a small town in Switzerland, close to my age, heading to Beijing. They likely saved my sanity as I was long overdue for some company on the road. And if there was any country where you might question your sanity, Turkmenistan was it.

CHAPTER 12
SAND, MOSQUES AND ALCOHOL

The Lada is by far the leading make of motor car in Turkmenistan, and you can take it for granted that someone will stop when hailed, hungry for a little foreign currency. The one that stopped for us had been souped-up, the driver taking obvious pride in his custom leather seats, tinted windows and a massively loud sound system pumping out gangsta rap. Two pairs of oversized furry dice hung from the rear-view mirror – it seemed we had got a lift with Turkmenistan's only boy racer and we signalled our appreciation with a thumbs up sign, pleasing the young driver immensely.

We cruised down wide empty boulevards passing exquisitely manicured lawns and landscaped parks, a thin green sliver of flora pinched between the yellow sand and mountains either side, whilst being pounded by the violent chords of 50 Cents' "Get Rich or Die Trying". The only person outside was the occasional policeman at a traffic-less intersection. Our driver quickly tuned into a Turkmen radio station whenever we passed one, switching back again when we were safely out of range. It was against the law for a Turkmen national to listen to foreign music.

First up was the Olympic stadium, covered in the Niyazov de rigueur white marble and utterly deserted. I doubt if it had ever seen the presence of athletes although I was sure it had held its fair share of tribute parades to the president.

"No photo! No photo!"

It was difficult to take pictures wherever we went; there was always a policeman, soldier or just some guy dressed in plain clothes telling us to stop, and none of us wanted to risk our cameras being confiscated for this. The sights after all, were not beautifully crafted monuments or anything of historical significance. They were wacky and gaudy vanity projects from the president's skewed imagination turned into concrete, marble and precious metals.

There was the infamous Monument to the Independence of Turkmenistan; as tall as Nelson's Column it was more informally known as The Toilet Plunger because it looked so uncannily like one, adorned lavishly in white marble and plate gold. However, we may easily have been mistaken because the same stick and suction cup design had been applied to a great many other monuments and shrines that littered this vast windswept concrete piazza. Dozens of plungers, hundreds of fountains, lightly cloaking me in a cool spray whenever the gusts of wind played in my favour. I remembered the old Star Trek episodes from my childhood: Captain Kirk always seemed to get beamed to places just like this.

It was easier to identify the Arch of Neutrality, a "magnificently awful structure" as the guidebook described it, an 80-metre tall tripod, obligatory marble plating and crowned at the very top with a twelve-metre-tall gold effigy of the president, rotating in time with the sun, his outstretched arm and wide-open palm declaring to his adorers: Look! I give you sunlight as well!

For a few *manat* the guard let us take a lift to the top of the tower. Below was the extensive complex of Independence Square, another chunk of Ashgabat given over to the adulation of the president; the blue domed Palace of Turkmenbashi had hundred-foot-high drapes sporting his friendly face rolled down between the quarter-mile long row of Corinthian columns that formed its extended portico. On the other side of the tower we could see the various government ministry buildings, including my personal favourite, the rather Orwellian sounding Ministry of Fairness. On the periphery, framed against the skyline, were cranes engaged in the process of constructing a few more vanity projects, and beyond that were the Karakum wastes, bare rust-coloured mountains sinking into the horizon. The view from here unequivocally affirmed that yes, this really is a city built in the middle of the desert, a Brave New World of half a million hidden souls.

That evening we returned to the area again, walking the length of Landmark Park as the last rays of the sun turned the fountains gold and the statues of Turkmenbashi looked down in sated contentment. The marble plungers had now been lit up, a fluorescence of colour slowly changing between shades of green, blue and pink every few seconds. Dare I say this was rather well done, and I enjoyed the free spectacle.

A few families strolled around the piazza and I guessed that these were the wives and kids of government officials, no doubt living in the adjoining complex of opulent apartment buildings. Almost everybody else lived in vast, dreary complexes of old Stalinist tower blocks on the city outskirts.

The president's palace, Ashgabat

THERE WAS REAL LIFE IN ASHGABAT IF YOU LOOKED HARD enough. The Russian market, tucked away in the outskirts behind concrete tower blocks, was bustling with people selling, buying, laughing, negotiating. The stalls were invariably run by women, hair pulled back under light paisley headscarves, and there was a colourful mix of everyday groceries as well as luxury imports from Russia – for me that meant some peanut butter. In the evening we found an outdoor restaurant, and people danced and sang with far more abandon than I'd find back home, a mixture of native Turkmen and ethnic Russians; the local women in their unfussy but colourful gowns, the Russians with their tight skirts and big hair. They didn't mix too much but I saw no animosity – for everyone this was one of the few moments they could forget about the rigid autocracy under which they lived, and the lights were dim enough that for once you couldn't see the smirking face of the president, watching you from some statue in the shadows.

Another antidote to central Ashgabat came in the form of the Tolkuchka Bazaar, the largest outdoor market in Asia, held once a fortnight on the edge of the city. A gigantic and chaotic dusty maze of thousands of stalls sprawled over miles of desert, selling everything you might ever need (in Turkmenistan at least). A long walk takes you past hundreds of scooters, cars and trucks, all for sale at the right price, including the bus you came in on. Turn into the market proper, navigate past trinket sellers, sweet vendors, makeshift bakeries and a dozen tea stalls. Now you're a little disorientated and it's getting hot. Pyramids of melons, bales of rice, mountains of bread and a veritable rainbow of fruit and vegetables. Jeans, T-shirts, skullcaps, shoes and cashmere hats (in this weather!). Pots, pans, laundry soap, carpets, Turkmen rugs. Cosmetics, watches, Lada spare parts laid out in the dirt (lots of these). Camels as well, in the animal market next door. I couldn't see them, but I could hear them and smell them. There was even a bicycle stall, a heap of old rusty parts and worn tyres that had been waiting for years in anticipation of a visitor like me.

Wandering amongst the walls of red carpet and through the dirt alleyways, a dozen vendors ambushed me with a score of propositions. I found brief refuge in the depth of a teashop, sipping my tea, hiding behind clouds of steam from boiling urns, continuing to watch this manic activity repeated on other patrons from a few yards away. With this much chaos there was hope for this country yet!

But was there hope for us? We had eight days to cycle 650 kilometres north to the border town of Turkmenabat, from where we would cross the river into Uzbekistan and go our separate ways. The director of the agency that sponsored our visas had turned up at the hotel to meet us, and it soon became apparent that she hadn't been informed of all the details of Dima's assignment. She was looking considerably flustered on hearing that he was to shepherd us on our bikes through the region's hottest, cruellest and deadliest desert.

"Nobody", she said, "travels through Turkmenistan in summer". Then making sure she made eye contact with every single one of us, she continued. "And absolutely *no one* rides a *bicycle!*"

Dima said something to her in Russian by way of an explanation, but this only exasperated her more and she chastised us all once again.

"Sure, sure!" she cried, "You cycle between 5 am and 10 am when it is... bearable. But what do you do between 10 am and sunset?" she questioned us all furiously.

"What do you do when it is fifty degrees in the SHADE?"

I RECALLED THIS WARNING AS I SAT UNDER A SOLITARY CONCRETE roof, a hundred or so kilometres out of Ashgabat, trying to fit beneath a thin sliver of weak shade as the mercury rose to 53 degrees centigrade in the midday sun. It was my first cycling day with the Swiss, and the first time I had cycled with anyone else since I'd met Sylvain on the road to Istanbul. It was wonderful to be able to chat to someone again on my own wavelength, share a laugh, and share the burden against a tough headwind. Maybe it was due to the long period without company, but I was secretly sizing myself up against my three new companions. Who was stronger? How many kilometres did they cycle in a day? Were they going to more exotic countries than me? Who had the better travel stories?

So, when the Swiss had suggested that we stop here for the day, this strange bus shelter-like construction in the middle of nowhere, I didn't particularly protest. I knew this place would get very hot, very quickly but I didn't want to display any shortcomings so early on in our alliance. However, right now, we were quietly competing for the limited rectangles of shade under the broken roof, re-manoeuvring ourselves subtly as the angle of the sun changed overhead. Every breath I took felt like I was inhaling from an open oven; the heat was starting to hurt our throats and our lungs, and our supplies of tepid water were disappearing much faster than expected. In the last ten minutes, several long lines of savage looking thick-bodied black ants had also appeared on the scene, no doubt anticipating a grand feast later.

Dima had warned us about this but we (well, the Swiss really) had stubbornly insisted that this was as good a place as any. So he left us alone to suffer, knowing that this was a lesson we all had to learn. When he eventually returned several hours later, we could barely hide our relief, and he his self-satisfaction. He was accompanied by a couple of perplexed local men, incredulous that anyone (especially tourists) would choose to stay outside in this oppressive heat. They had brought us coca cola and cold beer and insisted that we follow them in their truck to the next village, about ten miles away, where we could stay in a hunter's lodge. It was mid-afternoon by now, and those few miles to refuge were the hardest miles I think any of us had ever done. Dima knew that we would all behave from now on.

The lodge was basic, but it had an ancient air conditioner cranked up full. At 35 degrees in the torpid air it was still fiercely hot, but a damned sight cooler than outside. The owner was a local hunter of some repute, a grizzled Turkmen who could have been anywhere between forty and a hundred years old and to whom Dima showed obvious deference - he was the type of man who had a great deal of respect for hunting.

We sat on carpets around a low table while Dima took out a bottle of vodka from his cooler (it was almost lunchtime, after all) and translated the name for us – "Fire!". It had a picture of the smiling president on the label. As he poured us all a generous measure, the hunter brought out plates of boar liver. Dima explained how our host had tracked and killed the boar this very morning, and we all listened in reverent silence as he translated, keeping one wary eye on the chunks of semi-raw meat in front of us. On the conclusion of the story ("...with a final shot in the head...") we all raised our glasses to the hunter and downed the first shot. There was a ten-second pause as we waited en masse for our sinuses to clear, and our eyes to start focusing once again.

"The vodka is good for your body", announced Dima, slowly moving around the table and refilling our glasses while we nibbled on bits of boar gristle.

"It is antiseptic for the stomach", he explained. "Kills all bacteria!"

Seemed like a good enough reason, so we raised our glasses for a second toast. "To antiseptic!" we cheered, downing a glass of the president-branded vodka again.

There was actually some truth to this statement, as eating and drinking is not done in the most hygienic of conditions. Usually the meal is dumped onto a greasy mat, laid on the table for communal use by the diners, and everyone has their hands and fingers in it. Vegetables are washed in the nearby canal or stream, and meat has to be eaten pretty much as soon as it's slaughtered. Vodka is indeed the Alka-Seltzer of Central Asia.

Alex was not much of a drinker – he had only managed to down half the first shot, missed the second round, and was now taking short urgent sips to try to finish off his glass before the next one. Dima was getting more and more agitated and suddenly, patience exhausted, he pointed his finger accusingly at Alex.

"You", he pronounced, bristling with anger, "are an alcoholic".

We all looked perplexedly at Dima.

"You know why?" he asked, turning his gaze of disdain upon the rest of us while we shook our heads nervously. "Because taste of vodka is terrible! Only alcoholics like the taste of vodka enough to drink it slowly."

While we all pondered this lesson in Russian psychology, he refilled the rest of the glasses and we threw the shots back. There was another important reason for the vodka: sleep. Without this alcoholic assistance it would be just too damned hot to sleep, and there was certainly nothing else to do.

TODAY IT WAS 11 AM BEFORE WE FOUND ANY SIGN OF HABITATION – a teahouse by a bridge – and the heat was already unbearable. It is worth pointing out that a teahouse here is not a quaint rustic shop of antique furniture, deeply varnished wooden panelling and half a dozen varieties of scone on the menu; there are no embroidered cushions on heavy chairs and no crisp white dollies on the table. A teahouse of the Central Asian variety is a single storey rectangular dwelling, constructed from mud bricks if you're lucky or a hot flimsy wooden shed if you're not, sometimes split into two cramped rooms and likely hosting a camel-hair carpet or two outside on a bare wooden platform for seating and sleeping. And there will always be a couple of wizened old locals in the corner, whispering quietly to each other.

We spent the next nine hours here, in a stationary cycle of sweating and drinking fake Fanta and camel's milk, keeping any movement to an absolute minimum. This was madness! I wondered again, how on earth can people live like this? It was a dry brittle heat with zero humidity; I hand-washed my clothes in a bucket and they were bone dry within fifteen minutes of hanging them up.

In the evening it had cooled down enough to set up camp down by the canal, a few hundred yards away from the teahouse. The full moon and stars lit up everything in an eerie white glow. We pooled our food for dinner and the Swiss turned into a highly synchronised cooking automaton, pulling out pots and pans, knives, chopping boards and other bits and pieces; it was obvious they had been doing this for some time, so I peeled a few vegetables and left them to it. The breeze from the canal made the heat quite bearable and foiled the few mosquitos lurking in the air. It was actually a pleasant evening until I chose to make use of the outdoor toilet facilities of the teahouse further up the bank.

A dark mass of loud, rustling movement greeted me from the pit below, shafts of moonlight bouncing off the black shiny shells of a hundred thousand busy creatures four feet below me. I imagined the unseen antennae of some exotic desert-dwelling beetle stroking my exposed buttocks and had a sudden change of heart, doing my business in a self-made hole outside instead. Returning to the tent I double checked that my zip was properly fastened shut that night.

~

"IT'S TOO HOT TO WRITE ANYTHING."

This was the first and the last entry in my diary for the next two days. Mid-morning, we passed up the temptation of a shady grove of trees by a small brook – by now we had learnt enough to know that it would turn into a furnace in the next few hours – and we carried on until we found a teahouse, the considerable heat-retaining qualities of its cheap plasterboard and corrugated iron construction offset by a single fan rotating in a tortuously slow arc of 120 degrees, side to side. I became obsessed with the few moments I was blessed with a faint breeze at each rotation, unable to concentrate on anything except the thirty seconds I would have to wait before it fleetingly passed my way again. But at least this place had some entertainment, in the form of a portable TV and video unit; there was no aerial and only one warped and fuzzy video which we watched twice – Rolf Lundgren in Red Dragon, all the better for being dubbed into Russian.

Halfway through the second screening Dima picked up a small plank of wood, ushering us to keep still while he wandered over to the corner of the room. There was an almighty crash as he brought it down hard on the tiled floor, making us jump and even stirring the lethargic owner from her cot in the other corner.

"*Faranga*", he announced, satisfied, showing the still twitching corpse of an eight-inch-wide hairy yellow spider on the end of the piece of wood.

"Very poisonous. No vaccine. Probably die if bitten", he explained. "A very slow death", he added happily.

That night we camped outside, and I triple checked that the zip was properly fastened shut. Dima, as was his habit, unrolled a camel hair rug from the trunk of his car and slept on that.

YOU DON'T NEED TO SUFFER A SLOW PAINFUL DEATH TO BE annoyed by the bugs here. Mosquito bites, ant bites, bedbug bites, mite bites and a dozen other blood-sucking insect bites had my skin looking like an Aboriginal painting. I probably had fleas by now as well. Oh, and the flies! Swarms of them hovering around you, attacking anything moist.

"I feel like a damned horse", Pascal said dejectedly, waving his hands ineffectually around his head. "A ring of flies around my eyes, up my nose and another swarm of them buzzing around the corners of my mouth."

We made good time today, arriving in the main oasis town of Mary by mid-morning, having drafted the last thirty miles at speed behind a huge convoy of articulated lorries, transporting brand new combine harvesters to the north of the country. It was an exhilarating, surreal and sometimes scary experience, slipping in and out of the gaps between these agricultural behemoths, surrounded by clouds of dust, the smell of diesel and the sound of engines pulling heavy torque. We moved up and down the line of vehicles to locate each other as the half-mile long convoy speeded and slowed, and Pascal and I peeled off a few miles before our destination, taking a short break underneath a small cluster of skinny trees at a truck stop. We each bought a two-litre bottle of cold coke and greedily downed it, until the bubbles almost made us sick.

Mary was the launching point for trips to the ruins of Merv nearby, and for us it was a welcome day off. We had two nights booked in the salubrious Sanjar Hotel, a twelve storey Intourist facility from Soviet times, its prestige made all the more evident by a portrait of the president covering three of those storeys, leaning forward on one of his hands in a celebrity headshot, a wide Colgate smile and three volumes of the *Rukhnama* (yes, now three!) floating eerily behind him. Rather admirably, considering we were in the desert, my room was damp and mouldy rather than hot and dusty, but at least there was a functioning air conditioner, sounding like it contained a detail of miniature road workers plugging away on pneumatic drills.

The stopover in Merv was there to remind me that I was following the route of the Silk Roads. This had once been a major stopover on the way to the East, and for one brief period in the 12th century was reportedly the largest city in the world. It was rumoured to be the inspiration behind the tales of A Thousand and One Nights but there wasn't much left; this once splendid city had been put to the torch early in the 13th century in the name of Genghis Khan, his Mongol fighters following orders to decapitate 400 inhabitants each, slaughtering in total over a million men, women and children. Few structures survived this apocalypse.

The Mausoleum of Sultan Sanjar was an exception, a forty-

metre-tall domed cube, windowless and alone in the desert; it would
have been covered completely with blue turquoise in its day. The
interest for me was in the detail, both here and the other surviving
Silk Road sites; symbols of Islam lay alongside those of the khanate's
much older religion of Zoroastrianism, as well as Christian, Jewish
and even Buddhist emblems, showing how all religions had prospered here at one time. These and other ruins were for the most
part contained within the half mile wide enclosure of the Shahryar
Ark, the walls now just rounded mud ramparts and easy to climb to
get a better view of the empty desert-scape. Dromedaries lurked
half-hidden in patches of tall wiry grass, chewing contentedly on the
sparse offerings and viewing me with lazy-eyed insolence, while their
pre-adolescent herders whacked the errant ones back to the vicinity
of its companions.

Archaeology had become a passion of Dima's since he had
started to guide so many expeditions to the more remote regions of
this country, and he explained articulately about the remains and
the significance of some of the discoveries. He claimed that
although Mesopotamia (an area covering modern day Iraq, southern
Turkey and Iran) was commonly known as the cradle of civilisation,
the artefacts uncovered by the expeditions he had accompanied
here had thrown up a lot of new questions. Sites uncovered in the
area of Gonur Tepe, thirty miles south of here, dated from earlier
than 3,000 BC and already showed signs of domesticated horses,
carts, and ornate and intricate golden vases. This all pointed to
another, older civilisation, he said.

And this was probably the only subject (outside of hunting) that
exacted real emotion from Dima and offered us some insight into
his real feelings about the president.

"Excavations are badly underfunded, and most money goes to
government people", he said. "We could learn so much, but if we
find anything valuable it's immediately confiscated before any
analysis can be done. This is by orders of the president, for his own
private collection." He spat into the sand.

Turkmenistan was practically littered with ancient artefacts, he
said, and deep in the desert you can still find objects breaking
through the surface, untouched for centuries if not millennia. He
himself had uncovered two five-foot vases, each over a thousand

years old. He kept these in his own house, he admitted, which was strictly against the law.

"Better me than the president", he told us, defiantly.

In the evening we visited the local club in the hotel basement; a dark room, a single white strobe light and two large speakers... the bare minimum to meet the definition of nightclub. There were a number of young ladies in the flickering darkness, but we huddled close together, feeling suddenly quite vulnerable and naïve, suspecting that these were probably "working girls". Perhaps desperate to avoid the slightest suggestion that any of us might have some kind of world cycling sex tourist thing going on, we all made mighty efforts to avoid conversation with anyone else in the room, and left still unsure if they were really regular guests, and we had just unfairly labelled them professionals.

The next morning Dima put us right on this.

"Of course they are working! Ten dollars for the night, fifteen for a good one."

According to Dima, every receptionist, every cleaner, every shop assistant - they were all available for a bit of hard currency.

"I get best choice", he added, "because I have car."

He couldn't understand our delicate Western sensibilities on the simple transaction of exchanging money for sex. No big deal. In fact, Dima saw it as a way of spreading wealth, almost an altruistic action. His philosophy on this was quite simple.

"Once you reach thirty", he told us, "you should always pay for it."

The president and his Rukhnama collection

~

THERE WAS ONE VILLAGE AND ONE TEAHOUSE ALONG THE 260 kilometre stretch of road between Mary and Turkmenabat and nothing but the changing landscape to entertain us. The morning started with sweeping sand dunes, redolent of scenes from Lawrence of Arabia, later transforming into sparse, scattered tracts of trees. Stumpy, sorry-looking things, they had roots which delved as deep as forty metres underground, seeking out the barest hint of moisture for their survival.

The road undulated up and down, the effort wearing us thin and it was just after eleven o'clock when we arrived at the teahouse, overheated and close to collapse 120 kilometres later. Fortunately, Dima had negotiated the rental of an air conditioner from a house in the nearby village; as soon as he turned it on three boys from the village rushed in, threw themselves on the floor and immediately fell asleep.

Dinner was a ram, slaughtered outside with methodical efficiency as the sun slipped behind the dunes with a final orange flourish. The poor animal's legs were trussed together and it hung struggling over a thick vertical pole lodged in the ground while its throat was slit, and the blood drained into a bucket. After a swift cutting and sawing action the head was removed and the skin pulled off in one go, like a magic trick. A few more expert cuts and the butcher reached inside to remove the poisonous gall bladder, throwing it into the puddle of blood in the sand.

Still somewhat inebriated from the lunchtime vodka ration, we each took turns in fixing the head to our handlebars and riding a few laps in the dirt; only after we had splattered our bikes with blood and sinew did we realise it was a bad idea. That wasn't the only bad idea we'd had that day. During the lunchtime toasts we were making some unflattering comments about the smiling picture of the president on the label of the vodka bottle. Dima had got increasingly irritated, eventually slamming his palm down in the middle of the table and demanding in a hoarse whisper that we give it a rest.

"You should *never* talk like that", he warned us. "You don't know who is listening."

We were in a house made of mud bricks and corrugated iron

over a hundred kilometres from the nearest town, and the only other customer was an arthritic man of about ninety nursing a cup of tea, sitting huddled in the far corner of the room.

"Don't trust anybody", said Dima, oddly unnerved.

Camel herder, Merv

THE COMBINATION OF TWO BOTTLES OF VODKA, HALF A DOZEN cans of Baltika No.7 and one goat did nothing to help our progress the following morning. The headwind was the strongest I had yet experienced and also the hottest; every gust felt like my face was being shoved into an open oven while the miles of empty desert either side of me incinerated any fantasies of shade or water. Pascal and I cycled ahead of Evo and Alex, but the wind wore us down and we stopped at a teahouse which we knew was the only one between here and Tukmenabat. Pascal ordered a two-litre bottle of Fanta for each of us while I visited the latrines. It was the standard design, a square enclosure surrounded by a tall wooden fence and a plank of wood balanced over an open cesspit below, but what made it extraordinary was the pile of poo that rose twelve inches above the top of the hole. Just when do you decide enough is enough?

The searing heat and wind kept us inside the teahouse, sweating Fanta as fast as we could drink it. At this rate it would be mid-afternoon by the time we'd arrive in Turkmenabat - this was just theory of course, because the reality was that we would be dead, charred crusts by the side of the road by then. We asked the owner if there was any likelihood of getting a lift to Turkmenabat and he relayed the request to his clientele: of the three vehicles parked in this desolate outpost only one was going our way, but apparently we would have to drink a huge amount of vodka with the driver first. It was 10 am.

Further procrastination produced no more offers, so we reluctantly remounted our bikes and headed back into the torment of the desert, with the intention of getting a lift on the road. It was too risky to wait any longer; as the day gets hotter the number of vehicles rapidly decrease as most are old and their engines easily overheat. Nobody wants to risk being stranded, not out here.

Thirty minutes later we successfully flagged down a truck. This twelve-ton rig was at least twice as old as its most senior occupant, but at eighteen years old the driver was still four or five years older than his two companions. They were all excited, childish enthusiasm showing through in their smiles and jokes as they eagerly helped us load the bikes in the trailer and made room for us in the cabin. Our teenage driver had to yank the steering wheel hard to the left and hard to the right just to keep it in a straight line, but it was nice to see the endless sandy horizon pass by at a decent speed, and our young friends were easily entertained. They let us out a couple of miles before the next police checkpoint and waved goodbye from the window as we mounted our bikes for the final stretch.

Dima caught up with us as we approached the checkpoint, livid with anger.

"You idiots!" he shouted. "What happens if you get caught? You go to jail, they go to jail, maybe worse. Probably me as well. You are *my* responsibility until you leave this country. Remember that."

Evo and Pascal were sitting in the car, having got a lift with Dima after they had also succumbed to the heat. We hadn't thought it through and regretted now the danger we had put the young driver and his friends in; but looking at our fellow cyclists squeezed in the car, their baggage piled up high on their laps and the bikes sticking out the trunk of the car, I didn't see that we really had much choice.

Turkmenabat was the last Turkmen town on our route and marked an ancient intersection of the silk roads. Turn west for Khiva, once central Asia's largest trading town but now a long lonely drive into the desert, or continue straight ahead over the wide, silty Amu Darya river and onto Bukhara, now in modern day Uzbekistan.

It was a subdued final evening and even Dima lacked his usual verve in hounding Alex or suggesting prices for waitresses and receptionists. I imagined he was glad to be rid of us. Perhaps it was also an acknowledgement that we would be fending for ourselves once more, no local knowledge, no one to herd us through police checkpoints and no one to dispatch poisonous arachnids on our behalf. The Swiss had invited me to join them at least as far as Samarkand, but I knew I was wearing out my welcome: they were three old school friends on an adventure of a lifetime who happened to have picked up a stray Brit along the way. We cycled together, ate together, slept together and they always spoke in English for my sake. Worst was my abominable snoring and more than once I'd heard Pascal mutter that he hadn't slept well that night as he fixed me with a brief, aggrieved stare over breakfast.

The party was over. In Uzbekistan I would be on my own once more.

Faranga!

CHAPTER 13

PARTYING WITH THE (UZBEK) SOPRANOS

Surveying the fast-flowing Amu Darya river brought back memories of my conversation at the Iranian truck stop a couple of months earlier; as promised, there was indeed an old military floating bridge, ten-metre-long rusty iron slabs strung out in a snaking line across the river. At rest each plate bobbed up and down no more than a few inches but whenever a truck crossed, this would expand to a foot or more. We each timed the crossing of these gaps carefully with a wary eye on the trucks passing us, lifting our bikes up or down as necessary and making it safely to the opposite bank.

"Welcome to Uzbekistan", said the sign in huge letters strung across the border post. The guards kept asking us to fill in more forms while feral kids pinched things from our bikes. The wind was howling around us; the frames of derelict buildings and an arid, bitter panorama screamed desolation, and it was no small relief when we arrived at the tiny frontier town of Alat. There was a single basic restaurant and we negotiated the use of a storeroom above it and an electric fan for our night's sleeping quarters.

Lunch was a mistake. The heat of the day had roasted my brain to a point that I ordered with some excitement what I believed to be something similar to a Sainsbury's style chicken and mushroom soup (Here! In the desert!) but - shockingly apparent at the first mouthful - turned out to be a bowl of tepid clotted camel's milk. Finding it now somewhat difficult to downplay my initial enthusiasm in front of the delighted restaurant owner, I forced myself to finish it all off, upon which she immediately gave me a free refill, smiling her mouth of gold teeth at me. Two hours later I threw up in front of the same establishment then made a sudden dash for the village's primitive communal latrines, for a brutal series of orifice flushing episodes. A miserable day turned into a miserable night, and by morning I was a dehydrated husk, nursing a ferocious headache and a fever.

Bukhara, only 75 kilometres away, was on the tourist map and would be far more comfortable than a hot and stuffy storeroom. I couldn't contemplate spending another hour here, baking in this room while being cajoled into eating a range of camel-flavoured snacks, so I forced myself to pack up and set off with the Swiss. They rode in close formation around my bike, blocking me from the wind that attacked in searing gusts trying to topple us from our saddles, as I pushed the pedals around in a semi-conscious mechanical daze. I continued to swiftly deteriorate and when we came to a halt I was completely spent. I could barely talk with the waves of nausea welling up inside of me, my head pounding hotly at my burning temples and no energy left to stand, never mind cycle. For every minute in the sun, I felt a year closer to my death.

It felt an eternity before an old jalopy stopped for us; the driver was heading to Bukhara and agreed to take me with him. The Swiss loaded my bike and gear into the rear, me into the front, and I said an enfeebled farewell to Alex, Pascal and Evo. The quiet road eventually transformed into a busy highway and my driver swerved madly and haphazardly across all of its lanes, narrowly avoiding donkeys, carts, pedestrians and other vehicles, all the while barking questions at me first in Uzbek and then in Russian, and occasionally skidding to a sudden halt when it looked like I might throw up again. The parched scenery and his frustrated words swarmed in and around my consciousness, his agitated tones discharging pulses of heat and pain.

At one point he pulled over and dragged me from the car and into the carriageway, and I thought, *okay this is it, he's going to dump me here and drive off with all my stuff* - but he was just excited to show me the view of a famous minaret. After an abominably long time we arrived in Bukhara and he dropped me off at the first guesthouse we came across, only letting me stagger through the gates, half-pushing half-leaning against my bicycle, once I had emptied my pockets of dollars into his cupped palms. There would be no negotiation today.

A bed quickly assigned, and me collapsing into it. A brief *I don't want to die like this* thought-bubble, escaping my stupefied mind.

Dizziness.

Skin boiling to the touch.

"Someone, get a doctor."

A nurse, taking my temperature: "Forty-two."

I woke up in the same bed, soaking, and a concerned-looking lady was explaining in broken English that she was trying to bring my temperature down. Over the next twenty-four hours she visited me a half a dozen times, changing ice packs and supplementing my supplies with whatever medication she had been able to get hold of. To me, a Central Asian Florence Nightingale, whom I never did find again to thank properly.

The fever broke, and although I was still weak, the wave of post-illness euphoria encouraged me to venture outside. My lodgings were a traditional house, all rooms opening onto a large central courtyard where much of the daily business of the household was carried out by the women, while the men lazed around with cups of jasmine tea under the shade of grape trellises. It was a haven from whatever madness might be going on outside the walls, and I would spend a happy few days here recovering and getting my strength back.

BUKHARA IS PERHAPS THE MOST QUINTESSENTIAL CENTRAL ASIAN city there is, a veteran of the Silk Roads, having been a centre of trade, religious scholarship and artistic endeavour for well over two millennia. The old-town area of Bukhara was beyond words, an enchanting potpourri of old mud brick buildings, covered bazaars, mosques and minarets. The centrepiece was the Lyab-i-Hauz, a pond surrounded by mulberry trees and low-key waterside restaurants, framed by 16th century madrasahs. Their grand gateways were encrusted with hundreds of thousands of tiny azure blue tiles, interwoven with intricate geometric patterns.

A further wander through the labyrinth of alleyways brought me to a complex of mosques and more madrasahs, including the elaborately tiled Mir-i-Arab and the Kalyan Minaret, or "tower of death" which was employed in executing people by throwing them to their death fifty metres below, and was still being used extensively up to the 1920s. From this, the tallest structure in Bukhara, the domes of dozens of madrasahs and mosques shone like cobalt gems sprinkled on a sea of sand.

The fortunes of two of Britain's famous Great Game heroes, Charles Stoddart and Arthur Connolly, were brought to a brutal end here in 1841 in front of The Ark, the grand fortress city I was now approaching. After suffering for a year in the darkness of its water and vermin-filled underground pits while being subjected to various tortures at the whim of the Emir, they were at last pulled out - and then publicly beheaded in front of a cheering crowd.

The Ark itself had impenetrable looking mud walls, twenty metres in height and hundreds of metres in length. It was open to tourists and although there was no sign of the original underground pits, the dungeon had been restored and populated with life-sized and uncannily realistic wax models of emaciated prisoners chained to the wall, miserable in their soiled and ragged clothes.

I took a few photographs and showed them to a group of young American tourists many months later in China, when explaining how I'd cycled through Uzbekistan.

"Visa overstay", I announced severely, keeping a straight face. "I was bringing them some food."

The youngest girl almost burst into tears, while her friends looked on in shock. Backpackers – they just don't make them like they used to.

TALL TREES LINED THE ROAD FOR THE FIRST HALF OF THE morning, throwing welcome shade onto my side of the carriageway while cotton fields stretched for miles beyond. There was no shortage of bustling activity going on at the roadside, wooden stalls piled high with watermelons, hubcap-sized slabs of bread, packets of biscuits, boxes of cigarettes... I passed teahouses with weathered old regulars sitting outside, wearing black and white skullcaps to a man and chatting languidly with each other as they relaxed on the raised and carpeted wooden platforms. The women wore colourful one-piece gowns and paisley headscarves in an ubiquitous regional ensemble, appearing and disappearing into narrow tree-lined tracks adjoining the main road and generally trailed by a gaggle of kids chasing after their flapping robes.

It was midday when I arrived in Navoi, a large albeit nondescript town 110 kilometres further along the road to Samarkand. The road had been flat with a slight tailwind, but even this modest effort hit me hard after my few days of recovery in Bukhara, and it would take longer yet before I would fully have my strength back. Harder still, psychologically at least, was the fact that for the first time in over two weeks I was riding on my own, the decisions solely mine to make, the responsibility for adventure or misadventure in my hands alone.

Lunchtime, and no sooner had I stopped to investigate what looked like a restaurant behind the inviting shade of some trees, a man spotted me, shouted "Hey! Hey! Hello!" and motioned for me to come over to join his table. There were half a dozen blokes sitting there, hard eyes and open smiles, dressed mostly in suits and open necked shirts. It looked like a Sopranos set, Uzbek style, backgammon swapped for playing cards, jasmine tea in place of coffee.

"Welcome, welcome! My name is Assad. Where from? On *that*? Come, come, you join for lunch!" he said cheerily and introduced each of his friends by name.

He could speak a little English and his friends looked on, impressed. I was once again the involuntary centre of attention, no other companions to deflect the scrutiny, no omnipresent dictator for them to fear, no bustling city to offer a sanctuary of anonymity. They ordered up some food and while we ate, I showed them my maps and with a little help from Assad, used words of English, Russian and Turkish to piece together a conversation. I was surprised at how enjoyable it was to be the entertainer again, but I was also battling a fast-rising tide of fatigue. After a couple of huge pitchers of beer arrived in my honour, I explained my recent illness and tried to excuse myself from the revelries.

"Wait. I have apartment and it is empty; you can sleep there for free" Assad said. "I will take you later."

Everyone was united in agreement: yes, it would be crazy to spend money on a hotel. And these did not look like the type of guys whose generous offer you could brush off lightly. So with that decided, his friends got out a few bags of marijuana and started rolling joints on the table. This can't be good I thought. I knew that the penalties for drug possession in this part of the world were famously advertised as "extremely severe". I imagined the inside of an Uzbek prison cell – and it looked exactly like the one I'd seen with wax figures a few days ago in Bukhara.

Dogma was the bearded and surly looking man in the corner, who hadn't yet said any word in any language. He looked up, fixing me with a fierce stare, and smiled at me as if reading my mind.

"Fuck the Police", he said.

With some feigning of stomach pains, I tried to extricate myself from the situation. Thanks. Would love to stay but. Really need to get some rest. Not feeling good at all. Don't worry yourselves. Stay here and enjoy. Can get a hotel. No trouble at all.

"Okay, no problem no problem, I understand you sick", said Assad, seeing my distress. "So I take you to apartment - now!"

As I followed behind his car, navigating my bike through the backstreets of Navoi, I had an ominous feeling about the whole enterprise. I could escape his escort but where would I go, and would that be some kind of serious insult in their minds? It was not like there was a tourist mob to blend in with - I *was* the tourist mob. I really had no alternative, so followed Assad to the foot of a decrepit apartment block. At least people lived here, judging by lines of washing on stained balconies and unseen screaming babies. There was no lift of course, so we pushed and carried my loaded bike up six floors and he opened the door to a dingy apartment, mildew forming on an old leather sofa and another doorway into a bedroom, a crumpled mattress on the floor.

"Sleep, sleep!" he urged and gave me the keys. He was busy this afternoon, he explained ("business"), but would be back in a few hours. The inside of the door was reinforced with steel bars and a deadbolt, and it took a few attempts to understand what he was saying, as he repeated a pattern of knocks on the door until he was sure that I'd got it.

"Don't open to anyone but me."

THE SOUND OF ASSAD BANGING AND SHOUTING AT THE DOOR woke me up.

"Hello", he beamed. "I bring friends!"

Two ladies followed him in, the first a petite young woman in a tight-fitting body stocking hidden under a long shawl, and behind her a darker slightly older girl with a short skirt and jacket covering a pink boob tube... these were not the type of women I typically encountered in Central Asia. Coming up the stairs right behind them was a friend of Assad's, a portly smiling chap, red-faced from his exertions and carrying an ancient ghetto blaster and some beers. It was party time.

We settled around the table and started on small talk, which in my case was a concoction of a few Russian words, some gestures and a Central Asian phrasebook, but my new friends were very patient and with Assad's help kept me part of the conversation. The girl on my left was Afghan and had been working in Uzbekistan for three years now. On her upper arm was an eight-inch-long wound, bleeding and inflamed. Bloody hell, I exclaimed, what on earth had happened?

"Water snake", explained Assad.

"Where?" I asked again, impressed.

"In town swimming pool."

The conversation moved on to the subject of the police and I didn't have to speak Uzbek to understand how much they were despised. This proved to be a universal theme across the region, and I would hear many personal stories of intimidation, rampant corruption and abuses of power. It must have been impossible for the police to live or socialise in the same places as everyone else; the venom they inspired in their fellow citizens convinced me they would not survive long.

In Uzbekistan nerves were particularly raw as it had been only a few months since the infamous Andijan Massacre in the east of the country, a brutal government crackdown against protestors demonstrating against the regime. Official government figures put the numbers of dead at 187, whilst most outside agencies put the toll at several hundred killed and many more wounded; one anonymous government source had put the true figure closer to 1,500. This was also part of my planned route into Kyrgyzstan.

Assad's portly friend had loaded a cassette tape of upbeat tunes and was dancing, already bored with the conversation, swinging his pot belly in a wide arc and inviting us all to boogie with him. I had to decline - violent gyrations and hopping up and down were the last things I needed right now. After a few songs it petered out and everyone sat down again. There was a pause, and Assad turned to me.

"Sex okay?" he asked.

Four pairs of eager eyes stared at me, waiting. Here I was in a nondescript town in western Uzbekistan, Central Asian pop warbling on the stereo in a crumbling Soviet block of flats, being entertained by a likely local crime lord and cavorting with two working girls. Maybe this is what my guidebook had in mind when it espoused "Meet the locals" on its back cover? There was some eager prompting from Assad, gesturing to the next room while I thought rapidly for an excuse.

"Bad stomach", I said desperately to uncomprehending stares. "All that movement... you know... will make me sick again."

I tried to make my point by miming, eliciting amused looks and some misplaced cheering, but Assad was determined to satisfy his guest, no matter what it took. After a short conference with the ladies, he continued.

"How about", he said a little uncertainly, but in all seriousness, "I get you young boy instead?" The two prostitutes sitting on either side of me nodded sympathetically, while I furiously scrabbled through my English-Russian dictionary. When it was finally made clear that I was not interested in any of the options ("Not even quick hand-job then?") I waited on the sofa while Assad and his friend took turns on the mattress next door.

In the morning Assad picked me up from the flat and took me to meet his family on the other side of the city. He put my bike in the back of his car and accelerated up to 90 mph through the city centre, as I grabbed at the empty sockets where the seatbelts should have been.

We arrived at a traditional Uzbek townhouse in the suburbs, the anonymous rectangular walls of the outside completely at odds with the lush luxury of the interior. There was a raised polished wooden walkway surrounding a spacious courtyard open to the elements. Composed of carefully tended flowerbeds, grape vines, pear trees and herbs, it was a miniature paradise and his wife prepared jasmine tea for us while he played with his two young daughters. Towards late morning it was time for me to be heading off and after some protracted and emotional goodbyes, Assad finally let me go.

The Likely Lads, Navoi

FROM NAVOI THE ROAD TURNED EAST. I LOST THE SHADE OF THE trees and then the wind started, an abysmal, energy sapping wind, hitting me head-on and slowing me down to a morale destroying grind, barely above walking pace. Assad and the ladies had already alerted me of this last night, after their exertions.

"Wind get very strong around Samarkand, strongest in Uzbekistan. Only sound you hear is wind, like fighter jet", warned Assad. "Very tough on bicycle but probably not for you - you already cycle to my country from England" he said, stabbing Iceland decisively on my map laid out on the floor.

We were discussing my route through Central Asia, and the weather had been dismissed as the least of my problems.

"Tajikistan... dangerous. Kyrgyzstan... dangerous". They had all tut-tutted and shook their heads sadly. "Kazakhstan... dangerous".

Typical of so many people in this region, they were mistrustful and suspicious of their neighbours. With the population's movements closely controlled by authoritarian governments I supposed that they rarely had a chance to travel outside of their own borders. I was actually quite touched; they were genuinely concerned about my welfare, and we had talked happily late into the night about what other disasters might befall me.

And now this damned wind was turning my mood sour, the usual cheerful whistles from the kids working the fields somehow twisted into a high-pitched taunt grating on my nerves, and whenever the inevitable swarm of well-meaning locals enveloped me at every stop, I just didn't have the energy to reciprocate their friendliness. For two days it continued like this, a procession of parched cotton fields and bedraggled clusters of mud-brick bungalows, passing me by in slow motion while the wind tested every jot of resilience I had left.

I hadn't really noticed the changing landscape around me, how the bare dry hillocks had evolved into domed mosques, battered outhouses into multi-story brick buildings and the narrow potholed lanes into a busy carriageway, so it was with some astonishment when I looked up from the road and I saw that I was already deep into the city of Samarkand. From a mile away I could make out the Registan, a medieval congress of exquisitely tiled arches, turrets and domes, golden sunlight reflected from its many intricate surfaces like turquoise and sapphire jewels. Three ancient madrasahs dominated the far end of a vast public square and hundreds of people wandered across its precincts, local Uzbeks as well as tourists marvelling at one ornate building after another.

I thought back to my very first day of this journey, arriving in St. Albans late afternoon in front of its modest cathedral bordered by green lawns and well-tended flowerbeds. I was a little heavier then, and the bike and equipment pretentiously clean and unused. Less than four months later here I was, standing in front of one of the ancient wonders of the Silk Road, jersey flapping loosely around my waist, dusty bags piled in disarray on the rear of a serious looking machine. It was only with a strong dose of English restraint that I didn't punch my fists into the air and shout *I've done it. I have frigging well done it!*

It would be a lie to say there was no hint of a smug smile on my face as I wheeled my overloaded bike through the crowds, and I delighted in every look of disbelief from the tourists who stared at me (yep – I rode here on *this* thing, baby). Yet despite the people, despite the noise and the activity, there was a sense of peace about the place. For the next few hours, as I explored half-hidden corridors and courtyards and languidly followed mosaics of glazed blue tiles around the walls, I had forgotten all about my list of worries and concerns.

And considering that I was barely a third of the way through this venture, that was a very long list indeed.

SAMARKAND WAS A MAJOR STOP FOR ME, AS IT HAD BEEN FOR SILK Road travellers for well over a millennium. It was located perfectly between China and the West and had been the capital of the ancient Timurid empire, operating as a centre of Islamic study for many centuries. Nowadays it was the second largest city in Uzbekistan (after the capital Tashkent) and continued to attract travellers, mainly for its grand madrasahs and mausoleum.

Now that I was in a major city my guidebook finally had some relevant information and I made my way to a guesthouse they recommended; it was a convivial place where the guests gathered in a central courtyard to chat. Team Swiss were staying here – I saw their bikes locked up against a pillar in the yard – and I was told that they had left this morning by bus to Tashkent to arrange onward visas, something I would be doing shortly as well. There was another bike in the corner of the yard looking considerably worn and weathered even by world cyclist standards and I would later locate the owner as Al, riding his way back to the UK after three years on the road. Was this the Central Asian hub for round-the-world cyclists? I met him that afternoon as he was promoting the virtue of travelling light.

"Keep nothing but the bare essentials", he lectured.

That evening he pulled out half a dozen thick paperbacks from his panniers and gave them to me, adding another kilogram to my luggage.

Yet a good read was indeed a vital piece of kit. As I got deeper into the Stans and then China, the environment would never fail to be more alien and challenging, the excitement of getting far away from the proverbial beaten track marred by acute periods of melancholy and self-doubt. A book offered a welcome escape from the punishing reality.

I took a bus to Tashkent to arrange documentation for Kyrgyzstan, Kazakhstan and China. It was an impersonal modern city and the police stopped me repeatedly with their broken English and rotten bandit smiles. Relieved to get back to Samarkand, and with the final visas now indelibly stamped in my passport, I could now relax (relatively speaking). On a bike, it was all about the road and not so much the destination, so I never felt the pressure to tramp round the sights ticking them off one by one; there were already enough people doing that. I did, however, visit the mausoleum of Tamerlane, bribing the night watchman a few *som* to let me into the actual tomb at night, deep in the building's foundations.

Tamerlane was a military genius from the 14th century, a Turkic Mongolian often compared to Genghis Khan. He made Samarkand famous as the capital of his empire, the shaping of which his military campaigns are said to have caused the deaths of 17 million people – a terrifying five percent of the world's entire population at the time. It was quite chilling to be in the presence of his remains, and it was said that when his body was first exhumed in 1941 the inscription inside the tomb had said "Whomever opens my tomb shall unleash an invader more terrible than I". Two days later Nazi Germany invaded the USSR.

I was glad when the guard turned his torch back up towards the steps we'd come down.

"It is time to go", he said nervously, and I agreed. I couldn't get out of that place fast enough.

Samarkand was a wonderful city to while away the time and it was nice to hang out with Alex, Pascal and Evo again. It would be easy to spend weeks here I thought, or at the very least another five days, for this was when Team Swiss planned to leave and they were thinking of taking the same road as me, towards an uncertain border crossing with Tajikistan. The idea of facing Tajikistan alone was nerve racking: Uzbeks had already given me plenty of warnings ("The border's closed", "It's too dangerous", and the perennial "You can't trust a Tajik.") and the handful of comments in my guidebook that touched on this border area centred around words like "remote", "mountainous" and "bandits". Furthermore, the US State Department webpage warned of recent insurgent activity.

But this was my journey after all, and it was time again to face things alone. Any longer in this city and I might just never leave. If the lethargy didn't get me then the scorpions surely would; so far, I had killed two of them crawling along the bedroom floor.

In front of the Registan, Samarkand

CHAPTER 14

THE HOLY MAN OF THE
AYNI PASS

LONDON · (Tajikistan) · Ayni · Khojand · (Uzbekistan) · Fergana · Andijan · TOKYO

Early morning, Samarkand.

It had been a late night with the Swiss and some others from the guesthouse at an impromptu farewell party. The after-effects of half a dozen *Baltika No.5*s and a couple bottles of "anti-septic" (for old times' sake) were contributing to the fiercest hang-over of recent months, and with only three hours sleep I barged clumsily around the beds trying to get my stuff out the room and onto the bike, as quietly as possible. Thus it was with the minimum of self-awareness that I found myself on the road to Tajikistan. My head hurt, my stomach was in turmoil and my throat just got drier as the foliage thinned out and the intensity of the sun increased with the advancement of morning.

The road soon became devoid of most traffic – motor powered traffic that is – and the signs of population started to thin. I passed dusty fields, dirty green crops barely registering amongst the over-whelming yellows, browns and oranges. Through villages that were little more than a few plain mud-brick houses, I often found myself escorted by one or two local kids peddling furiously on rickety old bicycles, while village elders watched from under the ungenerous shade of a few stringy trees, sipping tea.

I barely noticed the border; it was just a small gate and a single square building in pretty much the middle of nowhere. The Uzbek guards were friendly, and the only demand made was for the sergeant to have a go on my bicycle. His colleagues laughed as he rode in a precarious figure of eight while I looked on nervously, worried he might fall and mangle my gears or worse, do himself an injury (and then the fun would definitely be over).

The border guard on the Tajik side was considerably less jovial.

"Fifteen dollars", he said flatly, glaring at me.

He wore a threadbare uniform of beige-green and sported an oversized peaked cap of cartoon proportions; a hammer and sickle were displayed prominently on the lapels of the jacket and in the centre of the cap, despite the fact that the Soviet Union had broken up almost fifteen years before. I knew that this was a huge amount of money - Tajikistan was still recovering from a bloody civil war which had ended only seven years earlier - and I asked him what the fifteen dollars was for. He spent some time in concentration, impressively retrieving some long forgotten English vocabulary.

"Road tax", he said, and we both looked at the cracked and crater-filled road leading away from his border post.

"No", I said, showing empty palms. "No cash."

The interesting thing about travelling in these countries by bicycle is that people don't really know what to make of you. They know that foreigners are invariably much richer than they themselves are, but they also know that people who ride bicycles only do so because they are too poor to afford a motor scooter. Cycling as a leisure activity is unheard of – who on earth would travel by a bicycle in these conditions if they had a choice!

"Empty your bags", he ordered half-heartedly, so I very slowly started pulling my panniers off the bike, lining them up in the dust. I had six litres of water and a couple days food – maybe I could camp here until he changed his mind, I thought. But thankfully it wasn't long before a bus arrived and he saw the opportunity for richer pickings, rather than hassling this odd foreign cyclist for an uncertain outcome. He resignedly stamped my passport and ushered me out of the trailer and over the border. A hundred yards later I paused to gather my thoughts and took stock of my situation: enormous mountains reared up in the northwest, mountains I would soon have to cross.

Mountains and gorges, Tajikistan

TAJIKISTAN WAS SOMEWHAT DIFFERENT TO THE OTHER COUNTRIES on my Central Asia agenda in that its culture and language was more Persian than Turkish. Not that this was particularly relevant to me as my strongest communicable language was neither of them – it was arguably Russian as I was now able to say, "Can I pitch my tent here tonight?" and "My bicycle has 24 gears". A staggering ninety percent of the country was mountainous and of that, half was over 3,000 metres in elevation. This fact posed something of more immediate relevance given that my map indicated this was the half I would be travelling in.

Afghanistan wasn't too far away to the south, making Tajikistan a popular transit point for drug smuggling across its porous border – a fifth of Afghanistan's heroin travelled these roads - and given the task ahead of me I wouldn't have said no to a performance enhancing product or two. I stocked up on (more conventional) supplies in Pendjikent, four large round flatbreads from the market and a pound of dried apricots. With a couple of jars of peanut butter that I'd been carrying with me since Turkmenistan and some other bits and pieces I was fairly confident that I had provisions enough for three or four days.

People were extremely friendly. I was mobbed by a group of kids when entering the town - in a good way, not a stone-throwing way –

and each took turns climbing up on my saddle and trying on my helmet. They chattered excitedly among themselves and a couple of them ran off to a cluster of houses a hundred yards away. Five minutes later they re-appeared leading two young ladies, both dressed in the richly coloured dresses typical of the region, enticed to come out and parade in front of the foreigner. One of them had a startling unibrow, a single black, bushy, rich and glossy eyebrow stretching across her forehead. In Tajikistan this was considered a symbol of femininity and purity and just as women in the West would spend time and money to pluck theirs away, any Tajik lady serious about her looks would encourage hers to meet in the middle.

She was friendly, trying to make conversation in Russian (and setting the kids off in uproar) but the chaperone on her arm – her conventionally eye-browed and consequently jealous sister – was very cool. There would be no Tajik nuptials for me.

I STRONGLY SUSPECTED THAT A PROMOTION AWAITED ME ONCE again in the ranks of adventure cycling. The horizon was rudely framed by tall jagged peaks stretching in a wide arc across my field of vision, and the brutal unpaved roads dissolved into monstrously deep shadows, the dark fingers of mountains tearing at the spartan land ahead. Oh bugger, I thought looking at my map, there would be no avoiding this.

First I had to cross an immense plain, a flat yellowed grassland, with patches of frayed and ragged green and the odd stunted tree, occasionally big enough to provide temporary shade against the sun. Judging by the dusty patches of crops and fields of drooping sunflowers there was certainly a living, if that's what it could be called, to be made from the arid soil, but as the road headed higher into the foothills it left the river behind and any subsequent hope of irrigation with it.

The road itself was punishing; unpaved, uneven and meandering up and down through small isolated villages of mud-brick houses. Women working the land by the roadside stopped to watch me, hands on hips and nonplussed while older folks offered polite greetings as I passed, their left hand pressed over their heart.

"*Salam alekum.*"

But it was so damned difficult to acknowledge anyone, and impossible to take a hand off the handlebars to place against my breast to say the customary *alekum salam* in return. It took all of my concentration just to stay on the bike, avoiding rocks, crater-sized potholes and crops laid out in the middle of the so-called road. There were also lots of kids, most just giggling and running beside me, while a few opportunistically tried to pull stuff from the rear rack whenever out of sight of their elders.

Mountains encircled me at a scale somewhat difficult to take in, and a closer look revealed the occasional narrow ledge a thousand feet up with some kind of dwelling and a few steep and parched-looking fields. How the hell did they get up there? It was all so wretchedly bare, brown-grey chunks of rock and sand, some chiselled into giant saw teeth, others polished smooth by the wind. Stark, empty, beautiful.

There was a coarse gravel road and I mused over its sudden and austere rise from the valley floor, simmering in the heat. A zigzagged upward trajectory had been blasted into the very rock face and I contemplated the absolute vulnerability of my situation – quite clearly, I was a long way from home. No medical facilities of any kind, no lodgings and certainly no other tourists. I contemplated the scarcity of water ahead, pulled out my water filter and scrambled down the riverbank with all my empty bottles. The first time I had used this thing was a test-run at my mother's house. After washing the dishes from a Christmas dinner I put the hose in the turbid washing-up bowl amid the floating turkey leftovers and pumped myself a glass. It tasted just as bad now as it did then.

Throughout this journey, looking for a meal often turned into an imaginative enterprise, but where there were people there was usually a place to eat. With enquiry, slurping noises and belly-rubbing (your own, not someone else's), you would usually be pointed to something, quite probably someone's kitchen after an entrepreneurial local had made a deal with the obliging household. But things did not look good for me here. Bald, steep hills... deep and dark ravines... rocky overhangs and monstrous slopes of granite scree... the only thing I could be assured of swallowing was dust from the road and a lot of flies.

However, late morning while struggling up a steep traverse, wheels slipping as I tried to stand and pedal, a small sun-scorched farmhouse appeared on the apex of one of the wider turns and a few weather-beaten Tajiks beckoned me to stop and come inside to sit with them. The single room was sparsely furnished, and the shelves were practically empty. While I explained my story to a patient audience, with a few more words of Russian (I noted pleased with myself) added to the conventional mix of gesture and drawing, the lady presented a pot of tea, a bowl of large uneven lumps of sugar and a pile of freshly baked naan flatbread. I was humbled by the generosity of people surviving on the edge of existence - even in these remote, empty mountain valleys there were still folks trying to eke out a living and I wouldn't die of thirst or hunger. There were far more exotic ways to meet your end in places like this.

It was late afternoon when I came across the first teahouse of the day and an ancient man of indeterminable years brought me *laghman*, the simple noodle broth available throughout central Asia. As food stops were becoming increasingly irregular, I was getting into the habit of eating whenever there was an opportunity, to make up for those periods when there wasn't. In this region it was advisable to forget a lifetime routine of breakfast, lunch and dinner and just eat whenever the chance presented itself. And inevitably I would be presented with bowl of *laghman*.

There was another customer, a younger fellow looking rather dubious in his dark glasses. He had turned up in an old Yugo – marking him as a rich man in this country - and he came over to my table pointing at my pot of tea asking me to share it. Whenever the owner was out of earshot, he badgered me for money.

"You give me 1,000 *somani*", he demanded. I shook my head. Pause. "How about 500 *somani*?" he countered. Again, I shook my head and his face turned a shade of red. "100 *somani* then!" he said, voice raised slightly. I kept calm and pointed at his car outside, a chance to practise some Tajik.

"How much *somani* was that?" I asked.

The old man came over and said a few sharp words to him; he left irate and sped off at speed - relatively speaking - in his clapped-out Yugo, throwing up a trail of dust in its wake. I imagined briefly what might happen if I met the same guy again later alone.

Back on the road shadows were starting to lengthen and I wondered where on earth I would sleep tonight. There was enough food and water stowed on my bike, so I left the decision to fate, finding myself traversing the side of a wide valley, a huge cleft in the earth with a fast foaming river a couple of hundred feet below and a green plateau of fields and trees far away on the other side. Mountains brown and grey towered over everything and the majesty of the view stopped me in my tracks. I had never seen anything like it and with a sense of awe that would linger for weeks, couldn't quite believe that I had cycled here.

The valley narrowed and the ribbon of road I was on dropped close to the valley floor. The cliffs closed in quickly and this road was now the only thing between the sheer scree slopes rising thousands of feet above to my right, and the violent blue-grey river bubbling down to my left, just a feeble scratch across the pedestal of an immense mountain range. In the middle of this barren backdrop, tucked in tightly at the next bend in the river, between the valley wall and the crumbling road was a teahouse perched precariously next to a waterfall, this splash of lush vegetation a small green fleck in the vastness of the colourless slopes above.

Shadows were moving quickly up the valley wall as the sun sunk lower and I knew fate had been listening... rest here tonight, she whispered. It looked deserted but an old man (they are always old men) appeared from the shadows of the place and prepared his last - or maybe his first - bowl of *laghman* for the day while I set up my tent on a small patch of flat land next to the falls above. The waterfall cascading down the mountainside next to me was deafening and I saw the valley winding away into the far distance. It looked like it had been chiselled from the raw rock and I watched until the last rays of daylight disappeared from the sky and the night was full of stars.

Teahouse, Tajikistan

THE ROAD TO THE AYNI PASS WAS AN UP-DOWN MONSTER AND MY map said it had an elevation of 3,378 metres, which was absurdly higher than where I was now. With a heavy bike, appalling road surface, a blazing sun and 40 plus degree heat, it was an especially cruel road. As any cyclist will readily acknowledge, there are few roads more disheartening than one that promises an honest climb with an honest descent, but instead delivers a series of false summits. Every metre of descent, you can't help but remind yourself, is another metre to be climbed again. There is an elevation account in your head and the strain to make a profit tortures you with every downward turn of the road.

I passed a huge apple orchid, this green oasis incongruous amongst a land of sand and rock and I almost considered camping here although it was barely mid-morning. The road dived precariously down to the valley floor, a deeply rutted track of red clay where I hugged the escarpment wall as closely as possible; if not careful I could find myself on an unintended shortcut. On crossing the bridge, hard clay transformed into deep sand and the violence of the descent was matched only by the sluggish grind up the other side. I struggled a few yards against the sand before the front wheel was enveloped and the bike overturned... I got up, dusted myself down, heaved the bike upright and got a little further before it happened again. Sometimes I would manage a few yards, sometimes a few hundred, but every good run on two wheels was inevitably concluded with some time on my arse.

Late morning, I arrived at some kind of crossroads; a couple of beat up Soviet-era trucks and an ancient Lada were all parked up and their occupants were spread amongst the two teahouses that straddled the road. Like me, they were headed over the Ayni Pass and onto Khojand in the north, though it would take considerably longer on my own human-powered transport. From the teahouse the road continued to follow the path of the river deeper into the valley until it eventually disappeared. The consequence of this geological fact was another road, thin and broken, that soared up the steep valley sides in a series of ascending hairpin turns and then tracked expertly across the acute contours of the upper reaches of the mountain.

I climbed and I looked back. The fertile valley bottom looked like it had been squeezed increasingly tight in a colossal vice of bluff mountain slopes. These were uniformly brown-black but for the occasional adolescent green fuss of vegetation, and the lower slopes fell over one another like dominoes. Beyond that (thirty miles away? fifty miles away?) were the fierce walls of another mountain range, sharp fissures and serrated ridges pushing up to snow covered peaks. Just how on earth had I managed to end up here? Any evidence that I may have started out from some civilised town or city had been conclusively and forensically wiped clean, the only record of my route being this gossamer thread of road which extended upwards like a thin white vine from the river far below.

As my water ran low, I started filling up bottles from the occasional murky roadside gully. I acquired a couple of local supporters, two small kids in ragged T-shirts and shorts who could keep up with my pace through a mixture of walking and jogging. Mainly through walking though, as in many places I had to dismount to push the bike through sand and rocks, sweating and swearing furiously in the heat. They were with me for a couple of hours and it was frustrating keeping them entertained with my three words of Tajik while I tried to make some kind of headway, but as they both carried eight-inch daggers – which passes for a toy in these parts – I thought it wise that I should.

This pass was not going to be conquered today, and as I started up the main climb towards the top it was clear that there were very few practical places to actually camp; on my left the brittle edge of the road and a sheer drop, and on my right, vertical sheets of rock stretching high into the heavens. Very occasionally, balanced on the serpentine curves between the road and the chasm below, would be a weathered old lady selling bags of raisins.

Through a low-level headache and increasingly laboured breathing I realised the altitude was getting to me and not far ahead, the dirt road was looking like a post-apocalypse ski-jump, rock-strewn and flayed of any reasonable riding surface. There was a narrow ravine perpendicular to the road, shrouded in deep shadow, and at its mouth was a rickety shack, a simple wooden platform set a few feet off the ground with a patched wooden roof. Sitting inside was an old man and he shouted across to me.

"Stop and have some tea!"

This was the best idea I'd heard for ages and I climbed up to join him. His name was Asfar and he asked his son to prepare some tea and bread while we sat cross legged on the carpet and watched the shadows crawl up the walls of the far side of the valley. We talked as best we could, through odd Russian words and gesture.

"I am here every day to sell these", he told me, pointing to a stack of biscuits, cigarettes and other provisions. He smiled gently. "But mainly I come here to teach my son to be a good man", he said, motioning to the young man preparing our tea.

Of the occasional vehicle on the road, most pulled in and stopped; the occupants would approach and remove their shoes, ask permission to step up onto the platform and greet him warmly, chatting and joking. After a few minutes the chatter suddenly tailed off into silence and they gathered closer around him, while he gave his assembled patrons a short sermon. They listened solemnly and when it was done, they all concluded the ceremony by placing their palms over their face and sweeping them down in front of their chest and out in an elegant arc. They placed money at his lap and went back on their way, now protected from the dangers of this perilous road.

He gave me the same blessing when they had gone, and I laid some cash at his feet copying what I had just observed; he refused and gave it back.

"What do I need with more money?" he said gently and grinned, showing me the bundles of *somani* notes stacked under the carpet.

I camped just a little further up the ravine on the bank of the stream, with a view over this little corner of the valley. From out of the hills and crags curious people appeared one by one, watching me set up my tent. By the time I had started cooking there was an audience of twenty smiling faces silently watching me, including the two boys from earlier. When I offered a young girl some of my meal, she shyly shook her head and backed away slightly. Wise decision, I thought. They were content just to watch and talk quietly with each other, and long after I had retired into the tent, I could see the silhouettes of my new friends on the tent walls until the light faded into black.

THE FIRST THING I SAW IN THE MORNING WAS MY BREATH IN front of me. It had been freezing last night and the discomfort was refreshing – when was the last time I had actually felt cold? The morning felt crisp and the valley was still draped in deep shadow as I skidded and slipped on the bike, negotiating the gravelly road, relishing the ice-cold air against my skin. A lone man huddled under layers of clothes on a downtrodden-looking mule; he was the only other visible sign of life at this hour and was heading down the valley.

"*Salem alekum*", he said as he passed.

The cold spurred me on and I made the pass in less than three hours; I was over two miles up and I couldn't believe I had ridden this heavy rig all the way up here. To the south-west was the brown-grey valley I had now beaten, pincered by sheer cliffs, and beyond this the snow-capped mountains of the Pamirs. To the north-east was another wide valley with an immensely long, gorgeous-looking descent directly in front of me. Well that's what it looked like - in reality it was a precariously steep, sandy and rock-strewn track clinging to the valley wall on one side, and the usual Central Asian plummet-to-a-certain-death on the other. I was not going much faster than I'd done coming up here.

But what the hell did I care! The air was like fine crystal and the more substantial delays came from shoving my tongue back in my mouth as I stopped again and again to absorb the views. I could see vast meadows of wildflowers far below, silver veins of remote rivers from frozen mountain peaks pulsing down countless valleys, tiny hamlets and villages, and the barely discernible dots of people and livestock. I was exquisitely alone, imagined master of this Shangri La.

The road improved somewhat over the next few hours and by late morning I could trust gravity to usher me through the lower slopes of the valley as green hillsides crowded closer around me and a wild colt and mare enjoyed some grown up delights in the sun. I reflected that it had been quite some time since I had enjoyed any such delights of my own, though with these roads it was doubtful that my battered loins would be much up to the job anyway.

Long climbs, Tajikistan

~

A TROUPE OF FOUR POLICEMEN CAME OUT TO GREET ME FROM their trailer. It was early afternoon and I had arrived at the first checkpoint on entering the Tajik lowlands. Each had a slightly different uniform to the others, some with lapels and some without, each one with a different shade of blue or grey shirt, and a couple with worn out trainers instead of boots. The portliest of their number wore a flamboyant peaked hat and a tin sheriff's badge pinned to his uniform of questionable official sanction, and the driver of every vehicle that arrived greeted him like an old friend, discreetly slipping him a few *somani* as they passed.

He was obviously the one in charge and his looks of suspicion and surprise melted into smiles and welcoming handshakes when I showed him my passport and explained where I'd started from.

"Sit down, sit down!" he said and ordered one of his subordinates to bring some watermelon while he attempted to ride my bike, giving up almost immediately, laughing as he came close to collapsing in a heap. His colleagues all fussed over me, insisting I help myself to another generous slice of melon as I explained my route and how I planned to finish in Japan. It was only after I had talked with each one of them, did I feel it polite to leave.

The last few weeks had evidently taken a visible toll on my appearance, for when I reached into my pocket to give the chief something for his hospitality, he stayed my arm, gazing at me intently with what I imagined to be a look of hurt. Instead he reached into his own pocket for a hundred *somani* note, pushed it into my palm and made me promise that I would use it to call my mother.

It was a straightforward, if somewhat bruising, descent to the plains, where the town of Ura Tybe was hosting a busy bazaar, bordered by a number of small restaurants and flophouses. I inevitably selected the worst, sharing a cramped room with two young and unwaveringly smiling Tajik traders and a toilet apparently shared by the entire bazaar. The room cost two dollars for the night and I felt ripped off, regretting that I hadn't cycled out of town and found a quiet place to camp.

These cramped lodgings meant that I couldn't park the bike in my line of sight. The closest place was downstairs in some back-room, secured against a solid looking pipe. The lock I carried was huge and weighed in at several kilograms, being the strongest I could find. A friend in Japan had advised me to wait until I was back in the UK before buying a lock - "an island of thieves, they know how to make good locks" - and it would indeed prove resistant to an attempted heist later that night, displaying a number of saw marks come morning.

It was clear the Tajiks in my room were immensely curious but acutely shy, talking to each other in quiet rapid whispers before one of them had been elected to ask me what my story was. When it emerged that I'd arrived here via Uzbekistan they both became highly animated.

"But Uzbekistan is so dangerous - especially now!" one of them exclaimed, and they talked heatedly of the Andijan massacre and the civilians shot down by the police and national guard. Seven thousand killed, they asserted, writing the number down on paper, the highest number that I had heard by far.

They were dismayed further still when I told them I would be continuing east into Uzbekistan again, and urged me to be careful.

"Remember" they warned, inevitably. "You can't trust an Uzbek."

The commotion attracted the owner's son who now invited himself into the room to meet the new curiosity. He was eighteen or nineteen and, having quickly caught up with the conversation, made some machine gun motions with his hands expecting to elicit some laughter from us. He was a typical Central Asian spiv; young, pseudo-business minded, and no doubt had some questionable contacts. He said to me that we should "do some business" together.

"What business?" I asked.

"Just business", he replied, and took me around the local bazaar to show off his new business partner, buying me a pack of cigarettes to seal the deal.

I left very early the next morning.

AFTER A CERTAIN TIME ON THE ROAD YOU BECOME QUIETLY seduced by daily familiarity with your environment and what was once thought of as fantastical retreats to the merely surprising, the surreal into the expected, and the exotica dwindle into just another day of cycling. Of this you must be careful.

Overweight men in skullcaps loping around on their sorry looking mules, whipping them in frantic hurried strokes... all taken for granted. The bright glint of gold teeth from the paisley robed and head-scarfed young woman working the field as she smiles at you... no longer teasing your imagination. And the raggedy old men, faces like burnished walnuts, hands outstretched from the side of the road holding writhing snakes for sale... you no longer question why. But then - with a sharp crack of wood - a roadside stall collapses, spilling dozens of watermelons across your path, and you swerve and brake and come off your bike in the middle of them.

Hundreds more are still piled up in child-high sized pyramids that line the road and as competing stall owners gather around, shouting prices, undeterred by the impracticality of selling you a 20-pound melon, you look up and focus on the scene unfolding in front of you. You take it in slowly, breathe it in deeply and you appreciate where you are once again - this is not your average day of cycling in Sussex.

Definitely not Sussex

❧

I WAS RIDING THROUGH THE VAST AND FERTILE FERGANA VALLEY, spanning Uzbekistan, Tajikistan and Kyrgyzstan. This wide basin had been an important sojourn on the Silk Road, offering replenishment and rest to travellers on their way to Europe after crossing the brutal passes from China. Now with cotton production on a massive scale, there had been little progress from the Soviet-era single crop economy, and I could see cotton fields extend mile after mile over the horizon.

It was early afternoon when I arrived in Khojand, the main city of northern Tajikistan. Situated on the banks of the wide Syr Darya river it lay at the foot of a stark-looking massif, the raw orange of its mountains contrasting violently with the azure blue waters of the river cutting below it. Khojand was a typically Soviet styled city for the most part but the wide leafy boulevards and small adjoining parks were a pleasant change. Although the buildings were cracked and the roads thoroughly potholed, it looked certainly more prosperous than what I had seen over the last week. With families living in makeshift homes of mud and rock, kids running around in rags and people with deep wounds or fractures patched up with dirty bandages and slings, Tajikistan still had a long way to develop.

Due to the arbitrary borders drawn up by the Soviets, to get into Kyrgyzstan I would have to enter Uzbekistan once again, a 100-kilometre ride eastwards. The road was well maintained and lined with trees; I passed cornfields and apricot orchards whilst blue reservoirs in the distance shimmied under the sun. This was a rich land, a Central Asian styled *Little House on the Prairie*, the road gently rising and descending over long, low hills. The road was straight and with totalitarian regularity I passed Soviet-era monuments off to the side: man-with-hammer-and-sickle, or woman-with-fist-raised-to-sky were the most common ones, but occasionally something of a more local flavour made an appearance, like the mural of a proud woman in her paisley dress carrying a basket of fruit, created from thousands of small coloured tiles. The only other interruption to this pleasant if unchanging scenery was the occasional ice cream stall set up on the verge and I stopped at every single one.

The border crossing offered a temporary break from the monotony and I was showered with curious questions and offers of tea I couldn't refuse. Then, before I knew it, I was in Uzbekistan for the second time, the only change being that I had picked up another cyclist, a very friendly Uzbek who worked at the border garrison and was riding home after his shift. For the next ten miles we chatted as we rode along a quiet dusty road, the lack of a common tongue making both of us increasingly reckless with hand gestures made from our moving bicycles. At the turn-off to his home he invited me to stay with him and his family, but it was still early in the afternoon and in my haste to push on I didn't take up his offer; when I later settled into a crumbling concrete hotel in Kokand with 150 kilometres on the clock I couldn't help kicking myself being for being so stupid, and scolding myself again about the point of this whole trip. It was not a race, I reminded myself.

But I was wrong – indeed it *was* a race. In the morning, I checked my visa stamp for Uzbekistan and my heart skipped a beat:

Holy Crap. It expires TODAY!

This was definitely not the kind of country to overstay your visa and I could not believe I had been so stupid. It occurred to me now that yesterday's border guard had actually warned me of this when he pointed at my passport and then held his forefinger in the air, repeating "One!" zealously a few times, until I had nodded and given him the thumbs up. I simply thought he was calling me Number One, presumably impressed by my bicycle heroics, but he had actually been warning me that I had only one day left on my visa.

So I was simply an idiot. A Number One idiot.

Rushing through the lush greenery of the Fergana Valley I only wished I had more time to enjoy it, but there were a hundred miles of ground to cover to the Kyrgyz border before dusk. The whole area was much more densely populated than what I was used to, and villages lined the route non-stop. It felt upbeat, the people outgoing and friendly, and I had to turn down countless invitations to stop and join them for *plov* or ice cream.

Travel warnings had advised that this area was a hotbed of Islamic militancy but here I was, sitting at the side of the road drinking tea, when a group of girls walked past, pointed at the state of me and howled with laughter. Clearly this was a good sign that the sombre state of affairs portrayed by official reports was somewhat exaggerated. Although, more gravely for me, it was not looking good for any romantic success.

There were only a few hours of daylight remaining when I arrived in Fergana city, a hundred oft-interrupted kilometres later, and I had to figure out the best way to get into Kyrgyzstan before my visa ran out that night. My map showed a minor crossing south of the city, but I couldn't get any consensus on whether it was open or not. If I got there and it was closed, then I would be out of time for alternatives. The image of a couple of burly Uzbek policemen tut-tutting at my passport and chuckling "No, no, we do not want your money..." was hard to dismiss from my mind, and I made a frantic call to my Man in Kazakhstan. In the year I'd been working with him, it was the first time we had actually spoken.

"Hey Steve, great to finally hear your voice", he said cheerfully, in fluent English (I had somehow expected a heavily accented Bond villain). "What's up?"

Then I told him my visa issue and his tone abruptly changed.

"Steve!" he snapped. "This is not a good situation. You must get the hell out of there – *immediately*. Pay someone to drive you to Andijan and cross at the border there. You have no choice."

After waving down a handful of random vehicles, I finally found a taxi willing to take me and my bike the remaining 60 kilometres to the main border crossing in Andijan. It was still only ten weeks since the massacre, and apparently the streets had been washed clean, repainted, and the bullet holes plastered over (and the bodies dumped in mass graves). I had a fellow passenger for the trip to Andijan and I asked him his job, trying to break the ice.

"Police captain", he said. We didn't talk much after that.

He got out at the city suburbs while I got out a few miles later at the border. There were long queues and it was getting dark by the time I got through, but at least I did – not long afterwards the border to Kyrgyzstan would be suddenly closed to stem the tide of Uzbeks fleeing their own country.

CHAPTER 15

STARDOM IN OSH

Kyrgyzstan was another country with a tumultuous recent history, if not quite so violent. In March the long-ruling authoritarian President Akayev had won yet another disputed term in office. Rigged elections were nothing new in this country, but what was different this time round was that the voters were not going to lie down quietly and accept it. Protests grew and after Georgia's Rose revolution in 2003 and Kiev's Orange revolution in 2004, there was now this, the Tulip revolution here in Kyrgyzstan. The opposition intensified and then even policemen joined their ranks, with stories of them discarding uniforms and crossing over to the lines of protesters. Akayev eventually fled into exile and Kyrgyzstan's first legitimate elections were held on the 10th July - only three weeks ago - and the opposition leader Bakiyez took 90% of the vote in an election praised by the international monitors. In time he too would become corrupt and power mad, but for now there was a new sense of optimism in the air.

Coasting downhill to the city of Osh I was interrupted enthusiastically a dozen times by locals eager to welcome me and received two invitations to stay in people's homes. Yet it wasn't the hospitality that was surprising, it was that suddenly most of the faces were oriental. In the fading half-light of dusk, coloured perhaps by a little loneliness, I almost thought that I was already back in Japan.

Until now I had never consciously registered a change in the ethnic makeup of the places that I'd cycled through but this time it was immediate and perhaps more so than the 7,000 plus kilometres on the clock, it made me realise just how far I'd come. And deceptively, but ever so welcomingly, it tricked me into thinking I was much closer to my goal that I really was.

~

IT TOOK A FEW MINUTES TO REALISE THAT I'D ENDED UP IN SOME strange kind of Central Asian beer garden with dozens of yurts set up in a municipal park. Strangers offered me beer and vodka and various unpalatable snacks made from sour horse milk, but all I wanted was to find a hotel, exhausted by hospitality and seven days uninterrupted cycling. I was looking forward to holing myself up in a room and interacting with as few people as possible. Spending some time unplugged from the world around me. Recovering physically. Recovering mentally.

Fortunately, it was not to be.

"Can you point me to this hotel?" I asked a lady in my best Russian, poking at an address in my guidebook.

I knew I was close, but the buildings here didn't really advertise if they were hotels or otherwise, with neither signs nor special markings. She was a harried looking woman but had a kind look about her; her young daughter held her hand and looked up at me from curious and intelligent eyes.

"Come!" she said firmly, insistent that she would lead me there herself. When we arrived at the hotel, I dragged the bike through the unmarked entrance while she asked the price at the reception and shook her head.

"Too expensive", she explained and started to bargain hard with the receptionist, who then called the manager who gave her a further discount.

"Still too expensive", she sighed, turning to me apologetically.

I'm okay with the price, I wanted to say, I can pay, I can pay! Refuge was so close, what did a couple of dollars matter! Her brows knitted as she thought through the situation for a few seconds, then her face relaxed and a decision was made.

"You will stay with us!"

These ex-Soviets have a way of making every offer sound like a command. I couldn't really refuse.

Gulya and her nine-year-old daughter Dinara lived in a modest apartment block with Gulya's older brother Shakir; they were all crammed together into two rooms and it was clear that life was not easy. Shakir was an educated man and spoke to me in decent English, the first time for him in ten years, he said, and this was a huge relief when it came to communicating with Gulya. When Shakir wasn't around I had Dinara to help me – smart, confident and mature beyond her nine years, I could explain things in simple Russian and she would nod her head in comprehension, immediately picking up on what I really wanted to say and translate into proper Russian for her mother.

"*Da, da...*", she would say impatiently, treating me like an imbecile. *Yes, yes, I know what you are saying so just hurry up and get on with it!*

Shakir and I talked long after Dinara had gone to bed and Gulya had fallen asleep on the rug, and his rusty English came back sentence by sentence. He told me how Dinara's father had left when she was a little girl, looking for work in Russia as many Kyrgyz men did, and never came back, leaving Gulya to raise her alone while holding down two jobs. Shakir himself had only been back in Osh two years, work having dried up in the former Soviet Union. We talked about corruption, a popular topic in this part of the world and unfortunately always relevant.

"You must be very careful of the police", he said. "If ever you are in trouble, go to anyone but the police."

I had been shaken down for bribes countless times but as a Western tourist I was privileged just to have it stop at that; the Andijan massacre had provided a rare insight to how the governments of these countries treated their own citizens. The next morning Shakir left the house early and came back looking particularly pleased with himself. He handed me a twelve-inch-tall, cone-shaped, black and white felt hat, with a long, braided tassel dangling from the top, and a wide upturned brim. I was worried that he might ask me to wear it.

"Wear this", he ordered.

This type of headwear was everyday attire for Kyrgyz people he explained, and it would help to disguise the fact that I was a tourist.

This was as dubious a statement as ever I'd heard but I had little choice - he waved me off from the balcony, which had a clear view of the half-mile walk up to the main road, so I had to wear this thing on my head and muster a forced smile, feeling like some nomadic Disneyland character, imagining people pointing and laughing.

The funny thing was that nobody gave me a second glance. I could walk down the street and not be molested by anybody. All the staring had stopped. I had put a foot-high, flamboyantly tasselled nomad's hat on my head and suddenly I had become invisible!

"You will be Kyrgyz", Shakir had said to me, and he was right.

MEETING UP WITH GULYA AND DINARA LATER, THEY LED ME UP the steep Solomon's Throne, a jagged orange rock that overlooked the city from its vantage point two hundred metres above ground. It was an ancient Muslim pilgrimage site, and under the scorching cloudless sky I received a blessing for my trouble from the imam sitting in a cave at the top. I was barely halfway to Japan and knew I needed every bit of good luck I could get. My previous blessing was from the imam on the Ayni Pass, to keep me safe on these dangerous roads. This one I hoped, as I similarly brought my hands down in an arc away from my closed eyes, was to keep me safe from the local constabulary.

Maybe I should have also asked for a minor charm against drowning as our next stop was a swim in the River Tar, a fast-flowing river that cut its way through the centre of the city. With wide grass banks lined by trees it was a paradise in these scorching temperatures and like the other small groups of people around us we stripped off to our underwear and, oblivious of the strong current and rapids, leapt into the shallows to cool off. Gulya was a full-figured lady and Dinara innocently grabbed a handful of her mother's breasts, encouraging me to do the same.

That evening after dinner Gulya broke down a little; it was hard bringing up a daughter with little money and two jobs. She was clearly a wonderful mother and I told her so. She clasped my hand and stared at me hard through teary eyes... and then Dinara walked in from the next room, unable to sleep.

My last day in Osh culminated in a feature for Osh TV, the BBC of southern Kyrgyzstan. Shakir was a well-connected man and had friends working in television, so he had set up an interview for me. We arrived at the designated meeting place in town and I was asked to perform a few cameos like riding towards the camera, parking my bike, looking at my map and doing some shopping. The cameras were set up in a small corner shop and I was asked to go and buy some water – so I entered the shop and asked for a bottle of water in Russian.

"No, no, don't speak Russian!" said the director, "Mime! Mime!"

I pointed at a pile of bottles and made a big gesture of pretending to drink one of them while the cameras rolled, and the bemused shopkeeper served me.

"Wear your hat!" he ordered while the interviewer, an attractive but bored looking woman in her twenties, reeled off a list of typical questions.

"Why are you doing this?" she eventually asked. And for the sake of me I couldn't think of an answer.

The afternoon was spent meeting some of Shakir's extended family, including one elegant old lady introduced as a famous Soviet theatre performer (before funds for the arts had dried up), and after half a dozen similar introductions Shakir and I eventually retreated to a park for tea.

The teahouse was in a quiet corner of the park and we sipped our drinks reclining on a *tapchan*. This carpeted wooden platform, about the size of a double-bed and festooned with cushions, is ubiquitous throughout Central Asia for eating, drinking, socialising or just sleeping. This one was under the shade of awnings and surrounded by dense trees; so very removed from the rudimentary teahouses I had experienced in the parched mountains of recent weeks. The river flowed lazily below us, sunlight flickering from its surface and I realised that I hadn't allowed myself many moments to just relax like this. The last couple of days had been fun but hardly restful and from tomorrow my obliging hosts and the beginnings of a Central Asian television career would be far behind. There was a long mountain ride to the capital Bishkek ahead of me, climbing out of the Fergana Valley and up into the Kyrgyz highlands with at least two passes over 3,000 metres on the way.

Why was I pushing myself so hard? Today was the first day of August and although there were visa dates to think about and the cooler months of autumn and winter ahead to consider, there was really no need to be so impatient to move on. But of course, I already knew the answer; if I slowed down now, I might never find the nerve to start again.

I stayed and ordered myself another tea while Shakir left to meet some friends.

With Gulya and Dinara

THERE WERE TEARS LAST NIGHT WHEN DINARA FOUND OUT THAT I was leaving in the morning. We solemnly exchanged teddies; I gave her Paddy, a small green Irish bear who had accompanied me all the way from London and was a gift from my mother. In return I received Mishka, a slightly startled-looking Russian bear who was Dinara's favourite. The tears started again this morning when I strapped Mishka in Paddy's grubby vacated spot below my handlebars.

Shakir had arranged for his uncle, the local imam, to see me off, but I felt terribly sorry for the old man when I saw him looking bewildered outside the block of flats.

"It is good luck for an older man to say farewell", explained Shakir as he introduced his frail 77-year-old uncle, helping him stand shakily in front of me. The man put a quivering hand to his heart in greeting and Shakir grinned at me.

"The older the better", he said.

Jalal-Abad was my last stop in the Fergana Valley before the serious mountains began and it was a day of pleasant if slightly monotonous scenes of cotton fields and watermelon vendors, the trees and bushes fighting a territorial war with the road. The first fifty kilometres were on a flat rutted road to a town called Uzgen and came very close to knocking those recent mountain tracks in Tajikistan off the top spot for Crappiest Roads in Central Asia. It was bestrewn with boulders, deep sand and gaping holes (I hesitate to say potholes, which would have only diminished the reality of these pool-sized craters).

There were no climbs, but I barely managed an average speed of 8 kph, little more than a brisk walk. Inevitably I also took a wrong turn, leading to a forty-kilometre detour so that I arrived in Jalal-Abad 140 brutalising kilometres later, weeping tears of frustration and pain. But mainly pain; with the aid of a mirror that night in the hotel, I discovered some intimate black and blue welts across my posterior. The next morning things were little better, so I booked another night. Today was an official rear-end recovery day.

Jalal-Abad was a pleasant place to spend a day; a university town with a thriving bazaar and several parks. I did a lot of walking (mainly because I couldn't do much sitting) and in the late afternoon, while struggling over the Cyrillic menu at an outdoor restaurant, an attractive lady who had been sitting opposite smiled and approached my table. My heart beat furiously as she approached, and I chastised myself for not wearing something cleaner. Or shaving. Or showering.

"Can I help?" she asked. "I am studying English at the University. My name is Chika."

She helped me decipher the limited menu and steered me away from having what would have been the same meal for a third time that day. Not that I would have cared - she was young, pretty and smart. We arranged to meet outside my hotel that evening.

I rushed through the rest of the meal and hurried back to the hotel room to clean up and make myself somewhat presentable. This could be the travel romance that had been due to me for far too long! I waited for her to turn up, more nervous than I had been at any checkpoint, but apprehension soon plummeted into disappointment when she turned up with a chaperone, a rather shy awkward young chap who followed us around morosely a few steps behind. We all went for ice cream and said goodnight early. Six months later I got an email from Chika – she'd married him.

After a disappointingly good night's sleep it was time to continue my progress north, passing a slew of small towns and villages. The day was punctuated by teahouses, where I would down bottle after bottle of cold drink for temporary relief against the furnace of the road. At one dilapidated establishment on a deserted dirt road, I stretched out on the *tapchan* under the shade of its awnings and surveyed the mountains in the singed, hazy distance before dozing off. The feeling of isolation and remoteness was eased somewhat surreally by George Michael's "Careless Whisper" being played over the crackly radio. The scenery remained dusty and unchanged but from late afternoon onwards I could see an ominous looking mountain range in the distance straight ahead.

The road changed from potholed horror to gravel and rock horror, and soon my tender backside was complaining badly, but it was too early to stop. Unbelievably, two figures on bicycles emerged from the dust ahead, a Belgian couple cycling home from New Zealand. Making as much distance as possible before nightfall was on all our minds, for despite the incongruity of meeting two other cyclists in the middle of the Kyrgyzstan savanna, we spoke for barely ten minutes before saying our goodbyes and continuing in opposite directions.

Shade from the lengthening shadows made it far more pleasant cycling at this time of day. The approaching mountains were illuminated by the soft orange glow of dusk but by 9 pm I had passed the small village of Tash-Komur and the last of the light had been extinguished from the wide-open skies. I found myself outside a tiny wooden teahouse. It was next to a flowing brook on the edge of a boundless expanse of farmland and the owner, a kindly looking old man in a colourful skullcap, invited me in. A single room extended away from the dirt road; this was also his home and behind that was a patch of ground where he grew vegetables and herbs and kept chickens. A trapdoor housed his "cellar", a couple of crates lowered into the stream to keep drinks cool and he had a car battery hooked up to a small portable television (I wondered if he had watched Osh TV recently). It was a low-tech version of any tiny counter-bar I might find in Japan except for the lack of alcohol.

He shared some bread and jasmine tea and I commented on the beautiful setting of this place.

"Yes, indeed, what more could I ask for?" he said. "I have this view of the mountains, a job I enjoy and my health". He smiled and showed me to a patch of ground next door where I could pitch my tent. He had run out of food so tonight I would have to cook myself, and as I set up the tent and prepared dinner, a constant stream of aged gentlemen dropped by for a chat with the owner, each one of them also greeting me with a hand on their heart and a softly spoken *"salaam alekum"*. Afterwards they disappeared back into the darkness of the fields.

I boiled up some pasta, adding a can of tuna and a pack of tomato sauce mix I had picked up at the Russian market in Ashgabat, many weeks ago. When I recoiled in a spluttering mess with the first mouthful, I realised that my tomato sauce mix was not tomato sauce but was in actual fact chilli. And the advised measure to add to a meal was one teaspoon, not the whole packet. However, by this point I had attracted an audience of half a dozen curious boys watching every movement of this once-in-a-lifetime spectacle, so I couldn't very well throw the stuff away. There was no choice but to eat the foul concoction, mustering a brave smile while my lips burnt and stomach lining ached and they looked on politely with sympathetic smiles.

It was a long night, much of it spent uncomfortably crouched in a field next door. Insects chattered quietly and the sky above me was clear. In the distance towards the mountains I saw fierce flashes of lightning lasting for much of the night. That's where I would be going.

Rocks, gravel & sand, Kyrgystan

THE FIRST THIRTY KILOMETRES OF ROAD WAS UNPAVED AND skirted the raised edge of an azure-coloured dam. The severity of the ride was matched only by the bare granite backdrop, but at least it was flat and far less a nuisance than the dogs. They had been getting increasingly aggressive since I'd entered this country. In Uzbekistan the dogs could not be bothered to rise up from their slumber, content just to stay curled up in the dirt and eye me lazily as I passed in front of them, but here the canine situation was decidedly more edgy. These dogs were vicious, teeth bared and oddly silent until I would hear their panting from just a few bike lengths away, putting all their energy into giving chase and launching themselves at me.

Ah, but the sport of it all! I found that the best way to confront these mangy mongrels was to direct angry bravado at them and perversely, I was getting to enjoy these confrontations. I always carried a few rocks in the outer pocket of my handlebar bag and whilst initially I might just pause my peddling and aim from the moving bike, increasingly I'd stop and dismount, face down my four-legged assailant and pursue him with a kind of war cry, letting loose a volley of stones from my hand. And if I saw a dog just sleeping obliviously on the side of the road as I approached, well, why not throw a bunch of rocks at him anyway. Just in case.

A deceptively straight line on the map turned into an unbroken series of wretched climbs, and whilst on paper it closely followed the course of the river, reality showed this relationship to be rather tenuous as it alternately spiralled high up into the valley and plunged down again to the riverside. I had an hour's nap at the only teahouse, waking up curiously enough to Alphaville's "Big in Japan", today's eighties hit on this increasingly bizarre Central Asian radio station. A bit optimistic, I said out aloud, taking some comfort in the only voice I had heard all day.

∾

"IF I HADN'T FULLY UNDERSTOOD WHAT PAIN WAS BEFORE TODAY", I had written in my diary, "then I definitely do so now."

I had stayed in Totogul, a scruffy looking village at the foot of a huge blue mountain range, and shared its rickety wooden guest-house with a team of Czech alpinists. They must have known something, because they left a huge bag of freeze-dried mountaineering food for me at the foot of my door in the morning (it would serve as my emergency supplies for the rest of this venture).

Today's initial ascent was through a steep narrow gorge lined with green foliage, nurtured by the blue-grey river cascading down its centre. Still early, it was bathed in shade, but as the morning advanced and the gorge widened into a valley, the trees quickly thinned out and I became a sitting target for the sun. Pedalling out of the saddle and struggling to propel myself any faster than an ambling walk, I passed an abundance of roadside stalls selling nothing but honey, hundreds of bottles of the stuff. They disappeared into the haze behind me as easily as they'd appeared, leaving me doubting their existence. I cooked lunch by the roadside and scrambled down the riverbank to fill up my water bottles, finding that I had attracted a couple of onlookers by the time I got back. They were content to watch silently as I cooked and ate.

The altitude was getting to me. I couldn't quench my thirst and the culmination of some intense climbing over the last few days was making my legs ache like they had never ached before. The valley opened further into high pasture, green velvet plains and knolls, ruled over by serrated snow-capped peaks behind. Here and there were yurts and the occasional dilapidated wooden railway carriage that had found a new lease of life, about as far away from any railway line as you could imagine.

Dozens of bottles of Fanta stacked on the roadside tortured me from afar, urging me to dig deeper in my efforts to get there - but when I did, it was actually horse butter, a putrid bright orange broth packed teasingly into two-litre plastic bottles. I fell for this cruel illusion more than once. The alternative was *kumis* - fermented horse milk - but after my last experience with camels' milk in Uzbekistan I was in no mood for further dairy experimentation.

There were lots of other sour, curdled snacks available along the road and while *kumis* could almost be called the Coca-Cola of the Kyrgyz plateau, *korut* – sheep's milk balls – seemed to be the local equivalent of the Mars Bar. For a hungry and thirsty cyclist, things really could have been better.

$\sim$

THE LAST FIVE MILES TO THE TOP OF THE ALA-BEL PASS WAS agonising, moving ten metres at a time and I was reaching deep into my panniers for some out-of-date energy bars to manage even that. There was rain now, hard and cold at this altitude, so I couldn't stay still for long. Rounding each bend in the road was a lesson in disappointment, the vast plateau surrounding me flattening my perspective of the road; it was impossible to figure out where the pass was and how far. The growing cold and legs that hurt enough to bring tears to my eyes stretched the last mile into an eternity. Any joy I should have felt at pedalling a 50-kilogram bike up to the top of a 3,175-metre pass were dispelled at the sight of a cheerless collection of half-a-dozen decrepit and deserted outbuildings there to greet me, rain-sodden and offering no shelter.

The thought of descending in this miserable weather was depressing and the fact that I had another of these bastards to do tomorrow was downright freaking morbid. I freewheeled at speed down into a vast soggy plain, icy rain needling me like air-gun pellets. Every metre down today, I unwillingly reminded myself, was another metre to climb tomorrow - but surely, I couldn't be as cold as I was right now. My raincoat kept out some of the weather but not all, and I was reluctant to put on extra layers as I needed to keep at least some of my clothes dry. Camping at this altitude it would turn even colder later.

There was a yurt a few hundred yards away from the road and, seeking a respite from the elements, I followed the dirt track leading up to it and hesitantly knocked on the door. Happily, the door opened, and I was invited in. Unhappily, I was presented with a large mug of *kumis*. By late afternoon I rolled into the town of Otmuk - I had learnt that a few scruffy trailers and wooden shacks huddled against the weather constituted a town in this part of the world. I camped behind a wall out of the wind, and it was all I could do to avoid the many types of turd when pitching my tent.

A man sat on his horse high on a nearby bluff and watched me for a long time. The light slowly faded as he turned to silhouette before galloping out of sight along the ridge. In the highlands at least, everyone rides a horse. Whole families on horseback would canter past me and young children could skilfully round up herds of sheep mounted on horses that were far too big for them. I looked clumsy and comical on my bike amongst these people.

The morning was dark and crowned with brooding clouds. The weight of a wet tent on the back of my bike was matched only by the weight of my legs and the heaviness of my heart as I hunkered down into a cold headwind towards the next pass. I was cycling through immense grass plains, the flat and silent expanse on either side of the road revealing nothing but the occasional yurt, wrapped up in dirty bandages like some unfortunate patient. It was uniquely bleak, achingly beautiful.

Savanna ousted green pasture as I climbed higher and a speck on the horizon materialised slowly into a draughty assembly of wood and tin. It served up *plov* and piping hot tea which I sipped gratefully. Then the road twisted skyward and the clouds parted fleetingly to reveal a single paralysing glimpse of the steppe marching south below. I was back above 3,000 metres when the pitch-black mouth of a tunnel entrance appeared in front of me, burrowing itself deep into the side of the mountain. A truck with a long wavering trailer laboured up the road and passed me; it took the full width of the tunnel and was swallowed by the hellish looking entrance in seconds, taillights extinguished, engine smothered.

"No bicycles, no bicycles!" A soldier was hurrying across to me from his post waving at me furiously to stop where I was.

"It is too dangerous for bicycle. You will die in there!" he pronounced adamantly, echoing rather closely my own tentative thoughts on the matter. I should hitch a ride with the next truck that came up the hill, he said.

No, no, I pleaded. I didn't want to wait for a lift and unload my sodden bike just to travel a couple of kilometres. It's not far and it even looks slightly downhill. I can ride through that thing! We went back and forth for some minutes before he finally relented.

"Okay, okay", he said after some thought. "It cost you five dollars."

Two things shocked me about this conversation as I reflected on it later. One, I genuinely wanted to ride into that tunnel. Two, I told him I wasn't going to pay the five dollars.

He led me to the guardhouse; I offered him a cigarette as we sat down in his chilly threadbare office and he stared at me resignedly. He had been stationed up here alone for three months, he said, watching this side of the tunnel while his colleague on the other side watched that. He showed me on the map where he was from – it was on the other side of the country – and showed me a photo of his wife and young daughter. We shared another smoke and he refused my offer of a couple of dollars as a gift, smiling as he gently pushed my hand away. He didn't really want my money, just something to break the monotony.

Making peace with the locals was not good for my health, but other than these occasions I had a strict rule of just one cigarette at the end of the day. Whether sitting at the door of my tent surveying the star-straddled Central Asian night sky, or squeezed onto the balcony of a cheap Chinese hotel, watching prostitutes touting for business below, I thought of this bad habit as a reward for the day's exertions - and a pack of Marlboro was easier to carry than a crate of beer. Rightly or wrongly I convinced myself it was good for stress, a tar and nicotine valve to release the trials of the previous 24 hours with a quick five-minute smoke. Maybe I should have done yoga, but that wasn't going to get me through the checkpoints.

The tunnel wasn't so bad in the end. The guard had radioed ahead to keep it clear and the only scary bit was cycling under the giant unseen ventilators, which rattled noisily in the darkness. Still, it was with some relief that I saw the pinhole of light in the distance, signalling my exit into the next valley. And what a sight that was! Mountains stretched neck-achingly high into the sky above and the road was a dream descent, squeezed between hard granite walls towering thousands of feet either side. It tracked the crystal-clear waters and rapids of a river with more twists and turns than a troupe of whirling dervishes.

I was breaking hard on the corners (*screeeech!*) and leaning deeply into the curves, exiting like the snap of a slingshot while my heavily loaded racks and panniers worked hard to dampen the gnarly and pitted road surface. When the gradient eventually eased, I could still coast downhill for another two hours as mountains softened into foothills and finally into plains. Fields stretched to the horizon in a glorious orange-gold blaze under the late afternoon sun.

Relieved that the highest mountains were now behind me I planned to enjoy some cosmopolitan comforts for a few days, so I joined the main road for Bishkek hoping to make as much distance as possible before nightfall. The last week in the wilds had deceived me; at most I was expecting to find a solitary teahouse amongst sparse prairie, but houses started appearing and people were strolling up and down an increasingly busy road. It was getting late, I was tired, and with already 150 kilometres on the clock there was no way I was up to cycling the remaining 50 kilometres into the city - and I knew from any number of travel warnings that Bishkek was not a place to start exploring once the sun went down.

SUNSET HAD COME AND GONE BY THE TIME I FOUND A SPOT IN A field, and a gnarly looking Russian farmer appeared out of the darkness to introduce himself as I was fixing the last of the tent pegs.

"*Zdravstvuyte!*" he boomed, and introduced himself, inquisitive blue eyes appraising me. "My name is Yura and this is my farm".

Oh no, he's going to tell me to move on I thought. But instead he broke into a wide grin.

"I welcome you to my field!"

Yura lived a hundred yards from where I'd pitched my tent and while I finished setting up, he prepared a campfire, some watermelon and two bottles of homemade vodka. We settled down in front of the fire, lounging in the grass and watching the flames in the pitch blackness while his wife walked to and from the farmhouse keeping us supplied with snacks. Yura was a man of few words and I of little Russian, so after the hardships of the mountains now behind me I positively embraced his suggestion of toasts with vodka shots. One and a half bottles later he passed out in the field and was dragged off home by a couple of local boys, while I managed to crawl the few feet to my tent and pass out there. I woke up at dawn with the moist black snout of a dairy cow nuzzling my neck through the tent opening, and I idly reflected that this was the best offer I'd had for months.

Soon after I'd packed up my tent Yura appeared with the remains of last night's vodka and I learnt the Russian for "hair of the dog". He gave me a tour of his farm insisting that I take photos of everything while he posed for the camera. The front of the house. The kitchen. The barn. The workshop. He enjoyed seeing the results on the camera's LCD display and we moved on to his goats and cows. They all had names and he introduced me to each of them in turn starting with the goats.

"This is Popo, always hungry."

"This one, Luigi, he is over fifteen years old."

I met them all while Yura affectionately stroked and patted each of them.

"They are my friends", he said, now starting on the bovine introductions. I spotted the one who had made my acquaintance earlier.

"Ah yes Juley, she is the friendliest of all!" and we took photos of every single one. Then we moved into the garden and I took photos of Yura in the cabbage patch, the flower bed, under the pear tree, next to the walnut tree, under the grape trellises and in front of his melons. Then I handed him the camera, swapped places and we did it all again.

Some considerable time had passed before we eventually said our goodbyes and I could retreat, making my way to a local cafeteria for breakfast. Yura showed up at the same place fifteen minutes later and we kicked off a whole new round of photographs with pictures of the place inside and out, and various combinations of the staff and customers. It was all done in good humour and everyone even managed to put together a Good Luck card for me during these shenanigans before waving me off on the road to Bishkek, physically restraining a teary-eyed Yura from running after me.

My best offer yet, Kyrgyzstan

CHAPTER 16
BLACKPOOL, KYRGYZSTAN

The road into Bishkek was dreary and busy and I observed increasing numbers of Russians as I got closer to the city, surprising me with their blonde hair and slab-white skin, blue eyes gazing blankly past me, or coldly and disparagingly at me. The miles went quickly, and I was in a Bishkek guesthouse by lunchtime. The friendly young Uzbek who ran the place booked me in and showed me my bunk. He had two eccentric uncles living in the garden, each of whom whispered to me in confiding tones that the other one was crazy.

Bishkek: Eastern Asian looks with Russian manners. You can stand at a shop counter empty of other customers and be completely ignored by the three people manning the registers as they talked amongst themselves. Your first couple of attempts to get their attention are met with contemptuous glances and you find yourself apologising for being a nuisance. With a snort of derision they finish up their conversation, talking quite obviously about you now, and after some insult said just loud enough to allow you only to hear half of it, one of them saunters over to the counter, snatches your money away and stares at you defiantly. And for some godforsaken reason, you say "Thank you".

The contrast between the Kyrgyz nomads of the highlands and the Russified attitude of the city was striking, but the mix of Orientals, Slavs and everything in-between offered me some welcome anonymity. It was marvellous to mingle with other travellers for the first time since Samarkand and a relief to just lounge around in the kitchen chatting with the other guests, catching up on email and reading. The city itself was pleasant enough with wide boulevards lined by trees and a few decent parks. The Ala-Too Mountains I had crossed to the south-east formed a spectacular backdrop to the city, and I looked upon them with particular satisfaction.

Mercifully there were no real sights as such, so no inner voice telling me I should be visiting such-and-such market or taking pictures of so-and-so madrasah. There were few chores either, no visas to arrange and no bike supplies to pick up. I took only one photograph in all my time there and that was on the day I arrived, of my bike propped up in front of the rather plain looking Ala-Too Square where Kyrgyzstan's Tulip revolution had been put in motion by thousands of protestors just a few months ago.

After that I had kept my eye on the pavement, careful not to fall down one of the many open manholes which had been deprived of their covers, stolen for scrap metal.

~

THE TRIALS OF THE ROAD HAD CAUGHT UP WITH ME AND I CAME down with a fever, vomiting and other unpleasantness, so it was close to a week before I said my farewells, looking forward to Lake Issyk-Kul and a few days of comfortably flat cycling. But it was not only the lake that I was anticipating; during my recuperation I had become friendly with an attractive French backpacker, enamoured with the romance of my biking adventures. She was stopping here for a few days before continuing to Karakol on the far side of the lake, to volunteer at an NGO located there.

"You have to visit me on your way to Karakol", she had told me in her rather intense manner, handing me the address as we figured out where it was on my map. "We must see each other again, Steve."

We parted with a brief kiss at the door of the crowded hostel, when she boarded her minibus. I followed on my bike as far as the end of the street where to my great surprise I was suddenly, and disconcertingly, violently sick. There was a familiar rumbling before my stomach cramped up, and I knew I had to get back to the guest-house double quick.

And that is where I lingered miserably into a second week, inca-pacitated in bed, the toilet or the garden. Calculating that it would take four days of cycling to reach René and knowing that she would be there for only one week, I saw my chance slipping away day by day until I reached the point where even a bus wouldn't get me there in time. Whilst life-endangering encounters and debilitating illnesses were straightforward enough, it seemed that romantic conquest would continue to prove an elusive milestone.

As I was in the garden readying my bike for departure, three young guys rolled in on their bikes and saw me with my tools and panniers on the ground.

"You're not Steve, are you?" one of them asked, and I tried to recall where on earth I may have known him from.

"We heard about you on the road to Bishkek when we stopped at a café. All they could talk about was you – Steve this, Steve that, Steve everything and then we were all invited to stay in 'Steve's Field'. You're famous!" he said.

They were three French friends cycling from Paris to Beijing. We swapped stories starting with my own recent setbacks, but they had seen worse luck than I. Passing up the offer of a night in Steve's Field they had cycled on a little further and camped in some urban woods. Whilst I had been assaulted by nothing more than rough vodka and a sizeable hangover, they had to give up their money and much of their gear at knifepoint.

However, they were in good spirits. I admired their camaraderie, reminding me of my short time cycling with Team Swiss and I realised somewhat morosely that I would be back on my own within a matter of hours. Yet at least I was leaving a legacy behind. Whilst Alexander the Great may have had magnificent cities named after him, I was more than satisfied with a field.

MY LEGS WERE FEELING THE WEIGHT OF THE BIKE AFTER MY TEN days of convalescence and the only amusement to be had was at a railway crossing, when half a dozen excited tourists leapt from a waiting minibus to take photos of a tired looking diesel locomotive. It has got to be a particularly specialist tour operator that provides trainspotting holidays to this part of the world.

I cleared the outlying towns and villages of the capital by mid-afternoon and found a secluded place to make camp in the spacious and overgrown grounds of a derelict factory. Surrounded by rusting oil tanks and huge arrays of steel piping, nature had already made swift work of reclaiming this space for itself, and the only other soul in this ruin was an elderly night watchman, who wished me good night before retiring into the dark abyss of the main building. I switched on my shortwave radio and tuned into the BBC World Service. It was a bulky device and the reception wasn't always that good - depending on the country the transmission might even be blocked - but tonight it worked and when I listened to the very British voices of an interview with Paul Weller, I felt not quite as far away from home as I was.

In the morning I pushed up through Shoestring Gorge, a long road which cut narrowly upwards through the Tian Shan mountains. My body was still somewhat rebelling against the sudden return to life fused to a bicycle frame, and there wasn't a part which didn't ache. However - I was enjoying myself! With a cool breeze, clear blue skies and a fiercely effervescent river tumbling down the side of the road, what was not to like?

Finishing lunch at a roadside stall I tried and actually failed to get up from the table. Stiff painful legs, a raw backside and now two painful knees; I was utterly exhausted, and it took all my remaining willpower to make it to the next town of Balykchy, suffering the torment of another long climb. The only hotel I could find was garishly decorated in some unnerving Jolly Roger theme and patrolled by shaven-skulled musclemen in shiny black suits. The rooms were priced from $40 to $100, a huge amount in local terms, and I was sure there were plenty of expensive sailor-themed entertainment options available as well, laid on for what I was certain would be a rather shady clientele. Fortunately, the concierge intercepted me and offered to let me stay with his family nearby for 100 *som* (about $2) instead.

Issyk-Kul is one of the largest lakes in the region, but I had a hard time finding it the next morning, ending up on the northern shore rather than the southern shore which I had aimed for. The cool blue waters of the lake were sparkling half a mile off to my right, separated by fields stretching down to the shore; in maddening contrast, scorched mountains rose up like an impenetrable wall to my left, radiating heat and separating Kyrgyzstan from her northern neighbour of Kazakhstan. I sure hope they get a little smaller I thought, knowing that I would be crossing these in a few more days. At least I found cause to celebrate my failed sense of direction. On the far side of the lake I could make out a vertically jagged road cut into bare cliffs and remembered how I had read many months ago that the southern route was full of "rugged ups and downs". Since I now had a pretty good idea of what "rugged" meant in these parts, I realised what a fortunate mistake I'd made.

A relaxed seaside atmosphere greeted me as the road passed through many small villages, usually a couple of scruffy shops and a boarding house on either side of a single street leading down to the beach. Big-boned Russian and Kyrgyz wives lolled on their towels a few yards from the water while their husbands tended to the barbeques at the back. The closer I got to the town of Cholpon-Ata the more people I saw on the roads and the more frenetic the atmosphere. I stopped for lunch at a busy row of roadside yurts and ordered a bowl of *laghman*. While waiting for it to arrive I heard a commotion from the yurt next door with raised voices, shouting and the crashing of pots and pans. The disturbance now escalated into screaming and the sound of splintering furniture. I peered my head around the corner just in time to see a bloke come rolling out of the door, saloon-bar style, to end up in a collapsed heap in the dust. Well, that explained the delay of my lunch - he was the cook.

There were a mass of shops selling inflatable armbands, snorkels and masks, buckets and spades, and the usual assortment of essential beach apparel as well as plenty of places renting out parasols, deckchairs, rubber dinghies and large billboards advertising banana-boat rides (albeit dodgy-looking homemade ones). And although I couldn't read Cyrillic, I was confident that what I saw written across the front of a multitude of headwear was the Russian for "Kiss me Quick". I didn't find a bingo hall but there was no doubt in my mind - Cholpon-Ata was the Blackpool of Central Asia.

The holiday atmosphere evaporated soon after I left town. The traffic thinned out and it became much quieter. There seemed to have been a turning point in the fortunes of the people out here, for the villages looked considerably poorer than before, with half-derelict homes and Kyrgyz men sitting around outside on their haunches, eyeing me as I rode past.

Yet that's not to say I didn't meet the locals; after the cook who had landed at my feet bloody and dazed in Cholpon-Ata, my next encounter was with a wide-eyed, mad-looking fellow on a rusty Honda Cub who buzzed around my bike, alternating between cutting me up, shoving me towards the ditch and swerving danger-ously across the full width of the road, whilst giving the finger to oncoming traffic and shouting obscenities at everyone else. After ten minutes of this, his scooter gave up, the exhaust exploded into a plume of black smoke and he came quickly to a halt. I saw his brow creased in puzzlement, his middle finger still raised defiantly, and I felt a little like some bicycle-riding Mad Max as my adversary got smaller in the rear-view mirror.

I felt uneasy cycling through these villages but at least I received an honest display of distain, the eyes (and sometime the yells) of the locals asking just what in the hell was I doing here. Instead of stop-ping at a farmhouse or *dacha* summer house to ask permission to camp, I continued to cycle until after sunset, looking for somewhere hidden to pitch my tent. The road closely followed the vast expanse of Issyk-Kul on my right, now a dark velvet hue in the twilight and apart from the occasional vehicle it was completely silent. Before the light disappeared completely and making sure that nobody was around to watch, I slipped into the next field, merging into the shadows and rolled my bike to a clump of trees well away from the road. I raced against the encroaching darkness to get my tent set up in time for me to collapse into an exhausted heap.

But it was a restless night. I was woken up by what sounded like a roll of thunder but was actually a horse and rider galloping through the darkness, passing within a few yards of my tent. I wasn't too sure what worried me most – whether he had seen me or whether indeed, he had not.

~

HOW WOULD YOU CHOOSE TO LIVE YOUR LIFE? A ROLLERCOASTER ride of ups and downs, anxious and fearful one moment but hollering with joy the next? Or careful navigation of life's surprises, teasing as much happiness from each day as you can. Probably somewhere in-between, I would guess. It is of course an analogy for traveling by bike, with the rollercoaster winning every time. And this is how it should be. The way good days and bad days constantly jostle for position would send any sane person mad in the real world but travelling this way gives you the opportunity to live like that. Whether you want to or not.

I woke up to a beautiful sunrise, ate a breakfast of bread and jam in the orange-yellow glow of dawn and packed up swiftly to a sere-nade of birdsong, pulling my bike up to the road before anyone was the wiser. I cycled through long colonnades of tall pines throwing cool shadows across the road, past fields abundant and colourful with ripened corn while the lake glittered in the sunlight like lazily scattered diamonds. Mountains reared up closely but today I felt more of their majesty and less of their menace, and the villages were well-kept with whitewashed cottages sporting sky-blue trimmings on the doors and windows. From among the morose stares I even received occasional smiles; one group of young girls spotted me and waved madly as I approached, and then jumped up and down with unrestrained excitement and mad giggles when I waved back.

Passing the eastern boundary of the lake I found myself arriving at Karakol in time for lunch, having already covered eighty kilome-tres relatively effortlessly. This is the fourth largest city in Kyrgyzs-tan, but the city centre was just a couple of streets crisscrossing each other, one or two acceptable places to eat and the now familiar pattern of half-bare general-purpose hardware and grocery stores. It was also the focus for a handful of trekking and climbing agencies and a plethora of signboards advertising "yurt stays".

I booked into a guesthouse for two nights and spent the next day resting up, giving my legs, knees and bum a chance to recover. I met a couple of doleful looking Polish high-altitude climbers; they were waiting for their flight home after an expedition had gone wrong and two of their party had been evacuated with frostbite.

It was my last stop before China and this time next week I would be on the road to Shanghai. Once more it was disquieting to imagine dealing with a new culture and people after spending the last few months traversing the countries of Central Asia. This loose amalgamation of ancient kingdoms had been conquered by Russia in the mid-19th century and had only regained their independence relatively recently, after the breakup of the Soviet Union in the nineties. Soviet rule represented little more than a hundred years in a history of thousands and it made for a colourful hotchpotch of Slavic values and nomadic customs. And just as I felt I was getting comfortable with the place it was time to move on. China would tax my personal resources once again.

The waitress interrupted my daydreaming and presented me with the bill for lunch while I was still chewing a chicken leg, slamming it down on the page of the book I was reading at that very moment. I was going to miss all this.

Hitting the road again, Kyrgyzstan

CHAPTER 17
NIGHT TERRORS IN KAZAKHSTAN

It would be September in a week and a cold and cloudy start to
the morning hinted that autumn was just around the corner. I
struck north-east via the village of Tup to the Kazakh border and
after all other side roads had vanished, found myself on one uninterrupted road, narrow and straight, leading me into a big, open and
lonely nowhere. Cloud-shrouded mountains waited for me in the far
distance, brooding over their approaching visitor.

On the plains at least, the sun had emerged, and I had the road
to myself bar a few horses and carts. There were no towns or
villages, just the odd hidden farmhouse, and the people I did meet
were good-natured, offering smiles and greetings rather than sneers
and swearing. Even the dogs surveyed me with a mild, even friendly
curiosity.

The rough road battered my body as the miles progressed but
the open prairie and the green, pine-filled valley that I was following
filled my vision and lifted my spirits. The river crashed over rapids
alongside me as Kyrgyz cowboys surveyed their livestock from the
surrounding knolls, directing their sheepdogs with shrill whistles
which echoed off the empty hillsides.

A family invited me into their ranch for tea. For the first time
since leaving Europe tea was now served with milk, though my
secret wish for some digestives was met instead with a plate of sour
milk balls. Their twelve-year-old son translated excited questions

from the rest of the family into a form I could understand; bits of Russian, gestures and some drawing on a notebook - it is of course always the kids who have the knack of communicating. His two baby sisters sat on the opposite side of the table frozen in motion and staring wide-eyed at me from grimy faces, soup dribbling from their open mouths.

Their father proudly showed me his horses, not locked in some paddock but roaming free on the surrounding pasture. He called out the name of one mare and she cantered up to him.

"You ride a bicycle every day", he said. "Now try a horse."

I mounted with some difficulty and clung on in embarrassed incompetence while the horse snorted distain, the boy looked on in mortal disappointment, and the father took back the reins and gave me the nod to dismount, which I did with a similar lack of dignity.

THE ROAD DETERIORATED COMPLETELY INTO GRAVEL AND ROCK and cut gently upwards through lush grasslands, like a narrow crease in a cloak of green velvet. I made out two solitary shapes in the distance coming my way - German cyclists riding home from China, on this road of all places. Is it only herders and the occasional mad cyclist who travels these backroads of Central Asia?

It was a long, flat run to the Kazakhstan border, but it was getting late and I was famished. Knowing how unpredictable these border crossings could be, I thought it prudent to prepare my dinner while it was still light, so set up my stove by the side of the road. It was a couple of hundred yards before the border post and a guard approached me after a few minutes. Unexpectedly he was smiling.

"Hey, why not come inside and cook in our kitchen? It is huge and there are only two of us", he said. "Use what you need."

He was a jovial chap and gave me some bread to supplement my pasta. While I cooked, he sat down to his own dinner and we chatted about my trip. He was friendly and laid-back and we could even share a few jokes, though he was somewhat mystified that I hadn't tried any Kyrgyz prostitutes. I assured him that I'd be sure to try plenty of Kazakh ones instead.

As I was sitting down to eat, his colleague joined us, having woken from his nap in the upstairs barracks. I didn't like the look of this one and if my new friend was good cop, then this guy was undoubtedly bad cop. Sure enough, after his partner had explained my story to him, his beady little eyes flickered with wicked opportunity and he held out his hand and fingered my watch. It was a good watch, including a compass, barometer and altimeter; this was before the days of the smartphone and it was invaluable to me.

"Present", he said flatly. It wasn't a question. It was a demand.

My strategy, I decided, would be delay and humour. I smiled back at his leering, clammy face and gave him a handshake.

"Present!" I replied in an overly chirpy voice.

Good Cop laughed appreciatively but Bad Cop stared at me coldly and continued to badger me for his "present" throughout my meal, while Good Cop told him to cut it out. I told him he would get something once I'd finished eating but I would have to look through my bags for it. This settled him somewhat while I cleared my plate, washed the dishes and stealthily packed everything back on the bike, wondering what I should do next. There was nothing I really didn't need here, and I certainly didn't want to produce any cash - who knew where that would lead. Humour, I said to myself again, placate him with humour. So I asked him to close his eyes, which surprisingly he did, and I put half-a-dozen walnuts in his open palms.

While his face slowly reddened, his jaw locked and he came close to cracking open those walnuts with his bare hands, Good Cop steered me quickly outside and helped me with my bike to the sentry box, stamped my passport and ushered me safely over to the Kazakh side.

"Good luck", he said, and I think he meant it.

The Kazakh guards were obnoxious, spotty-faced teenagers with guns who mocked my Russian. Reflecting on the results of my recent comedic recklessness, I judged it best not to crack any jokes.

It was dusk by the time I got through the border checks and the last rays of the sun bathed the Tian Shan in orange fire. Negotiating this appalling road in darkness would be madness so I pushed the bike up a grassy hill and pitched my tent in an empty pasture. It wasn't empty for long though, as horses were soon trotting nonchalantly past my tent door as if it was some kind of equestrian cross-roads. It was almost dark so I quickly packed and pushed further up another hill, where I found a Kazakh rancher's cottage; the family inside said I could use their wagon, another of those baffling old wooden railway carriages, like a shed on wheels, that was set up next door. They invited me into the house for dinner and after success-fully dodging curdled horse-milk products for an entire month in Kyrgyzstan, I was now faced with a large meal in which that dreaded substance formed the main ingredient of every single dish.

Later I stood outside and looked up at the night sky. There were no towns or cities for nearly a hundred miles and until this moment, I had never appreciated that there were so many stars and that they could be so astonishingly bright. I watched as shooting stars competed for my attention, late into the night.

Kazakh grasslands

CHOPSTICKS ON THE TABLE AT LUNCHTIME TRIGGERED A RUSH OF excitement; it was the first solid sign that I was nearing China, the border only a couple of days away. I had been gaining elevation slowly since Lake Issyk-Kul and my altimeter told me I was at over 2,000 metres. Pasture had been usurped by arid savanna and

Kazakh cowboys by windblown brush and tumbleweed; bar the snow-capped mountains encircling me at great distance, I was alone on a limitless desert plain.

The featureless steppe removed all sense of gradient, and my bike started to freewheel and then accelerate along what looked like a thoroughly flat road. I hurtled downwards into a dry narrow gorge that cut like a knife through the desiccated skin of the land; rock and soil grew taller on either side of me, before the road imperceptibly levelled off and turned upwards, forcing one more climb on me before resurfacing onto the steppe. I didn't see another vehicle the whole time apart from a few pick-up trucks parked in the village of Shonzhy, the last place I passed before pulling off the road for the night. Dry sandy plains transformed into scrubland and marsh, and the first place I choose for a campsite resulted in two dozen mosquitos firmly attached to my arm. It took some time to find a place somewhat less infested, but it was a moot point in the end - neither option could have prevented the terrifying night ahead.

From the door of my tent I watched the early evening sky turn from blue to black, and the stars were swiftly extinguished. It took no more than a few seconds before there were ominous flashes overhead, igniting the whole clearing in a snapshot of electric light, trees and brush surrounding me in menacing silhouette. Oh my God, I thought, what if I was hit by lightning? But before I could even begin to brood over that peril, my eardrums were suddenly assaulted by what seemed to be the furious revving of a V12 engine, right outside my tent door.

And then all hell broke loose.

Diabolical blasts of wind flattened my tent, with me inside it, slamming the walls from one side to the other. Bags and belongings flew all over the place as a demonic whirlwind tried to rip up the floor from beneath me. My bike was pushed and dragged across the ground outside as ear-piercing screams and wails circled my tent like vengeful wraiths.

It looked inevitable that the tent would be devoured, along with everything in it, but much more terrifying was the premonition that I too would be swept up with the whole bloody lot as well, sucked up into some despicable Wizard of Oz tornado. I pulled everything, including my bike, into a tight bundle around me, and hoped that in aggregate we would be heavy enough to remain anchored to the ground.

At that moment I had never felt so alone, had never felt so frightened. I clasped with white knuckles the small silver medallion around my neck of Saint Christopher, the patron saint of travellers, uttering prayers under my breath. My mother had given it to me for good luck and now I was rapidly rediscovering a faith unvisited since my first Holy Communion.

The wind buffered me relentlessly for two hours, until it calmed as abruptly as it had begun. A crystal-clear starlit sky appeared above me bordered by dense cloud; I supposed this was what is meant by the eye of the storm, because I was woken up an hour later by the wind howling and violent gusts trying to pull me away again. However, by now I had some idea of what to expect and could rein in the worst of my fears. I could also appreciate that this was one strong tent.

THANKFUL TO BE IN ONE PIECE AND ACTUALLY GRATEFUL TO gravity for a change, the rough night was followed by a dog-tired day, not helped by the monotonous scrubland, dark skies and the usual array of dismal border towns to ride through. In one of these towns I stopped for lunch and a grizzled old man surprised me by introducing himself in English.

"May I sit down next to you?" he asked politely and queried me about my journey. I explained that I was heading into China.

"I see. So you will cross at Khorgas and travel through Xinjiang - my motherland. I am Uighur, and maybe you have heard of our struggle?" he asked, watching for my reaction.

"The Chinese steal our land and treat us no better than animals. If we try to be good Muslims, they put us in prison, torture and then execute us."

Xinjiang province was China's Wild West, a huge autonomous region encompassing the vast Taklamakan and Gobi deserts. For over two millennia this part of the world was cut off from ancient China by the Great Wall. It was home to the Uighur people, ethnically and culturally far closer to the peoples of Central Asia than

China, but apart from occasional and short-lived declarations of independence, it had been an unwilling appendage to China since the 18th century. And since the 1950s there had been large scale migration of Chinese into the region, taking advantage of new industries built around its massive oil and gas deposits.

The spoils of this new gold rush inherently go to the Chinese migrants, whilst the Uighur are excluded. They tend to get the lowest paid jobs, live in the most dismal conditions and suffer constant restrictions against their traditions and religion. Protests are suppressed and any signs of dissent dealt with firmly. A low-level violent insurgency has grown out of this discontent, and with that comes regular crackdowns against suspected "terrorists" which always casts a wide net. The situation was bleak, and this old man complained bitterly about the occupation of his homeland; it was a precursor to the long list of injustices I would hear a lot about over the next couple of thousand kilometres.

Not far from the border town of Khorgas it started to rain and soon turned into a torrential onslaught soaking me thoroughly in a matter of minutes, a cold, penetrating rain that taught me how to shiver again. A long and soggy crowd of people were laying siege to the customs post and it was absolute chaos, mainly small-time Chinese traders jostling with each other for position, returning home for an upcoming three-day public holiday. These people knew how to jump queues, and unsurprisingly I was the very last person through immigration that evening.

When I wheeled my bike through the last checkpoint it was 9 pm Beijing time (7 pm Xinjiang time) and also the first occasion I had ever stepped into mainland China. My port of entry was unusual - an obscure border town in the extreme north-west, far beyond the Great Wall, even beyond the Gobi Desert.

Uighur men in skullcaps and women in paisley dresses reminded me I was barely out of Central Asia and although they outnumbered the Chinese on the street, there was nevertheless an immediate and overriding culture shock; the road was lined by a hundred small restaurants, stalls and shops, all decorated in garish bright red signs and people packed shoulder to shoulder. The severe backdrop of the northern Tian Shan's ice-capped peaks did little to soothe the sensory attack of colours, smells and a thousand voices shouting to each other all at once in a dozen new languages. Brightly coloured signs in Chinese, Arabic and Russian confronted me from every angle, three-wheeled "moto taxis" scuttled back and forth along the road, and a dozen random faces approached me offering a myriad of goods and services.

I was already looking forward to getting back to the desert.

Probably not a Kazakh horseman

CHAPTER 18

XINJIANG AND THE NORTHWEST FRONTIER

My first meal in China was the best meal I had eaten in months, a plethora of rice, steamed vegetables, marinated chicken and spicy tofu. I was in a starkly lit concrete-floored room, the grandiose sign and decoration outside belying a bare functional interior. The waitress looked at me sour-faced and I wasn't surprised when she immediately walked away, refusing to serve me because I couldn't speak the language. I had to wait half-an-hour for someone else to come back to deal with me.

A neighbouring table hosted the only other customers, a group of Uighur men, throwing themselves into singing what I guessed was a Uighur folk song, a few quite emotional and one or two falling over my table and then being helped up by apologetic friends. I'll have to learn some Uighur rebel songs myself, I thought, still smarting at the attitude of the waitress. However, the food was very good; it was just going to take some time to get used to reading the menu. In Central Asia things were so much easier – you just didn't get a choice.

I spent a day in Khorgas to learn some survival vocabulary, clean up my bike, and try to get a feel for what I'd be dealing with over the next couple of months. My first goal was Jiyuguan, the western-most outpost of the Great Wall. It would take two thousand parched kilometres to get here, skirting the northern edge of the Taklamakan Desert and cutting through the Gobi Desert.

A chain of well-populated oasis towns, known as the Hexi Corridor, would then signal the slow transition from desert to agriculture, and eventually usher me into Xi'an. One of China's ancient capitals, the city of Xi'an also marked the end of the Silk Road.

Finally was Shanghai, a parade of the past and future, the metamorphosis of a country of farmers into an industrial superpower. The isolation of the desert will have never seemed so far away when I'd finally roll into Shanghai, population fourteen million and counting.

China was a mammoth undertaking: no matter how I split up this journey, no matter how many times I looked at the map... I still had no sense of nearing the end of it.

LAST NIGHT I NOTICED WITH SOME DISMAY THAT NOT everything was documented on my map; there was a 200-kilometre gap which neither my Central Asia nor my Western China map covered. It took me two hours in an internet café to find the missing piece on an obscure academic website (this was before the days of Google Maps). However, it took me only two minutes to copy by hand - when you are this far away from anywhere, you just don't get that many roads to choose from.

It was a beautiful morning. Rows of tall trees bordered lush green fields and families on overladen bicycles wavered left to right in front of me. Corn was being harvested and had been laid down on the road to dry in the sun, a bright yellow strip extending for miles ahead. Some people smiled and some gave me the thumbs up, but most just stared in utter bemusement. Stone distance markers started appearing on the roadside: shaped portentously like little tombstones, the first one showed a shocking 4950 km... it was the distance left to Shanghai.

The road climbed the serpentine slopes of a gorge, the sun-burnished plain below now dotted with yurts. I came across a long row of stalls selling nothing but honey, hundreds of bottles of the stuff. A young Uighur couple called me over to one of the stalls and treated me to freshly baked bread and honey.

"Please help yourself to some tea as well!" they urged, pouring me a cup of Jasmine tea and refilling it before I had drunk it all. Black tea had been succeeded by Jasmine tea in China, and I savoured its fragrance while waiting for the cup to cool. They showed me the calling card of a German couple.

"We met them a few month ago, travelling this road by horse. Do you know them perhaps?" they asked.

Herds of cows and sheep took the full width of the road, the herders lazily smacking their charges into some kind of order as they spurred them down the mountain. I almost got knocked off my bike by one inquisitive camel, saddled-up but with no rider on board; he had probably been thrown and abandoned a few miles back I reckoned, as this one didn't look like the type to obey orders.

It took me the full morning to reach the top of the pass and I looked back with satisfaction over the valley below. The mountains were carpeted in swathes of tall pines and green pasture, while the road I had climbed zigzagged its way along the course of a cobalt-blue river. Mountain goats perched on rocky precipices joined me in silent regard of this majestic panorama.

Lake Sayram greeted me on the other side of pass, enveloped by a ring of mountains. A sign advertised hot food by the lake, so I turned off the road, barely managing to control my bike on the damp grass slopes leading down there. It was decidedly chilly and on the shore were rows of flimsy looking wooden shacks in badly chipped red paint. Overlooking this eyesore from a hillside above were a few yurts and as I surveyed these rather grim surroundings, I realised I was in some kind of Chinese lake resort.

Food was served in one of the yurts. I was promised a huge lamb stew, so I paid the extortionate sum requested by the local spiv and settled down inside. It took an hour for a small plate of bread and cucumber to arrive and after dumbly waiting for another thirty minutes, now ravenous with hunger, I had to stand over the cook's shoulder and make sure he supplemented it with lamb. It was dark by the time I got my dinner and then it started to rain – there was now no choice but to stay the night in a bloody tourist yurt.

"This sleeps four people", smiled the charlatan who had no doubt planned this all along. "So you must pay for four people."

In the shacks by the lake, appalling singers were belting out crap karaoke love songs, and as I listened to the toneless wailings of inebriated Chinese holiday-makers, I felt a little homesick for Tokyo, where inebriated salarymen would be doing the exact same thing right now.

Later that night I was woken up by a commotion at the entrance to the yurt. I had used my bike as a wedge against the door but now there were some people trying to get in – it was the dodgy owner and three other blokes.

"I am sorry, but my brothers have just arrived after a long journey and need somewhere to sleep", he said. "Can they please stay here tonight?"

It was absolutely freezing out there and raining really hard. They were all stinking drunk and whoever they were, it was my guess that their wives had locked them out. I smiled sympathetically, pulled the door tightly shut, deployed my bike lock for good measure and then went back to sleep, a little happier now than when I'd woken up.

Western Xinjiang, China

DAWN WAS A DULL BATTLESHIP GREY, LIGHT DRIZZLE alternating with driving rain. The lake was all but invisible and I sealed myself against the elements as best I could: rain trousers, thermal jacket, Gore-Tex top, plastic bags on my feet and full-length gloves on my hands. After half an hour my hands and feet were soaked through and I was deliberating whether to just find some refuge until the weather cleared. At the eastern point of the lake I came across a rickety wooden structure and approached the open door. Rotten shutters snapped back and forth with the violent gusts of wind and the colourless surface of the lake was just about visible through smeared windows, filling the cold bare room with a weak, limpid blue-grey light. It was, of course, another Chinese resort hotel. I found it more welcoming outside.

There was a descent of nearly 2,000 metres from the lake, my fingers were frozen numb and my face stinging from hard drops of rain pelting me like stones. By the time the road flattened out almost an hour later I was shaking uncontrollably. There was no feeling left in my fingers and I struggled for several minutes to get my useless gloves off my frozen hands. What was borderline hypothermia, I shrugged off with some hot food and a nice cup of tea at a muddy roadside stall, got back on my bike and carried on.

I was tougher now than I had ever been in my life!

My spirits were lifted when the rain ceased and the sun came out, but the villages I passed through were depressing lines of featureless single-storey buildings, heavy iron grills covering small windows and padlocked steel doors. The only distinguishing mark might be a few Chinese characters painted on the wall – I didn't know if they were homes, shops or something else, but the lengths people had gone to protect some very modest real estate wasn't exactly reassuring for a man in a tent.

From the mysterious to the surreal: the road abruptly turned into a smoothly surfaced motorway with vivid green crash barriers and pristinely painted white lines, separating six lanes of asphalt disappearing over the horizon. There was practically nobody else on it. Once in a while I would meet a car, sometimes on the proper side of the road, sometimes not, the driver seemingly unaware how to deal with such choice, whilst elaborate flyovers had been built to service half-derelict villages of a dozen mud-brick houses in the desert. In this, the most remote province of China, there was a colossal construction effort in progress, and it was clear that the Chinese government was serious about promoting migration into the north-west. If the local Uighur population were struggling to retain some autonomy today, then their future looked increasingly bleak.

Everything ended as unexpectedly as it had begun, fizzling out into a bumpy lane, making me question if the whole thing had been imagined. I ordered *laghman* at a Uighur truck stop, a line of makeshift stalls and restaurants spilling into the road, while I sat back on the straining plastic chair to watch grainy Uzbek pop videos playing on a television and VCR set up outside. The people were relaxed and friendly and during the course of a meal I imagined I was back in Central Asia, oddly easing my homesickness.

It was still light when I got to Jinghe, despite a hundred miles on the clock. It was a small but bustling town, and I soon found a hotel. The room was basic but clean enough and I shared it with two other guys and my bike; the toilets, however, lived up to the horror stories and I was disheartened by the rotten aim of so many of the guests.

That night there was some remarkable hawking and spitting going on in the corridor outside my room, and I had to navigate my bicycle through its remnants the next morning more gingerly than any fast-flowing stream or puddle-filled track. This habit of hocking up all you've got was something I would never get used to in China. Indoors, outdoors, it didn't seem to matter, and maybe I'm old fashioned, but when I see an attractive woman doing it with such impressive nonchalance then I know something is not right with the world.

Travelling the outskirts of the Taklamakan desert, hours of smooth empty miles and unchanging waterless savanna exasperated me to the point that I turned off the highway and on to a rutted side road just to break the monotony. This also went on endlessly, but just more painfully. I passed one bedraggled-looking man lumbering along in the middle of the road, face plastered in dirt and sand. Where had he come from? What was he *doing*? Once in a while there was a dirt road going north, turning off perpendicular into the hazy desert but there was nothing there! Where was it heading? What purpose did it serve?

Todak was a town being built in this wilderness, a chaotic street of hastily erected buildings, restaurants and noisy workshops on either side of a half-finished, salmon-pink ten storey building which seemed to contain government offices and apartments. The centrepiece of all this was, most aptly, the bank. Despite the hubbub of activity around me and some very surprised stares, I could sit down to lunch and eat it undisturbed by anyone. One thing I liked about China was the respect paid to a meal; only once I had finished would everyone swarm around, bombard me with questions, squeeze the tyres and prod my legs.

On the highway, groups of women carted heavy bags of sand in wheelbarrows, mixed cement and laid long stretches of tarmac under the punishing sun. I saw numerous chain gangs, prisoners providing hard labour in the service of the government's construction boom, warily watched over by machine-gun toting prison guards in mirrored sunglasses.

Everybody seemed to be working on this freaking highway!

A little before sunset, another hundred-mile day completed, I turned off into the surrounding plain, the ground so dry and brittle that my tyre left a trail of fine sand floating in the air. The surface was scarred with shallow, crumbling gullies which had not seen rain for a very long time, and I had to manhandle my bike through several of the deeper ones before I was comfortably out of sight of the road. That night, camped in a gully, I dreamt of escaped convicts in black and white striped uniforms running by my tent.

THE MORNING STARTED PAINFULLY WHEN A FLASK OF HOT TEA AT a roadside stall shattered in my hands, scalding my arms and legs while a devilish headwind brewed outside. I turned onto a dirt track which fizzled out at a wide gravel flood plain; it was covered as far as the eye could see with piles of red peppers, a huge mosaic the colour of the burns on my arms. I got out my camera and one of the workers came running over.

"Wait, wait! Let me gather my friends together first", he told me, hollered over to his mates to join him, and they all lined up in front of the bundles of peppers to get their photograph taken.

All day I kept my head down and pushed through the wind, the arid landscape remaining unchanged for hours on end and my face etched into a perpetual grimace. I was grateful to have made it to the small town of Savan as dusk approached, enjoying a muscle-repairing broth of noodles, vegetables, eggs and meat at a street stall as I watched people waiting their turn at the karaoke machines set up outside. I was particularly pleased with myself today because I had negotiated a half-price discount with the hotel manager, explaining that I'd cycled all the way from England to stay here and proved it by showing him the route on my map.

However, more surprising than my bargaining success was the fact that he actually understood just how far I had come. One thing that becomes apparent when traveling through the Chinese hinter-land is just how few of its citizens know anything of their own vast country, never mind the wider world. An account of my ride here from England and the countries I had journeyed through would usually elicit a disappointingly lukewarm reaction, something along the lines of "Well done, mate" or "Not bad, not bad". It was only when I'd mention the name of a town that I may have cycled through two days earlier that I would then really get open-mouthed looks of disbelief, congratulatory slaps on the back and enthusiastic calls for free tea.

I started to hawk and spit, the result of a heavy cold and increas-ingly bad air pollution the closer I got to the provincial capital Urumqi. I was grateful for a tailwind that carried me into the outlying town of Hutubi, coughing and spluttering, where I found a little Kazakh restaurant and ordered my dinner in Russian. The following morning, I woke up feeling like someone had sat on my head all night, and I was now spitting up so much phlegm that I perturbed even some of the locals. I felt feverish under the piercing sunshine and faced a devastating headwind all the way to Urumqi, finding myself back on the motorway and now fighting with cars, trucks and other bicycles on a ride that never ended.

Urumqi was my first experience of a Chinese city and with its crisscrossing roads, urban expressways and miles of buildings in various stages of construction (or demolition) it was difficult to know precisely where it started, and I spent two hours on its complex, traffic-besieged roads trying to find some place that looked like a city centre.

By some truly fortuitous fluke I halted, in tears of frustration, outside the city's main post office. My sister-in-law had dispatched a package two months earlier, addressed to "Poste Restante, Urumqi" (in Chinese characters I had choppily prepared by hand) – and by a further miracle it was there waiting for me. Enclosed were novels and a few spares, but most importantly there were maps for Central and Eastern China – I was now set up for maps right through to Shanghai. The luck continued as I was pointed to a pleasant youth hostel where I could recover over the next few days, paying some tender loving care to my bike (the only likely recipient of such attentions, I had concluded by now) and doing a little exploration on foot.

New buildings were popping up everywhere, multi-storey utilitarian oblongs with minimum time-wasting architectural embellishments, unerringly painted in pastel shades of yellow, pink or green. A few upmarket stores sold Prada, Chanel and all the other obligatory signs of upward mobility and their joyless-looking clientele were exercising their right to drop a small fortune on branded trinkets and handbags. A marble-floored department store was still under construction but already open for business, and a few expensive cars sat parked on the road outside. Build it and they will come – that seemed to be the plan, while outside a withered old man knelt in the middle of the pavement, arms outstretched to the heavens, begging for a few *yuan*.

Urumqi was a stark mix of old and new. Among the rusty agricultural vehicles and diesel-spouting trucks on the road were new Toyotas and tinted-windowed luxury coaches. Weaving in between were all kinds of bicycles hauling all kinds of things from small flatbeds of vegetables to a full household of goods. A three-piece-suite and refrigerator were all being moved under the stream of one wiry old fellow, cigarette hanging from the corner of his mouth, pushing hard on the pedals to get the whole unstable edifice moving. I looked on in some awe, embarrassed by my own modest load.

Between the People's Park and a luxury supermarket lived the night market, reassuringly chaotic with a dazzling array of stalls and food stands, brash illuminated signs sticking above a sea of people and bicycles manoeuvring through the melee. I sat back on a crate with a Chinese beer in hand, while fat rats scuttled under the tables and chairs. In front of me, a girl stepped on some exposed electrical cabling with her high heels, short circuiting a row of lights in a flurry of lively blue sparks.

Room with a view, Xinjiang, China

THE ROAD FROM URUMQI TO TURPAN FOLLOWS A NATURAL WIND tunnel; the surrounding mountains channel gales of such ferocity down its narrow length, that it is as much feared by modern day truck and train drivers (their trailers and railcars prone to overturning) as it was by the Silk Road merchant caravans of centuries past. It cuts through the massive complex of Dabancheng, the largest wind farm in Asia, where hundreds of enormous turbines stretched into the hazy distance either side of me while the roar of their rotors cut through the air above, a diligent army of gigantic white alloy windmills set against a clear blue sky.

I came to a long gorge and the road became squeezed between vertical rock walls. My speed was rapidly increasing: 50kph, 60kph,

70kph... I anxiously applied the brakes, wary of going faster. It felt like a generous descent on a steep downhill, but this road was almost flat, and only when I tried to stop the bike did I grasp the full awfulness of the situation.

Keeping the brake levers squeezed as hard as possible, I stopped and tried to lean the bike against a wall as the wind shrieked and howled malevolently around me, but it was a losing battle to even keep hold of the handlebars. The wind kept shunting the bike forward a yard or two at a time, like some enraged poltergeist on steroids – that was over 50 kilograms of metal and luggage slipping helplessly through my hands. I had no choice but to get back on the bloody thing and go with it. And as if the bike had a mind of its own, I was rapidly in motion and accelerating hard once again.

HELLLLLLP!

Traveling at speed through a bleak and rocky desert plain, the road curved subtly to my left and what was once a manageable if ungodly tailwind, now turned into a personal hurricane, attacking me from over my shoulder, propelling me forward and trying to punch me off the bike at the same time. It was appalling; just to stay on the road I had to hang off the side of my bike and twist the handlebars perilously towards the centre line. Thus I was sucked into the slipstream of every bus and truck that passed, and then - as I wrestled to straighten the bars - spat back out. There was never any warning – the demonic howls of the wind were the only thing I could hear – and if at all I slowed down, it would endeavour to topple me into the ditch at the side of the road instead.

Turpan town is the centre of the famous Turpan Depression; at 150 metres below sea-level it is the lowest point in China, and a respite from the punishing winds of the long desert crossing. It was an increasingly popular stop on the Southeast Asia backpacker circuit, famous for its vineyards. For me it should have been a relaxing day off, a place to hang out and join the washed masses on comfortable guided tours. Yet my morning began with a three-hour bus ride back to Urumqi the same way I had come, carrying my bike's rear-wheel. Although I had survived a hundred-odd kilometres of purgatory, my bike had been less fortunate, and the hub of the wheel had cracked.

While local repair options had centred around a sand-blown

street commandeered by a half a dozen guys with foot-pumps and hammers, in Urumqi I had actually found a proper bike store, optimistically placed to capture the beginnings of a small middle-class (I was the only visitor). The mechanic was mute; it was easier communicating with him than with most people right now, as both of us were effectively fluent in mime. We had a long if somewhat athletic chat, while he unearthed a compatible hub and rebuilt the wheel.

By late afternoon I was back on the bus back to Turpan. The driver was a fidgeter, continually wiping the dashboard, re-combing his greasy hair over a shiny bald spot, rearranging ornaments and half-finished flasks of tea and water around him, eating corn-on-the cob, leaning far back in his seat to catch a glance at the on-board television... and occasionally watching the road ahead.

Proper cycling, Urumqi

"YOU CAN ENTER BUT NEVER LEAVE".

This is the literal meaning of the Taklamakan Desert, and with these fierce winds I now understood why. There was a wall of early-morning mist across the sand, splintered with the long shadows of petrified trees in the dawn light. The villages were unmistakably Uighur, large rectangular houses with tall mud walls and central

open courtyards hidden within, and a welcome reappearance of the
tapchan daises, so reminiscent of Central Asia. Clusters of miniature
mudbrick houses with tiny doors were used for drying some of
those famous Turpan grapes into raisins.

An old lady sold me a drink from a roadside stall; she ritually
waved the *yuan* notes I gave her over her goods before hiding them
away in the folds of her dress. Later, a watermelon seller ran out
towards me from his flimsy stall, waving me to stop.

"Slow down", he yelled, "Slow down! I can speak English! Come
over here and rest for a while". His name was Mamud and he urged
me to try some melon. "They are the best in China - you cannot
leave without trying any."

I was getting close to the ancient oasis town of Hami, famous
for the sweetness of its watermelons and praised by Marco Polo in
his travels 700 years earlier. More recently Hami had also gained
prominence for its abundance of natural resources: metals, natural
gas, oil and coal. This explained why ethnic Uighur now made up
less than 20% of the local population whilst Han Chinese counted
for almost 70%.

"I am actually a qualified English teacher", Mamud told me, "but
I am 27 years old and never had a teaching job."

Being Uighur, he explained, meant that he had always been
passed over in favour of a Chinese candidate.

"So, I look after this stall, like my father did, and his father did
before him."

I stopped in Shanshan for dinner. It was a Uighur town and the
place was buzzing, the bazaar offering dozens of food stalls, an
amazing array of colours and noise and exotic aromas. I washed it
down with several beers; like the vodka drinking Stans, religious
piety was somewhat mollified here in Xinjiang. Most people seemed
to drink alcohol. I never once heard the Muslim call to prayer, and
more so than madrassas or mosques the quiet backstreets housed
softly lit massage parlours offering more immediate earthbound
pleasures. The Soviets and the Chinese may not have succeeded in
completely suppressing religious worship, but they had made a
damned good effort at watering it down.

CHAPTER 19

WINDS OF THE GOBI, WINDS OF CHANGE

LONDON

(China) · Hami · Dunhuang
· Anxi · Jiyuguan

TOKYO

A team of Uighur truck drivers treated me to breakfast and lamented the plight of their people while we all attacked a heap of naan bread and *plov*. No opportunities for the young. Persecution of our religion. Exploitation of our natural resources. The friendly joviality of my four new friends turned into unexpected melancholy as they recounted their disputes with China. One of them was still struggling to hold back his tears when I said my farewells.

Out on the road a scattering of small oasis towns abruptly gave way to desert all too soon. It was unexpectedly hilly and a surprisingly dirty black. This was the infamous colour of the Gobi Desert and I knew then that my flirtation with the Taklamakan was over and the affair with the Gobi had begun. Stretching across large tracts of China and Mongolia, the Gobi is the largest desert in Asia and it is made up of far more gravel plains and rocky bluffs than golden dunes of sand.

There was nowhere to hide from the barrage of headwinds, crosswinds and tailwinds, and I had trouble believing what I now felt: drops of icy rain. This desert also had one of the most extreme climates in the world and even sudden snowstorms in the middle of summer were not unknown. But black sand, yellow sand or flaming pink sand – confronted by an unchanging view and a singularly screaming wind laying siege to your eardrums all day long, it still becomes teeth-grindingly monotonous. However, I would discover some company over the next few days.

My messenger was a lone motorcyclist, appearing and disappearing over the sandy brows of this windswept road as he slowly got closer, finally pulling up in front of me and removing his helmet. He was Israeli, living in some central Chinese city with his Chinese girlfriend and out on a solo road trip through Xinjiang.

"I saw a cyclist about thirty minutes back, heading east", he told me. "A woman", he added, with a subtle lift of his eyebrows, "in her early twenties I think."

Well I couldn't very well be hanging around here for small-talk - I had some serious cycling to do!

If I pushed harder and took no further breaks, then I reckoned I could catch up with this mysterious lady cyclist in just a few hours. I had already eaten a chunk of bread and jam, but I was fuelled by something far more substantial than a sandwich – imagination! I raced ahead, shedding miles effortlessly, and after a couple of hours I saw a dot in the far distance.

In another fifteen minutes I was a hundred yards behind, seeing the slender figure in front of me gamely bashing away at the pedals, long wild hair escaping from underneath her helmet and further unfurled by the wind. An orchestra was playing out the final climatic chords of Ravel's *Bolero* in my head as I pulled up alongside thirty seconds later, trying to catch my breath, and beaming a winning "What are the odds, eh?" smile in her direction. But it came to a sudden and premature halt, needle scratching across an imagined turntable, when I glanced across. "She" was a he.

Taiichi was a young Japanese cyclist and we talked in a halting mixture of English and Japanese, both of us rusty in our second language. He had recently graduated medical school, he said, and was taking a break before starting his internship. This was impressive in itself; taking a gap year after university was unheard of in Japan. And then to spend it cycling across distant deserts... well, this was way off the scale.

"It took a long time to get offered a job once they found out what I planned to do", he told me. "No interviewer could understand why on earth I wouldn't want to start work right away. At the beginning I had the choice of all the top hospitals, but by the end of the whole process, only one small hospital in Yokohama was willing to give me the chance. So I took it!"

He smiled; he had got six months of freedom and he was making the most of it. I admired his attitude and his optimism. Especially his optimism. Mugged in Portugal, bike stolen in Tashkent, blown off his bike by winds in the Gobi... he was probably the unluckiest cyclist I had ever met but he always kept smiling. We would cycle the next few days side by side, before losing sight of each other, and continue to meet like this on the road again a couple more times before Shanghai.

The sun was low on the horizon and our long shadows danced madly ahead of us as we pedalled. We found shelter as dusk fell, a solitary ramshackle restaurant of mudbrick walls and a corrugated iron roof where a Uighur family eked out an existence repairing trucks, serving food and selling cigarettes. They rustled up a basic meal and as we finished up, a small group of exhausted-looking road workers walked in, smothered in a thick layer of sand. They settled down to watch a grainy video, the pinnacle of entertainment for miles around.

Taiichi and I had agreed our night's lodgings with the proprietors; the barn next door. It was unused and quite filthy, with one uncluttered workbench and a bit of space on the ground.

"Please, you choose first", he asked politely, and I selected the bug-ridden bench over the vermin infested floor. Oh, the advantages of seniority.

AT DAWN WE LOADED OUR BIKES AND HEADED OUT AS THE STARK mountains to the north of us glowed a fierce orange. The winds were ridiculous and compounded by a long climb out of a wide basin; the sharp jagged spines of mountains encroached along the plain and crept menacingly behind us, like an advancing army.

The desert had been sprinkled with sparse patches of green shrubs and moss, a feast to the eyes after the monochrome landscape of yesterday, but it didn't last. Apart from a single oasis, a verdant strip of agriculture barely a mile long and looking uncomfortably out of place, we faced the black sands of the Gobi Desert all day. Occasionally we would see a crumbling fortress far off into the desert with the cragged backdrop of the Karlyk-Tagh mountains far behind. Relics of another age.

A jovial truck driver gave us directions to a truck-stop where we could get a basic room and dinner. Not that it was difficult to find; it was the only building we'd seen in over five hours and with its barred and opaque windows, crumbling walls and the inviting demeanour of a small gulag, we knew that we had located our lodgings for the night.

There was a vicious dog, musclebound with bloodshot eyes and foaming jaws, chained to a stake in the backyard on the way to the latrines. Ingeniously, the chain was just the right length so that if you carefully shuffled by with your back right up against the wall of the kitchen, you could pass by without your groin making contact with his capable-looking jaws. He would continue in a cycle of leaping toward you and being violently restrained by the chain mid-air, recovering and doing it again, making himself increasingly angrier. One day that chain will break, I thought.

Four young and friendly women ran the place and judging by the rather garish clothes they wore and the saucy way they teased the customers I think they did more than just the cooking and cleaning. They let their hands linger on the legs of the truck drivers who playfully slapped their bums in return. One lady was quite taken with Taiichi.

"Sit here pretty boy, you much nicer than this rough man", she said, poking one of the guests playfully in his ribs. "Maybe want drink pretty boy? Ah, but you so young!"

Later that night there was a knock on the door, and Taiichi looked at me, petrified. We held our breath until the footsteps moved on to the next room.

FANATICAL JAPANESE SOLDIERS WERE SHOOTING WOMEN AND children. A prison guard slowly tortured his prisoner, cut by cut. A labourer was run through with a samurai sword. We were flicking through the local TV channels after calling a halt at Hami Town, having pooled our resources for a decent hotel after a morning of devastating headwinds. There were an awful lot of programs showing the Japanese doing something inexplicably cruel to the Chinese.

Yesterday when some Uighur truck drivers found that Taiichi was from Japan, they threw themselves wholeheartedly into a good-natured imitation of sword-slashing and machine-gunning while he looked down at the floor in embarrassment. The constant stream of ham-fisted TV dramas about Japanese aggression against the Chinese, along with the general anti-Japanese sentiment throughout the media, added up to make them the most popular nationality in certain parts of Xinjiang.

Not to be left out, the British also got a good shake. I watched a film about Great Game related espionage set in Tibet in the 19th century; it was well produced with realistic sets and proper period costume. In one scene British army generals and Buddhist monks were arguing, the dialogue refreshingly in English with Chinese subtitles:

"No, no! You imperialist dogs will not make us part of the British Empire", the Tibetan monk announced in fiery conviction to the British aggressor. "We are Chinese!"

Desert and tumbleweed, Xinjiang, China

I left Taiichi behind at a truck-stop mid-morning, eager to push on. Despite all my whining about loneliness I realised that sometimes I just relished the solitude of the desert. By now I was starting the mornings with ten litres of drinking water loaded on my bike whenever possible, and although I rarely came close to exhausting it, today I was glad of the precaution. But for that bedraggled truck-stop, the road stretched uninterrupted for 200 kilometres and it would be my longest day yet.

Although the map had indicated a village at the halfway point, it materialised into just two signposts separated by a hundred yards of sand, and a long vacillating line of dust devils slowly traversing the road like a row of Space Invaders, uprooting everything in a whirl-wind of dust and tumbleweeds. I timed their progress, waited for a gap and then sprinted through, trying not to get caught up in one of them. Glancing nervously over my shoulder to make sure that they were not following, I paid little attention to a dense cloud of sand ahead until it was right upon me.

Except it wasn't a cloud of sand - it was a swarm of wasps!

Scores of them bounced off my chest, buzzed ominously around my head and latched onto my bike and luggage. I *hate* wasps! What business were they doing in the middle of the bloody *desert*? The air was already rife with them and they were swirling in a frenzy around me, like I'd just been rolled in treacle.

I was wearing my typical desert ensemble, protected head-to-foot against the sun with hat, long-sleeved top, trousers, gloves, and a face mask to keep out the sand. However, there was a gap between the mask and my sunglasses - a tiny exposed piece of flesh - and it was to this that the evil little bastards launched themselves. I stum-bled off my bike in a blind panic, running up and down the road in a shimmering cloak of wasps, trying to get them off me and waving my arms around like a maniac at a passing truck in an effort to get it to stop. The bemused driver waved back and gave me the thumbs-up. I was now slapping every part of my body in a frenzied game of pat-a-cake gone shockingly off kilter, killing and stunning dozens of them, and causing enough of an alarming spectacle to provoke the only other vehicle I saw to speed up as he passed.

I'll outrun them I thought, and heaved the bike off the ground, adrenaline helping me push the pedals as hard as I could. It felt like some terrible B-movie, a horrible insect variant on Alfred Hitchcock's The Birds, and as I sped up, they sped up with me, stinging me repeatedly before I finally lost the last one five miles later. I could already feel my left eye slowly sealing up from the swelling, as the pain subsided into a low-level throb and then eventually numbness. I couldn't see a great deal out of it, but my other eye was fine, and miles of dismal desert convinced me I wasn't missing out on much. Now I knew why that place didn't make it beyond a couple of signposts.

I took few breaks after that, convinced as I was that a line of tornados or swarm of killer insects was not far behind, and it was dusk when I arrived at the entrance to a rocky canyon, the road turning definitively upwards. I wasn't going to camp here and wait for the next biblical episode to happen, so I pushed on up a tough ten-mile climb in fading light to Xiaxiaxing, a gritty village on the border with the next province, Gansu. There wasn't much apart from a canteen, a couple of truck workshops and a dosshouse, but it had offered me a blur of light to aim for in the darkness, and a welcome bed for the night.

THE WINDS WERE FLAYING ME ALIVE; I HADN'T BEEN BATTERED and pummelled like this since half a dozen teenagers had set upon me outside a Bristol nightclub, many years ago. The sun throbbed insufferably above me and turned my steel-framed bike into a hot radiator, while my skin felt like ancient parchment, and my mouth like I had swallowed a bag of sawdust – followed by the saw. And then I thought I was hallucinating: out of the haze ahead emerged a group of middle-aged Chinese men and women on touring bikes, and as we stopped and marvelled at each other, a couple more guys came up behind them five minutes later - two British cyclists on their way home to the UK from Beijing. If you are old enough to remember the Twilight Zone, you will understand when I say that I had just entered it.

We took pictures of each other while the wind blustered around us and a truck lay overturned further up the road, a reminder of how these winds can quickly turn nasty. This really was no place to hang around and chat.

"So, what happened to the eye?" asked one of the Brits tentatively, as we were about to part. I told them of the wasps and tornados, which somewhat dampened the mood.

It was late afternoon when I turned off the main road south for the oasis town of Dunhuang. A meeting point for the northern and southern branches of the Silk Road, Dunhuang had long prospered from the trade between East and West; it was also home to the Mogao Caves, attracting growing numbers of tourists to peruse these ancient Buddhist grottos. The wind was full against me as the narrow road wound through an undulating sea of black dunes, and although I tried to find shelter amongst them to camp, the wind, howling and screaming, always found a way in. The southern sky was being rapidly wiped of its colour – a sandstorm was approaching – so I mounted my bike to return the way I'd come, the vanguard of the storm carrying me into Hongliuyuan where I got a grimy bed for the night in a trucker's dormitory.

When I caught sight of myself in the mirror that night, I got a shock. To be fair, that was happening quite a lot recently, but when I looked at the gaunt, sunburnt and wind-ravaged ghoul staring back at me, I also saw that the skin around my left eye had swollen to child-frightening proportions, leaving nothing but a narrow slit of puffy flesh to peer out of.

The wild headwinds had subsided, and the view of black dunes to the horizon was much more pleasing the next day when I knew I didn't have to put up a tent behind them. A half-mile west across the desert I saw the sandblasted remains of an old fortress, and on my map was written "End of the Great Wall". Was this ruin part of it? Was this my first glimpse? This clump of weather-beaten bulwarks made my spine tingle, and I imagined the ground beneath me tremble from a camel train of traders, wind billowing around their silken robes, sunlight glinting from the scimitars of their armed escort.

By lunchtime I had reached the outskirts of Dunhuang, the desert mercifully replaced by phenomenally green fields, prosperous looking villages of well-kept mudbrick houses, tree-lined shadow-draped lanes and an unending stream of people cruising along on bicycles and scooters. It was easy to imagine the relief of those earlier travellers when they arrived here after enduring so many weeks of desert.

However, for the modern-day tourist, Dunhuang was much more than just a brief refuge from the hardships of the road... or more accurately, the hardships of a fully air-conditioned, plushily upholstered modern coach. I saw dozens of them in the spacious car park and hundreds of sightseers, mainly Chinese and Japanese, clambering over the enormous Singing Sand Dunes, so called because of the low whistling that arises from breezes that race across their slopes. The dunes didn't sing to me, but maybe that was because my attention was diverted by long camel trains of camera-toting tourists, jeep rides, toboggan runs down the side of the dunes, paragliding, microlight rides (with a purpose-built runway across the sands) and even a shooting range. Yet despite all this, the dunes were singularly impressive, stretching for many miles and some more than a vertigo-inducing hundred metres tall. The shadows in the fading daylight accentuated the sweeping curves of their long ridges, and the tourist hordes didn't seem quite so bad anymore.

I spent a couple of nights in Dunhuang and toured the Mogao Grottos, a multi-storey complex of hundreds of cells carved into the cliff face. They held an exhaustive collection of Buddhist artefacts, from murals on the wall to carvings and statues stretching from the 4th century through to the Middle Ages. There were far too many rooms to explore properly, a great majority were shut, and the popular ones had crowds squeezing into them and tour guides providing commentary in multiple languages. It was a treasure trove of Buddhist art but I soon tired of the melee involved in entering each cave, tourists ignoring the "No Flash Photography" signs and agitated backpackers running in and out of the caves at speed, determined to tick each one off their list.

This in a way summed up Dunhuang for me. It was another must-see sight listed in every guidebook on China, both high-brow and budget, but was small enough that the impact of tourism running full steam ahead was overwhelming. I just didn't get a sense of the town's true personality; far more than any weight in sand, it was smothered beneath an unyielding layer of commercialism.

Barely viable roads, Xinjiang, China

THE ROAD SOUTH FROM DUNHUANG WOULD STEER YOU BACK towards Europe, the southern Silk Road route skirting the perimeter of the Taklamakan desert and carrying on west to Kashgar and beyond, an extravagant U-turn that I was not going to entertain. I continued eastwards, the monotony interrupted by the occasional crumbling fortress from which I could sometimes eke out a little shade; these were the remains of the first Great Wall built around 200 BC, a thousand years before the Ming Dynasty and the main era of construction. Their once sharp and intimidating angles were now just a weather-eroded outline but they struck me with a very real sense of wonder, sitting out here alone in the sands and the raging winds, more impressive than any restored and preserved monument in a city.

There were also a number of simple modern graves; mounds of earth marked simply by plastic flowers tied to a bamboo frame and stuck into the ground. Were these unknown travellers, buried where they fell? The graves of migrants working on this never-ending road? It was a lonely resting place but once this highway is opened and trucks start hauling mineral wealth east, then maybe the souls lying here will yearn for their lost seclusion.

I ran into Taiichi again in the town of Anxi, amongst a

cacophony of dusty two and three storey buildings and garish shrines, and after we'd stocked up with supplies we headed back out into the desert. My guidebook described this place as the windiest in China but this evening, at least, the air was completely still. At dusk we pulled off the road, walked our bikes a long way into the desert and camped under an immense full moon that dominated the night sky.

∽

AN ATROCIOUS NARROW TRACK OF JAGGED ROCK, GRAVEL AND sand cut feebly through the desert while the wind blustered violently around us, buffeting the bikes from side to side and rising to a banshee-like wail. The wind was allied with a long uphill and a barrage of manic trucks overtaking us by a whisker of a gap, and it took all my strength and concentration just to keep the bike upright. I struggled with the handlebars and pedals, pulling with my whole body left to right, to and fro, like some over-caffeinated disco dancer, manoeuvring through pockets of deep sand and random patches of gravel and hidden rocks.

Then the sandstorms started, and everything was reduced to an orange-brown twilight. The eerie faint glow of the sun was disseminated through the trillions of sand particles entrapping us, leaving nothing but a few metres of road visible ahead. Vehicles appeared quietly out of the soupy air like ghosts materialising into worldly form, and progress became painful and slow. It took ten tense hours of cycling to travel barely 70 kilometres, finishing in the small wind-blown village of Qiawan.

Physically shattered and by now encrusted in a thick layer of white sand, we headed directly to the village canteen where the owner read our minds with uncanny accuracy, and without a single word exchanged, placed two bottles of beer on the table. I knew we would be going no further today, and slept as I was, in a room out the back of the restaurant, dead to the world.

By morning sand had found its way into everything that wasn't completely sealed, turning my breakfast of bread and jam into something unexpectedly crunchy, and the chamois of my cycling shorts into a shocking approximation of sandpaper. However, the storm had passed and although the headwind was still there in all its vitality, the skies were clear. As we cycled out of the village and looked south there was something odd with the horizon, or rather there was something in front of it, spanning across our field of vision as far as we could see. It was something truly colossal, running parallel to the road many miles away. We could not quite believe our eyes.

It was our first sight of the Great Wall.

The Wall and the road converged to within a mile of each other as the day wore on, and from the top of a small pass I could see far enough south to watch its tall, thick mass extend in an astonishing straight line as far as the eye could see. It cut the desert into two decisive halves, reminding me that until a few hundred years ago I would most definitely have been standing in the wrong half, the domain of Mongolian warlords and other marauders and mortal threats from across the steppe. Nowadays at least, my enemy was just the wind, and the mortal threats the occasional truck that roared by me ever so closely.

Up close there was a long deep trench showing some solid foundations, but over the years, settlers had dug down and removed materials for their own use. Above ground some sections had collapsed into little more than earth and rubble; desertification and the accompanying surge in sandstorms had contributed disproportionately over the last fifty years to erode large lengths of it. I felt humbled to witness something that was still uniquely inspiring, but also a little sad. It was said that in another twenty to thirty years, not even this would be left.

We hit an asphalt section which had us nodding and agreeing with each other that the worst was over; as soon as we did, it degenerated into an abysmal stretch of concrete, with random sharp rocks sticking out at all angles like a gym climbing wall fallen on its side. In the clouds of dust and gravel thrown up by passing trucks I became separated from Taiichi once again.

For lunch I stopped in a Uighur restaurant, its ethnicity obvious from the large Uighur writing eclipsing the Chinese characters on a sign outside. These places were becoming rarer since I left Xinjiang province almost a week ago, but 6,000 kilometres on from Turkey I was still encountering places where Turkish was spoken. The lady who ran the place seemed to appreciate my embarrassing attempts at the language and refused payment, waving me off with a smile.

That evening the wind picked up to a terrifying pitch and I looked hard for accommodation. In the absence of any human dwellings, I found some long-abandoned outhouses and set up camp in the stables just as the sandstorm closed in. The deep long groans of the elements outside turned into a lonely lullaby that ushered me quickly into an exhausted sleep.

JIYUGUAN PASS WAS A KEY FORTRESS ON THE GREAT WALL AND, as its westernmost outpost, was historically the gateway between wilderness and civilisation. Nowadays it marked the entrance to a modern city, but the road I followed was little more than a track scraped between the rolling dunes of the desert. With a surface of sand, of varying viscosity depending on its depth, and serving surprise jolts to bike and body depending on the size and shape of the rocks hidden underneath, it took a full array of cycling skills just to remain upright. Trucks left me in a cloud of dust and sand, riding blind for a few seconds before it all cleared so the next truck could do exactly the same thing. I noticed waves and thumbs-ups and shouts of encouragement from the drivers in their cabs, but it was all I could do to keep the bike upright and manoeuvre safely through it all.

There was a newer paved road that I found out about later, but I didn't really mind; it felt true to the weight of history that I had endured a certain level of suffering to earn my right to enter China proper. It was all too clear to me now why this fort had also been called the Gate of Sighs; it was from here that unfortunate citizens, be they disgraced officials, criminals or anyone else who may have displeased the authorities, were dispatched in the opposite direction, exiled to the ungoverned wastelands outside. With the snow-capped Quilian Mountains in the distance and the mighty Great Wall sloping majestically out across the desert to meet them, it was a formidable and intimidating sight.

I, an unwashed, ill-attired barbarian from the Gobi Badlands, had conquered the desert and had officially crossed the Chinese border of a millennium ago. I had witnessed the haphazard line drawn on a world map over eighteen months earlier turn into a real-life record of my progress, once unfamiliar and unpronounceable names of cities turn into all-encompassing mantras, and an inch-long stroke of the pen reveal a pleasant few days on fast European roads, or a week struggling up mountains and over windblown and rock-strewn tracks. My days were a rich potpourri of encounters with remarkable people, and long expanses of loneliness and self-doubt.

It was the beginning of the end of the desert, and part two of my passage across China. I had a thousand miles to ride to Xi'an, the ancient capital of this enormous country – and for the very first time, I felt I was ready.

The Great Wall, seen from Jiyuguan fortress

CHAPTER 20

THE END OF THE SILK ROAD

W hat a transformation!

Bustling towns and villages, industrious citizens rushing about their business, luscious green fields of crops lining the road, tangible shade from the occasional clump of trees and even the absence of a soul-crushing headwind – perhaps civilisation really does start at Jiyuguan. With 170 kilometres covered it had been a long day and with it came the end of my isolation, as oasis towns increasingly broke up the savannah and slowly the landscape turned into one of agriculture. I was an apparent magnet for mini-tractor drivers, single-stroke, oversized lawnmowers splattered in mud and sand, the farmer upfront steering with a kind of rudder and his wife and kids in the trailer at the back. They would hover right in front of me, pointing and laughing for a few miles before turning off and being replaced by another amused family.

The road was smooth asphalt for the most part and I could quite easily have done more distance, but there were always at least a couple of people within sight of me and I could find no secluded spot to pitch a tent. At the next one-horse town, I rolled my bike into the local hotel and the half-dozen girls chattering to each other at the reception went suddenly silent, spent a brief moment in shock and puzzlement, and then burst into giggles at the sight of me.

The early mornings were now noticeably cooler. It was late

September and I could feel the chill on my skin at last. Surrounded by fields of ripened corn, the only sign of the desert were the occasional dunes I could see beyond the wide strip of fields. The solitude was clearly gone. Whenever I stopped for lunch, a dozen people would gather around, watching me intently, commenting to each other on the way I used chopsticks. Grown-ups would giggle childishly to each other and throw me a "Hello!" or "Goodbye!" to get an easy laugh out of their friends. I lamented the end of those lonely desert teahouses where the only other customer might be a solitary truck driver, staring into the middle distance, solemnly smoking his way through a carton of cigarettes.

Zhangye had been an important garrison town on the Hexi Corridor, protecting this important fertile tract of the Silk Road. It was huge and I had a hard time finding my bearings; I wandered for over an hour through a major thoroughfare that had a hundred mobile phone shops lined up next to one another and tall buildings with nothing but China Telecom or China Mobile plastered over them. Thousands of people were in a rush to get somewhere. Some streets were full of glitzy high-end clothes shops, others crammed full of electronic shops and another full of banks. Certainly, this is what I had imagined of a modern Chinese city... but not this far west, not barely out of the desert.

Yet not all had been consumed by this malaise. A few wizened old men sat on portable chairs around an upturned cardboard box, playing an impromptu game of *mah-jong* in the middle of the pavement, ignoring the maelstrom of people flowing around them.

The old town had been thankfully preserved, attractive streets of elaborate Chinese storefronts and the curling, tiled roofs of tiny red temples squeezed in-between. Bicycles were absolutely everywhere, and the whole panorama was caressed by a colonnade of weeping willows. It was picture postcard perfect, the Chinese provincial town of my imagination and a world away from the rest of the city; Marco Polo was said to have lived here contentedly for a year of his life.

It was also home to the Reclining Buddha, the largest in China (or Asia, or the World, depending on which information board you referred to) and although the actual Buddha was covered in scaffolding, the temple complex was spacious and uncluttered, with walkways leading me to several exhibitions in the outlying temples. I passed a pleasant couple of hours in unaccustomed tranquillity and it made me think of Kyoto in Japan, with its thousands of temples and shrines, not quite believing that Japan was little more than a month away.

The ancient streets were as soothing during the day as the television was strangely mesmerising at night. I was transfixed by the commercials, dramas and inane variety shows that were now available over a multitude of channels. What was it with all this over-acted, teary-eyed emotion on one hand, and crass slapstick humour on the other? Many of the female celebrities had a disquieting caught-in-the-headlights stare; it took me a while to realise that they'd had cosmetic surgery to widen their eyes. In combination with some over-the-top clothing choices and rather severe makeup, they resembled Japanese *anime* characters more than real-life people.

Something a little closer to what I expected, and certainly more entertaining, was shown later on CCTV Channel 7; a competition pitting army teams against each other, testing strength, teamwork and skill across a varied range of obstacles. It reminded me a little of the *It's a Knockout!* show from my childhood, which would have opposing teams dress up in silly costumes and compete over a course of bouncy castles, slides and water-canon. However, this Chinese version was a little more robust, and had the contestants fire mortars at targets, drive jeeps over self-made bridges and tackle obstacle courses ringed with spiked walls and barbed wire. There were two teams, red and blue, their uniformed supporters sitting stiffly on army-issued camp chairs and waving little coloured flags in strict synchronisation whenever their team won a point. Nobody seemed to be enjoying themselves.

The whole program was hosted by a stern, though not unattractive, female officer shouting out commands and demanding answers to her quiz questions, eyeing the cadets with distain and mocking them mercilessly when they got a question wrong. Oddly enough, she featured in a dream of mine later that night, putting me through my paces...

∽

The Great Wall, Gansu Province

SEMI-DESERT TRANSFORMED INTO ROUGH GRAZING LAND AND THE hills, dotted with parched vegetation, became longer and higher. I was cycling right next to the Great Wall and the scale of it continued to astound me; huge sections were over six metres tall and many of the fortresses were almost twice that height, despite the ravaging of the centuries. I came across a large and well-preserved fort, surprising a trio of old Uighur men sitting in the shade of the main gate, drinking their jasmine tea.

"*Salaam alekum*", I said, and guarded looks gave way to surprise.

"*Alekum salaam*", said one of them in return, and a brief account of my trip convinced him to fish deep in his robes for a key to let me in. It was a large open space, a hundred metres square and murals were painted on one of the walls, still impressively intact.

That evening, dinner was a large bowl of noodles, mince and tofu, a plate of meat and vegetables and a bottle of beer which together cost 7 *yuan* (70 cents), watched studiously from the doorway by two smiling young boys and a girl with snot streaming from their noses. The room where I stayed was surprisingly clean and the place even had a toilet; most of these lodgings expect you to find a spot in the surrounding scrub. Unfortunately, I didn't find out about this until I was leaving, and the landlady berated me for bespoiling her backyard.

Calls of nature were now becoming fraught occasions. In the

desert I had the choice of a thousand dunes, but with the change in surroundings it was becoming increasingly difficult to find a private patch of ground to do one's business.

~

PROTRACTED CLIMBS AND SWEEPING DESCENTS USHERED ME through green-sloped valleys of fields; long rectangles of land hosting thousands of bales of buckwheat stacked in perfect formation, lost to the horizon. I used to obsess about knocking out hundred-mile days but now I'd lost count. There were a few eyesores – it wouldn't be rural China without the sporadic smoke-belching factory complex – but as the road ascended to 3,000 metres these ramshackle signs of industry were left behind and a sole Buddhist stupa marked the top of the pass, hinting at the Tibetan community that lived in these highlands. The descent was glorious, taking me through swathes of fertile farmland as fields were being worked with bullocks and wooden ploughs.

In the next rather dour-looking town I noticed another language supplemented the Chinese characters on shop-signs, and there were more than a few people wearing some extravagant and colourful headwear. People smiled at me easily and it felt very different from the rude intrusive staring I was used to of late.

When I turned the corner, it was like turning a page in a children's storybook.

I heard the unmistakable din of Tibetan hornpipes and found myself surrounded by dozens of laughing, joking faces, and a long line of people standing one behind the other performing what can only be accurately described as "the conga". It was a Tibetan funeral procession, and people gathered excitedly around, eager to ply me with some exceptionally strong alcohol, while I posed for photographs and pulled out my maps to help field a barrage of the usual questions. The moonshine was flowing freely, and I built up quite a crowd of admirers in a very short time. When I could finally push my bike through the throngs of cheerful faces - quite unsteady on my feet by now - there were well over a hundred villagers waving me off, the effects of the concoction I had been drinking only adding to the intensity of the whole dreamlike experience.

It started raining, hard and cold, single raindrops soon turning into a proper downpour. I looked at the abysmally rutted track ahead of me, puddles growing deeper by the minute, and smiled. That potent Tibetan firewater would continue to exercise its magic for some time yet.

After so many months of heat and sand, these grey drizzly skies now held some novelty value, and I approached the miserable looking and deeply muddied roads with an oddly placed sense of optimism. I took a toll road – completely empty – to Langzhou, which undulated up and down through a misty landscape of small hills and narrow canyons, resembling a perfect Chinese watercolour.

Langzhou is the regional capital of Gansu province, terminus to the Hexi Corridor of the desert and springboard for the eastward approach to the old capital of Xi'an and the provinces of middle China. The buildings were cheap and utilitarian in design, and the long approach to the city centre was lined with the usual assortment of unruly shopfronts, dosshouses and dilapidated family apartment blocks. But it was a real city, and with no obvious tourist sights to distract me it was a perfect place to sleep, eat and do nothing for a couple of days.

Langzhou perhaps epitomised both what I came to love and hate about Chinese cities. By day it was ugly, dilapidated and architecturally barren, the entire population outside my hotel room banging their car-horns. However, after sundown came the night markets, popping up along the meandering lanes, an endless succession of shops and stalls selling anything from shoes, books and dodgy DVDs through to serving a seven course Peking Duck banquet. An enchanted world with a menagerie of hole-in-the-wall shops and restaurants, fruit and vegetables, fresh meat, clothes and a deluge of cheap knick-knacks transforming the light of low-powered lightbulbs strung along frayed wires into a beautiful kaleidoscope of colour. The soft, almost romantic pink glow of the brothels, hordes of people, pedicabs and bicycles miraculously avoiding deadly pileups, traffic-lights more for decoration than utility, and mechanics casually welding broken appliances in the middle of the busy pavement.

Tibetan funeral party, Gansu Province

TODAY WAS THE FIRST DAY OF OCTOBER AND FELT LIKE AN English autumn. Dark clouds and rain continued to follow me all day as I gradually lost feeling in my fingers and toes, and I stopped frequently at roadside canteens, drinking hot tea to warm up. The road into Ninxia province took me over two fabulously scenic passes and through some spectacular terraced hillsides. Lush rice paddies rose hundreds of metres high, stretching as far as the eye could see.

The work put into engineering this landscape had taken centuries and had been accomplished all by hand, by countless generations of farmers living in the small villages at the foot of the hills; a mix of modest mud-brick houses and peculiar *yádòng* dwellings carved out of the side of a hill, looking like something out of Tolkien's The Hobbit.

Stone distance markers for Shanghai were now fiendishly placed at single kilometre intervals along the roadside. Rolling through the muddy streets of Jieshipu, they informed me I had 1,945 kilometres still left for Shanghai.

"Stop please! Stop please!"

A small group of uniformed high school students had spotted me and were now waving rather excitedly. I paused in front of them.

"Come to our school and teach us English", one of them said, the others nodding vigorously in agreement, while one boy was dispatched to the school to get the teacher.

My legs still felt fresh and told me to keep moving, but these kids were very persuasive. When I countered that there was nowhere for me to sleep, one boy led me to his home and excitedly suggested that I could stay with him there. He showed me a tiny square shed with a narrow bed, alone in the middle of very muddy field: no electricity, no plumbing, no toilet. The teacher from the school turned up just in time, and he greeted me as enthusiastically as his pupils.

"Hello! And welcome!" he clamoured. "We are very lucky to meet you!". His English was excellent, and he fired a volley of questions at me, before moving onto the topic at hand.

"So, will you not stay here tonight?" he asked. "It would be wonderful for our students if you can come to the school and teach a lesson this evening". I hesitated in my answer, mulling over the miles I still had left to do. He continued:

"They have never met a native English speaker. And as you are from England, you speak the best English of all."

He was obviously a highly educated man – of course I would stay!

My almost-to-be roommate looked a little deflated when his teacher said that he would arrange accommodation for the night, and we walked towards the town centre. He ushered me between a maze of high walls leading eventually through a gate and into a small courtyard, with cramped rooms jammed in around the sides. All four generations of the same family lived here, and for the princely sum of 5 *yuan* (50 cents) I could stay with the great grandparents. My sleeping arrangements were discussed and concluded - I would be sharing a bed with the great grandfather. I felt this was somewhat more socially acceptable than sharing it with a teenage boy.

With no time for dinner I was whisked off to the school and put in front of fifty high school students who were studying for their university entrance exams, hastily assembled for this special, extra-curricular opportunity. A long time ago I had spent a year teaching English, but never had I encountered a class so enthusiastic and interactive as this one. The lesson plan was of course the tale of my travels from the UK to China, and with everything I said a dozen arms shot up in the air, ready to answer or ask a question. It was great fun, but they were also clearly very diligent, with books full of notes and a good grasp of the language; I admired their teacher for instilling such a passion for study. And they laughed at all my jokes - full marks all round.

After the lesson had ended the teacher asked if I could sign everyone's notebook with a message of encouragement. Dozens of eager pupils crowded around, books thrust at me from all directions.

"Dear Ming, good luck on your upcoming university entrance exam", I wrote. Easy.

"Dear Yun, study hard and pass with full marks!". Nice.

The others swarmed around the first few recipients, excitedly pointing at my remarks and pushed their notebooks even harder at me. They each wanted their own personal message.

"Dear Wen, very nice to meet you and I hope we can meet again in the future."

"Dear Wu, I hope you get your dream job."

This was exhausting.

"Dear Chian, I am very impressed with your English. Keep studying hard!"

"Dear Jun, all the very best to you."

"Dear Lei, all the best."

"Dear Shan, all the best."

"Dear Wei, all the best."

It didn't matter, they all loved what I'd written and showed each other my sage words, chattering excitedly and even letting escape a few squeals of joy. I felt like a rock star! There was even someone waiting in bed for me back at the hotel.

That night I dreamt I was transported six months into the future, dressed in a shirt and tie, sitting at an office desk and typing diligently away at a computer. I woke up miserable.

CHINA HAS AN OLD, HOMEGROWN RELIGION CALLED *DAOISM*, ITS philosophy of *yin* and *yang*, shaping much of Chinese culture from the practice of Tai Chi through to traditional Chinese medicine. I had planned to tackle one of its sacred mountains, the Kongtong Shan, on my bicycle. The ticket attendants looked at me with some wonder when I slapped my thighs and gave them a self-assured thumbs-up signal as I cycled away from their ticket booth, but two corners later the road shot almost vertically upwards. They laughed at me when I reappeared in front of them a couple of minutes later.

So I climbed the thing on foot, dumping my bike at the attendant's cabin and starting the hike through muddy forest trails and hundreds of slippery, moss-covered stone steps in my cycling shoes. There was a total of 38 temples perched high on precipitous misty cliffs amongst the clouds, all requiring further considerable ascents on steep uneven steps while dozens of tour groups pushed past me on their way down – it was the Chinese "golden week" holiday and one of the busiest times of the year. I had hoped for peace and maybe some opportunity for quiet reflection, but the mountain retreat echoed with the blast of car and bus horns, random shouting and an unending barrage of monkey impersonations.

That night I stayed in Jingchuan, a provincial town of uniformly drab beige and grey buildings, where the citizens dressed in beige and grey trousers, jackets and caps, and rode or wheeled heavy bicycles weighed down with beige and grey sacks. A mist had started to envelop the town, smothering any other colour apart from the flamboyant red of the communist party slogans that bordered the town square and hung at intervals across the street.

By morning a dense fog had settled across the town, and even after a hard climb up to a wide plateau there was no change in the thick white mist surrounding me. I could see no further than the side of the road, making it difficult to know if I was cycling through a village or across open countryside. It was captivating and hypnotic as faint images appeared briefly out of the mist, making me question whether I was seeing them or just imagining them. A group of people huddled in a tight circle by the roadside... an old man crouched over a long bamboo opium pipe... a pastiche of faces looking at me with curiosity and occasionally suspicion... I heard a sudden, shocking squeal ahead of me, and watched as a piglet strapped to the back of a kid's bicycle came into focus through the fog, and then disappeared behind me as I passed.

Dozens of caves pockmarked a long cliff face on my left, and many of the entrances were bordered with elaborately carved figures. I pulled off the road to take a closer look and saw that there were more wall carvings inside. Steps in the rock led to another elevated opening further up and as my eyes adjusted to the gloom, I spotted the dark outline of a statue within – *but then it moved!* It was a wild-eyed bearded man, crouched down and chewing on a strip of blue plastic - he turned to me and smiled. I bolted down the steps and leapt back onto my bike.

The roads were getting crowded now. The town of Bin Xian, now less than a hundred miles from Xi'an, was a veritable hotspot for heavy goods vehicles, hundreds of trucks parked up in the town centre and cruising around the main square. The air was thick with a new type of fog, suffocating diesel fumes and all manner of pollutants; I could taste the toxic air as it seared my throat and stung my eyes. The road climbed for a long time through beautiful green hills, but I was sharing it with articulated lorries and now a new breed of vehicle; three-wheeled trucks belching foul-smelling fumes from their two-stroke engines. These were becoming increasingly numerous, an unwelcome upgrade from the spruced-up lawnmowers I had been content to share my road space with up until now.

It was baking hot, but how much of that was climate versus chemical, I wasn't sure, and I ended the day covered heat to foot in a greasy layer of soot, dirt and God-knows-what.

CHAPTER 21

SOMETHING IN THE AIR – XI'AN
TO KAIFENG

On the road into Xi'an I met Taiichi once more, and we cycled into the city together, taking pictures of each other posing triumphantly in front of the West Gate: two scraggly-haired, unshaven oddities on overloaded and mud-splattered bicycles at the end of the Silk Road. I spotted a MacDonald's and I cracked. It was the first one since Azerbaijan and I always avoid these places, but this time I was drawn in to order a Big Mac. They shook their heads and said they'd sold out. I almost cried.

This is a huge city and its population of 8 million makes it one of the largest in China. Glass-fronted skyscrapers dominated the skyline and many more multi-storey apartment buildings lined the roads which actually looked quite liveable. The whole place had a convincing veneer of order and structure that I hadn't seen in other Chinese cities, and despite the roads being rammed full of traffic it was also unusually quiet. All the cars, buses, lorries, and scooters moved along the lanes and through the roundabouts without the usual obnoxious symphony of noise. This was due to a remarkable city regulation that had banned horns in this part of town. I tested it by riding in front of a minibus – nothing, but for some swearing from the driver behind me. Amazing!

It is of course, the famous buried army of terracotta warriors that has put Xi'an on the tourist map. There are 8,000 of them, along with hundreds of sculptures of horses and chariots, interned with the emperor Qin Shi Huang in 200 BC. This huge tomb was on the outskirts of the city and on my route east. However, my immediate mission was to find a decent bike shop to replace my chain, rear cassette and chain ring, all of which had worn prematurely from the thousands of desert miles they had seen. It took a full morning of searching and many animated conversations with strangers before a local bike enthusiast took me down a maze of alleyways to a street exclusively populated with bike shops. They replaced the components, realigned the wheels and even sprayed all the accumulated mud and sand off - the bike looked cleaner and more presentable than I did.

The Great Mosque was the only sight I visited within the city; it was a sanctuary from the noise and chaos of the streets outside and I spent a couple of hours wandering around its grounds. The architecture was almost exclusively Chinese. It looked and felt more a temple than a mosque, despite the number of men in skullcaps making their way to the main hall of worship. I imagined the Chinese would not take kindly to such overt religious emblems as domes and minarets in their ancient capital.

At the gates to Xi'an, Shaanxi Province

IT WAS A RARE SUNNY DAY WHEN I LEFT XI'AN AND IT WASN'T too difficult to figure out the way to the Terracotta Army. All I had to do was follow the line of stonemasons with life-size copies of terracotta soldiers for sale, all with their heads missing, presumably to be added with a likeness of the buyer upon purchase.

I had a huge palaver with my bike once I got there; the guards wouldn't let me take it in and neither would they look after it. The commotion attracted a horde of cheap pottery hawkers who were suddenly all over it, pulling brake and gear levers, opening saddle bags and playing with the cycle computer. One fat bellicose woman had her hands deep into my handlebar bag while her toothless friend was asking for a ridiculous amount of money to "take care of it". Thankfully, because it was plain black and lacking any ostentatious accessories like huge suspension springs or gaudy graphics, they concluded it was worthless and soon lost interest. I quietly left it at a friendly taxi stand.

Once inside, the first surprise was the babble of American accents. I hadn't come across such a concentration of American tourists before, and the sudden exposure to a sea of Western tour groups was, ironically enough, a bit of a culture shock. Where had they all been hiding? From the entrance it was quite a distance to the vaults that housed the statues and I started to suspect that the long walk, spacious grounds and various marble-clad buildings were there to encourage visitors to believe they had got their money's worth. Each statue is said to have its own unique face and expression... maybe I was tired, or maybe I had overly high expectations of something I had dreamed of visiting since I was a child, but after a while, one 2,200-year-old terracotta soldier with a goatee starts to look like any other.

After three different vaults of warriors with their horses, cattle and wagons there was a huge shiny building, entered via an ornate winding marble staircase, and requiring the final and largest hole yet to be punched out of my ticket. This has got to be good, I thought, feeling a tremble of excitement and looked down eagerly into the centre of the vaulted chamber. It housed a bronze figurine of... a duck. A life-sized duck. Or maybe it was a goose.

Faced again with the mêlée of street vendors, I barely escaped the grounds with my bike unscathed, but back on the road the smiles of countless strangers and the shouted cries of encouragement went far to revive my flagging spirits. I do wonder what the average tourist makes of the Chinese, if all those they meet are aggressively trying to flog them something at each and every sightseeing spot.

Crickets chirped musically as I wound up and down through green terraced valleys, and people leisurely worked the fields soaked in the soft orange light of late afternoon. I found a room in a small village and wheeled my bike through the muddy yard as the last sliver of light disappeared completely from the sky.

THE LARGE ORANGE BOWL OF THE SUN CLIMBED SLOWLY OVER THE silhouette of a broad mountain range ahead, and a mist-speckled ride of shallow ups and downs ended fifty kilometres later at the foot of the sacred Dao peak of Hua Shan. Daoists believe the god of the underworld lives in this place, and the path to the top is infamous for being notoriously steep, crumbling and decidedly treacherous, devouring a number of souls every year. In the past, pilgrims attempted the ascent at night, considering it safer in the dark for the simple reason that they couldn't see the terrifying and precipitous drop into oblivion below. Nowadays there was a safer and far less arduous alternative available – an expensive cable-car. I got out my wallet.

In the same manner as Kongton Shan, tourists visiting Hua Shan liked to break the irritating silence and tranquillity of the place by swapping hoots and howls with each other from the clifftops. The scenery, however, soon made me forget the couple on either side bellowing into my earholes. It was singularly spectacular, with sheer white granite cliffs soaring over a mile into the air, swathes of forest deep in the valley below, puffs of green foliage bursting out of the cliff walls and a legion of mountains ahead as far as the eye could see. I saw a rickety and meandering walkway stapled across the vertical cliff face on the other side of the vertiginous gap in front of me, like temporary scaffolding put up haphazardly by some dodgy building contractor, and I understood why there were so many deaths on this mountain. The god of the underworld had chosen some prime real estate indeed.

The terraced valleys were enveloped in a blanket of orange and shadow under the late afternoon sun, and I pushed through some short hard climbs and technical descents, captivated by the real-life Chinese watercolour enveloping me. Farmers had covered the road with their harvest, spreading the crops carefully over the width of the asphalt with pitchforks, and leaving it in the path of oncoming trucks, cars and motorcycles which would help in the task of threshing by running it over. It amazed me that all this work was still carried out manually (albeit with some vehicular help), by men in clean shirts and pressed slacks, and women dressed immaculately - and absolutely everyone with a mobile phone in their hand.

My first choice in accommodation was generally a basic *ju-su*. Not mentioned in the guidebooks, banned to foreigners and found only down unsavoury narrow and cluttered backstreets, they might be marked by a scruffy handwritten sign (I recognised the characters by now). Usually with basic shared rooms, no shower and highly questionable toilets, they were very cheap (less than a dollar), friendly, and had no problem with me wheeling my mud-splattered machine into the room. It was always a great relief not to unload the bike and make several trips up to some room four or five floors above.

After a day of heavy rain, I arrived in Sanmenxia, the prefectural capital of Henan, and chose the first *ju-su* I found. It was reached through a warren of dimly lit underground corridors that led to a row of gloomy dormitories. Most rooms were clouded in shadow except one that was pleasantly decorated in pink, with three female residents who didn't look like guests and definitely didn't look like they cooked or cleaned.

∼

THE MORNING WAS HEAVY WITH MIST, LASTING THROUGH TO evening, and although I faced some stiff climbs the scenes of rural life floating by were comfortably distracting. I had noticed that whilst a few fortunate farmers had tractors (or at least a motorbike rigged up to some kind of trailer) the majority just piled up everything they needed into a cart, wrapped a rope around their chest and hauled it all between fields by hand. It was the same with the way they worked the land, heaving and pulling a heavy iron plough through a muddy field, with neither bullocks nor horses to do the work for them.

At dusk I found myself in the town of Luoyang and was pleasantly surprised by its generous tree-lined boulevards, reminding me of those ex-Soviet cities in the Ferghana valley – that all seemed so long ago now. But before I got too nostalgic, I felt a hard slap on my back, knocking the wind out of me and almost dislodging me from my saddle. A short stocky man of around fifty overtook me on an old bone shaker of a bicycle, looked back - smiling or growling I wasn't sure - and hollered something excitedly at me. What had I done? Was he going to mug me? Would anyone step in to help?

We had both stopped our bikes by now and before I knew it, he had my map of China off the top of my handlebar bag and laid out on pavement, prodding at it with his finger and asking me a rash of quick-fire questions in Chinese. I nervously traced my route for him and pulled out another map to show that I had started in England. His semi-scowl turned into a grin and then a wide beaming smile. I breathed a sigh of relief, as did the crowd of onlookers now gathered around us. He jabbed my shoulder with every question and for every answer I gave, he broadcasted it to the now considerable crowd. This elicited gasps, one or two cheers, and more questions (and shoulder jabs).

I had just been introduced to the dynamic Mr Lu Song Tao.

"You will stay at my house tonight!" he barked at me in Chinese, and I reflexively answered yes. I can't imagine anyone has ever refused Mr Lu.

He then went systematically through the crowd, stopping random passers-by and interrogating anyone who looked of university age, until he found a young man who was studying English.

"My house, tonight, 8 pm sharp", he told the overwhelmed student, giving him his address and swapping mobile phone numbers. "You will be our translator!"

He led me home in a high-speed kaleidoscopic tour-de-force through half a dozen open-air night markets. First up was the poultry market where Mr Lu bought a duck. Then down another alley and across a busy road for the vegetables, followed by a confusing series of sharp lefts, rights and a U-turn that took us into the market selling sweets. These were secrets of the city I would never have found alone, and we weaved through cars, scooters and dozens of other bicycles coming from all directions in the dimly lit streets. I ducked under the eaves of weeping willows lining long alleyways, through bazaars illuminated by rainbows of coloured lightbulbs, hole-in-the wall noodle sellers, aged men standing by with floor-pumps, sauces and spices and rows upon rows of water-melons. This was how you toured a Chinese city.

We arrived at Mr Lu's house, newly built and three storeys high, and he told me proudly this was all his. His young wife and five-year-old son met us graciously at the door, with minimum fuss, despite the unannounced visit of this rather odd guest. Mr Lu was no doubt in the habit of springing surprises. While he led us upstairs to the living room, excitedly explaining my story to his family, Mrs Lu discreetly gestured at the bathroom, indicating that perhaps I would like to wash up before dinner. When I looked in the mirror, I understood why; I had the face of a coal miner after a twelve-hour shift.

This was no normal mist I had been cycling through all day.

The university student Liu turned up as arranged, along with his mother, but by then Mr Lu and I had already settled into a pattern where we could somehow get along. And it soon became clear that Mr Lu was no ordinary man. Twenty-three years ago, he had done something quite extraordinary.

"LIKE EVERYONE ELSE, I LEFT SCHOOL AT FIFTEEN AND WENT TO work in a factory. Although I stuck it for a few years and saved some money, I was so very bored doing the same thing day in day out. Here I was, living in a vast country, but I knew little beyond my town", he explained. "That seemed to be enough for most people, but it was not enough for *me*."

Contrary to all the advice from family and friends, he quit his job and embarked on an eighteen-month journey around China – on his bike.

"That kind of thing was unthinkable in China twenty years ago. Unthinkable!" and he grinned at the recollection. "I cycled to Tibet, around Xinjiang and the whole of the Northwest. I learnt more about China this way than any academic sitting in his library, or the countless documentaries that you can watch on TV nowadays."

Old black and white photographs showed a Chinese one-speed bicycle with a couple of bags tied to the handlebars and a much younger and thinner Mr Lu standing next to it, engulfed in a woollen great coat two sizes too big for him. The backdrop was of endless snowy plains.

"*That* is why I was so excited to find you", he said. "Only you and I know what real travel is; we are not like everyone else who just hop on a comfortable bus to take them from one place to another! Ha ha! Eat! Drink!"

Mr Lu had since gone on to make his fortune, first by supplying feed for chickens and then working hard over the years to eventually become the owner of a modern factory producing agricultural parts. The catalyst for all this, he said, was the day he decided to leave his job and cycle around his country – and now at last he had found someone who could genuinely appreciate his story.

We talked late into the night, long after our obliging student Liu and his mother had departed, and the next morning we were up early for a trip to the Longmen Grottos. This was probably the most famous of all Buddhist cave complexes in China and the only reason for tourists to pass through an industrial city like Luoyang. It was a good eight miles south of the city and not far off my planned route; the best way to get there was, of course, by bicycle.

Cycling through the early rush hour traffic was done at a frantic pace, overtaking other bicycles and motorcycles, skimming through narrow gaps between overloaded lorries, their wavering cargos leaning precariously above us, and cutting up busses moving errati-cally between lanes. Mr Lu was a man on a mission, and it was only when we had at last reached the remote suburbs that I could pull alongside him – and stop praying under my breath to any god who might listen.

There were dozens of tall apartment blocks under construction and wide roads almost devoid of traffic, with an immaculately attired policeman at every intersection directing a bare trickle of vehicles. Meanwhile, only a couple of miles away, the traffic lights were out of order, the roads gridlocked in absolute chaos and not a single traffic cop was to be seen anywhere.

Entrance into the Longmen Grottos was expensive and I implored Mr Lu to let me pay for something, but a quick and surprising burst of anger put stop to that – "You are my guest!" – and there was no question that I would be allowed to spend a single *yuan*. After the rather claustrophobic experience of the Mogao grottos at Dunhuang, I was not expecting much from Longmen, but I could not have been more mistaken.

"This valley is made up of two mountains, Xiangshan and Long-menshan. Both are covered with many sacred caves." Mr Lu pointed out the caves dotted along the across the hillsides of two mountains.

"They are called the Grottos of the Dragon's Gate", explained Mr Lu. "The caves are the dragon's teeth, and the River Yi that runs between the mountains is the dragon's tongue."

The valley had been chiselled out and widened by hand; hundreds of caves contained thousands of Buddhist carvings and statues, running a mile along the valley sides. It had taken 400 years to complete and, unlike Mogao, almost everything was open and visible. The vista of caves scattered all over the slopes presented an incredible sight.

However, it was all seen in a flash, as Mr Lu led me around at a frantic pace. It was my fault, as I'd told him I wanted to be back on the road by noon in order to make it to the next town before dark. And true to his word, after treating me to lunch, thrusting a bag of food into my hands, and wishing me a long and prosperous life, I was on my way shortly after midday. We had no language in common but somehow, we had managed to communicate in depth the previous night and all through this morning. A remarkable man. Thank you, Mr Lu.

Back on the road, the absence of my new friend left me with a pang of loneliness and a little sadness; that evening I rode into the town of Xingyang with barely any memory of the 140 kilometres I had cycled that day. The whole route had been ridden in a haze, both figuratively and literally; when I caught sight of myself in a mirror that evening there it was again, the coal miner's face looking right back at me.

With Mr Lu at Longmen Grottos, Henan Province

KAIFENG WAS BARELY A HUNDRED KILOMETRES AWAY, BUT I FIRST had to navigate through Zhengzhou; with an urban population of six million people it was several stressful hours before I found myself on the right road. Kaifeng was on an order of magnitude worse than this, as it seemed to have the same number of people crammed into a fraction of the space.

A rabble of diesel and human powered transport zoomed past in all directions, and I followed an old man peddling a tricycle with an aviary of songbirds, as he threaded his way around trucks and mopeds with more skill and poise than I would ever be able to summon. I checked into a basic hotel and carried my bike up three flight of stairs to my room, collapsing onto the bed, senses saturated, nerves shattered, unable and unwilling to face anybody for the next four hours.

When at last I did, I had the restaurant owner's eight-year-old son to deal with.

"OKAY!" he shouted, "HEY!" he screamed in my face as I ate,

trying to ignore him while his mother and the other customers just chuckled and looked on indulgently.

I was experiencing Little Emperor Syndrome, an unfortunate outcome of China's one-child policy, where the only child is brought up with far too much pampering attention from their parents and grandparents. I paid his mother and she handed him the change to pass back to me; he pocketed it for himself, slapping my hands out the way and strutting back to the counter, whistling. I appealed to his mother, but she was just surprised that I wasn't laughing along with her loveable little joker. Meanwhile the pint-sized tyrant was now showing his arse and then gyrating his crotch at me, antics which only got a further approving chortle from his parents.

Kaifeng was the capital of China many dynasties ago, and has a history going back to 700 BC. It is most famous for its "Iron Pagoda", touted on the information board with typical Chinese modesty as "Officially the Best Pagoda in the World". It was completely covered in thousands of glazed tiles, the colour a rusty red (hence its name) and each tile was intricately engraved; as well as images of the Buddha there were pictures of nobles going about their business in court and scenes of daily village life. Despite my short attention span for works of art, I found myself spending two hours examining them in detail.

The pagoda was set in spacious landscaped grounds with temples and ponds. Considering the mayhem of the streets nearby it was surprisingly peaceful. There was no rush to get things done, no miles to kill, no routes to map out, no provisions to buy. I wandered around until well after dusk, watching the final deep orange flush of sunset until everything was bathed in the phosphorescent light of the full moon, and the temple's guardians – a pair of monstrously sized half-dog-half-demon statues – glared back at me from the deepening darkness.

Kaifeng recharged me for the final stretch to Shanghai. It also marked a decisive transformation of the roads I had ridden over the last few weeks. The dramatic landscapes of the deserts of Xinjiang had developed into an increasingly prosperous montage of villages and towns, with bustling businesses and restaurants lining the road. Mountains had softened into rolling hills, untamed steppe into sculpted rice terraces, and I had to contend with rain and mud instead of perilous winds and sandstorms.

Autumnal mornings turned into smog-filled afternoons and the days were noticeably shorter, but the biggest change was that I was never alone. Tiny dots on the map that once marked a windswept village now exposed a sprawling modern city, and the towns in-between - they were uncountable.

CHAPTER 22

A SLOW BOAT FROM CHINA

Sunlight glistened off the many roadside streams used to irrigate fields of corn and cotton. Trees lined the road, half-naked from the seasonal loss of leaves, but the trunks and branches still threw some welcome slivers of shade across my path, offering partial respite from the harsh sun still low on the horizon. My company on the road was a stream of rickety tricycles, powered steadily along by gnarled old men with their equally gnarled old spouses dozing in the trailer on the back. On the roadside I passed groups of women sitting in semi-circles on the ground, knitting furiously.

After ordering lunch at a roadside stall, I saw a bicycle pass by with a trussed-up dog howling and struggling on the rear rack. That's a little harsh, I thought to myself. Finishing up my noodles twenty minutes later and sipping on a cup of jasmine tea, I saw the same bicycle with the same dog coming back the other way. But this time he was a lot quieter - the poor blighter had been skinned.

I called it a day at Shangqiu and found a place to stay on the outskirts. It was a basic dormitory (cardboard windows and crickets chirping in my room) and a communal toilet with character. I had barely rolled the bike into the room when a stream of people from the neighbourhood started wandering in, and there were soon two dozen people crammed into the room with others leaning in through the window (the cardboard shutters not doing a good job here). Everyone had something to ask me.

The usual questions were hurled at me in rapid Chinese, and by now I was familiar enough with this that I could even scrape by on some responses with minimal theatrics. One girl knew a few words of English and was clearly desperate to join the conversation, finally getting the chance to ask her question.

"What... did... you... *eat?*" she asked somewhat hesitantly, and I gave her a run-down of what had fuelled me for the last half year or so, not too sure how much she was actually understanding, as she stared at me intently. When I mentioned chicken she immediately brightened up, raising her hand to interrupt me, while everyone looked on in awe at their neighbour's hidden language prowess.

"How many?" she asked.

A long pause.

"Twenty", I replied, and she smiled, satisfied with my answer.

Two eager kids showed me around the food stalls outside, found me a stool and bartered with an old lady serving up noodles, securing me an extra helping and a couple of boiled eggs, as they topped up my tea as quickly as I could drink it. It was a welcome contrast to the Little Emperor of Kaifeng.

When I got back to my room, I was utterly exhausted and I still hadn't changed out of the clothes I'd been riding in for the best part of a hundred miles. As I collapsed on the bed there was knock at the door – it was the local newspaper. The reporter walked in with a photographer and two assistants, and of course the entire neighbourhood followed behind. An attractive woman in her twenties, the reporter spoke decent English and we talked for over an hour while she made notes and the photographer took pictures. I enthusiastically agreed to her suggestion of an early morning photoshoot.

At 5 am the photographer and his assistant had turned up, but no attractive newspaper lady. It no longer seemed quite as much fun as I'd envisioned but, as agreed, I followed them behind their motorbike to Shangqiu Old Town. The Old Town was garrisoned by a square mile of perfectly preserved brick ramparts with an elaborate gatehouse set in the middle of each of its four sides. It was further surrounded by a wide moat, one of only four in China, the photographer informed me.

In spite of the manic din of scooters and trucks, here was the China that you have always imagined. The narrow streets were lined with weeping willows, ornately roofed houses, stone courtyards and row upon row of small shops, their contents spilling out onto the pavement. I performed a montage of scenes for the camera, circling the busy roundabout in the centre of town, riding in and out of the gates at all four walls and repeatedly up and down a number of shopping streets, all in the midst of some thoroughly chaotic traffic.

"Raise your hand! V for victory! V for victory! Smile at the camera!" yelled the photographer again and again as I tried to avoid the string of two, three, four and twelve wheeled vehicles coming straight at me.

Once it was all over, they sent me on my way to the next town, recommending a quiet rural backroad over the busy highway. This also happened to be the formula for Instant Celebrity: select local road, add foreign bicycle tourist and... *voila*! Every time I stopped to check the map people swarmed around me. At one point the crowds of onlookers completely blocked up one side of a dual carriageway and I was a little worried about the oncoming traffic. But it was fine – they stopped their cars and joined in as well!

DESPITE THE BUSY MORNING I HAD COVERED ALMOST A HUNDRED miles by late afternoon and had crossed from Henan into Anhui province. Here the farms were larger and distinctly more prosperous, with more tractors at work on the land rather than farmworkers with hoes and harnesses, and I saw many elaborate and well-kept ancestral tombs. However, there was nothing prosperous about my lodgings for the night; on the edge of a muddy courtyard, my room was directly across from a battery of concrete pigsties and next to that, the gloomy opening into some type of warehouse, from the depths of which I could hear vicious barks and growls from some devil hound.

An awful-smelling, haggard old man in rags shuffled into my room, sat on the foot of my bed and started smoking an opium pipe, unaware or unconcerned about my presence right next to him, as he hawked and spat at the floor. Oblivious to my verbal protests I had to physically push him out of the room, and I wedged my bike up against the door before going to sleep. He woke me up in the early hours trying to force open the door, until I chased him away again.

A foul headwind harassed me throughout the next day putting me in an equally foul mood. Whenever and wherever I stopped people flocked to me, competing with each other to ask questions. It reminded me of Central Asia in some ways, but with more people and considerably less restraint. They were especially intrusive here, snatching away a book I might be reading over lunch, trying to unzip my bags, crowding around and staring at me while I ate.

When I lumbered into Sixian I was so exhausted that I decided to find a decent hotel with a comfortable bed, my own clean bathroom, and a television (Tuesday night was English movie night on channel CTV6). In a city this size such hotels are usually everywhere you look, but today of all days, I had to spend two hours trying to locate one. There were plenty of signs advertising "crap room available", "dosshouse round back", "cockroach motel" and "cesspit disguised as room" (my reading of Chinese characters had considerably improved), but none for a regular hotel. It was after dark when I eventually found a run-down looking *binguan*, gladly checked in and settled down for a long-anticipated evening of television followed by a thoroughly good night's sleep.

Alas, there was a power cut as soon as I got to the room, lasting through to morning. And with the way that the receptionist was casually handing out candles to guests in this plasterboard firetrap of a building, I didn't exactly sleep too soundly either.

~

TODAY I SAW A LOT OF PIGS HAVING SEX. A SMALL VILLAGE CROWD would generally gather around the action, amongst the mud and rubbish, while the owner of the "stud pig" looked on delightedly as his pride and joy got on with the job. The spectators watched studiously, adding expert commentary on the proceedings, while young schoolgirls pointed in puzzlement and whispered furiously to each other. It must be the season, I supposed.

Women scrubbed their clothes clean by the riverbanks and for the first time I saw water buffalo being used to haul ploughs through the furrowed rice paddies. The road rose and fell through forests, a welcome change, as a headwind doesn't bite nearly so hard when you're already slowed down by the climbs. Making his own slow journey, a Buddhist priest was on the roadside, face like a burnished walnut, kneeling, prostrating, rising and repeating the same operation again one step later. I felt humbled, and for once didn't moan about my aches and pains at the end of another hundred-mile day.

I made up for it the next morning though; this road was the worst stretch of asphalt I had ever ridden. Deep ridges and ruts ran across the width of the road and random lumps of concrete protruded several inches from the surface, turning this into 40 kilometres of the most deviously designed speedbumps you could ever imagine.

Nanjing was the biggest Chinese city to date that I had come across. From the city limits to the centre it stretched over 30 kilometres, a huge and thriving modern city. I couldn't imagine what cycling into Shanghai would be like. I was looking forward to ticking off some sights like any regular tourist and booked into a youth hostel for a couple of nights. I scanned the lounge – wow, this place was young. The guests here were mainly European and North Americans in their late teens or early twenties; energetic, excited, full of enthusiasm. Fifteen years ago that might have been me and I also would have been staring at the weary-looking bloke in the corner thinking: who is that boring old duffer, sitting quietly reading a book? Well my boy, that's you... fifteen years on!

The first stop on my itinerary was also the grimmest: the "Memorial to the Victims of the Nanjing Massacre by the Japanese Invaders". This was unfortunately the only reason I had heard of this city and the Nanjing Massacre had always been a thorn in the side of Sino-Japanese relations, the Japanese always disputing the level of brutality and the number of victims. Visiting the museum, I could understand why; the exhibits and photographs were truly appalling, and the accounts of atrocities from survivors made harrowing reading. I walked away shocked. But I also saw that exhibits on the Japanese surrender avoided any mention of the atomic bombing of Hiroshima and Nagasaki by the Americans, and the horrors inflicted on civilians there. Feelings were clearly still raw, which likely accounted for the distinct absence of Japanese tourists.

I rode my bike east out of the city, skirting the ancient city walls before heading further into the hills to Purple Gold Mountain, a beautiful, densely wooded mountain retreat on the eastern outskirts of the city. There were a number of must-see sights out here, but I preferred the relative tranquillity of the forest, dotted with small lakes, temples and statues, and the wide steps of the Xiaoling Mausoleum snaking their way up into the far reaches of the green mountainside.

Nanjing is pleasantly green, a city endowed with well-tended leafy avenues, parks, lakes and canals - and it's clean, showing no signs of the urban detritus I saw clogging up the streets of most towns. There are modern shops, restaurants, a Starbucks even, and judging by those bloody youngsters rolling into the hostel at four-thirty in the morning, a seemingly lively nightlife as well. It was the first Chinese city I had come across that I wouldn't outright burst into tears at the thought of living in.

YELLOW RIPENED FIELDS OF WHEAT JOSTLED WITH FACTORIES AND industrial parks. The scenery was becoming blander and the roads busier the closer I got to Shanghai. But at least the Shanghai distance markers that had mocked me for so long were now down to three digits rather than four.

The rules of the road are simple here. Look out only for the guy in front of you and assume the guy behind is doing the same; do not glance over your shoulder, as you really don't want to know. Navigating through Changzhou my nerves were really put to the test; haulage trucks, coaches, buses, cars, motorbikes (with three generations of the same family squeezed on board), pedal-tricycles, motor-tricycles, pedicabs, three-wheeled lorries, pick-up trucks, dump trucks, road-rollers, and of course bicycles, coming from everywhere, most using the full width of the road and pavement, and many in the wrong lane. On one stretch of road the surface was being dug up haphazardly by an excavator; it spilled a couple of pumpkin-sized rocks into the carriageway that just missed the car next to me and rolled past my back wheel.

Nerves jangling but commendably still alive, I found myself in a small town a little short of Wuxi, another hundred-mile day completed. With the help of a winning smile, the map of my route, a couple of locals I had just befriended, and a bit of pleading, I bargained the price for a room down from 180 *yuan* to 100 *yuan* (7 dollars). It was also the nicest and cleanest hotel I had stayed in yet. That evening the restaurant would not even accept payment; it was on the house they said, seemingly delighted with the idea of a British tourist stopping the night in this nondescript town when there were so many popular tourist alternatives to choose from.

Another long day of mad traffic and gritted-teeth cycling took me to Suzhou, the "Venice of the Orient". I was in spitting distance of Shanghai and it was with some considerable self-control that I took the following day off, to make sure I could explore the place and enjoy the novelty of staying in another Chinese city that was clean, modern and pleasing to the eye. As well as canals and bridges, Suzhou is known for its expertly sculptured classical gardens, a favourite being the famous Lion Grove Garden full of oddly shaped rocks (the "lions"), creating a maze around a central pond. It all came together in an ingenious illusion, as paths led bewilderingly over and under other paths, leading you to somewhere you did not expect, or taking you back to where you started. Not unlike many of the roads, I thought.

It was in Suzhou that I had my third haircut of the trip (the last one had been in Uzbekistan) and I decided to pamper myself by going to one of the nicer looking establishments in the tourist area. Thirty minutes in and they were still on the head massage when, suddenly, the chatter of the lowly team of hair-washers and apprentices fell into a reverential silence and they moved aside in unison. The stylist appeared in front of me (possibly with a flash of white smoke) carrying a shiny aluminium briefcase. Waiting a couple of moments to let the magnitude of his arrival register with all assembled and with one final contemptuous stare, he laid down the case, flung open the lid, threw his arms open wide... and pulled out a pink floral-patterned apron, laying it over me in an artistic flourish.

I got a short back and sides.

THERE IS NOTHING LIKE THE RUSH OF EARLY MORNING TOXIC

smog through your hair and diesel fumes in your lungs, pollution clinging to your face like a gritty mask. Little compares to the thrill of high-speed psychopathic truck drivers trying to run you down like a dog, the excitement of opportunistic pushing and shoving from motorcyclists and the delight of sneers, hurled abuse and spittle from pedestrians. It just doesn't get much better than this!

My original plan was to meander through the back roads to Shanghai, taking in a few sights over a couple of days, but I was now just so damned close after all these months of cycling that my patience was shot. To hell with it, I wanted to take the most direct, traffic-clogged, ugly road I could find. Endless half-built industrial estates... dismal looking concrete blocks of flats... soot-smeared, rickety roadside garages and ill-looking shop proprietors... so this was China's economic miracle. I crossed over a river, the water black and stagnant, and saw a barge lined up against the muddy banks with its cargo of bricks being unloaded by hand, the two dozen labourers moving in nail-biting synchronisation over precarious bamboo planks, a hundredweight of bricks balanced on their shoulders. They bounced to the shore, unloaded their cargo and repeated the process again and again in an unending loop.

And then, without fanfare, I was unexpectedly in downtown Shanghai, multi-storey buildings rising up high on either side of claustrophobic streets and a skyline of skyscrapers ahead, a dense mass of humanity teeming along at a frantic pace. For the first time I saw "No Cycling" signs and unbelievably, after everything I had seen in this country, they were actually enforced. Police ordered me to wheel my bike on the pavement, and whenever I got back on the road, there would soon be another one blowing his whistle at me.

What the hell was going on? Was this not China, land of the bicycle? Two wheels, three wheels it doesn't matter; trailered-up or trailer-less, with improvised diesel motor or without... it's still a bloody bike, carrying a family, a week's groceries or even the contents of a house. This economy has been built by millions of Chinese plying their wares back and forth on the back of a bike for Chrissakes! I have ridden my bike halfway around the world, and now they have the nerve to proclaim No Cycling?

However, Shanghai makes it very clear that this is no place for the bicycle. The car is king and the bicycle an embarrassment, a reminder of the past, an anomaly. This city has eyes focused only on the future.

∿

SO, WHERE DID THE TIME GO? I HAD ALMOST A WEEK TO WAIT FOR the next ferry to Japan but it was over all too quickly. Had I done enough? More than once I entertained the idea of heading south through Thailand, Vietnam and Malaysia – why not finish in Australia instead? It seemed almost crazy that now I'd got all the hard stuff out the way, I wasn't heading to the banana pancake-rich resorts of Southeast Asia for some well-deserved relaxation.

But I also knew that wasn't the point. It had been a decade of flying back and forth between London and Tokyo, a life somehow split between the UK and Japan, that had precipitated the idea of this journey in the first place and resonated strongly enough to drive me this far. The plan was good. I just had to finish it.

Shanghai was more cosmopolitan than anywhere I had seen in China. The average person I passed on the street was young, professional and seemed to ooze sophistication, with a mobile phone permanently hanging off one ear. The men had their hair gelled carefully into place and the women were beautiful, expensively attired in brand name fashions. I felt more out of place here than in any of the nameless villages I had stayed in over the last two months.

After treating myself to a new T-shirt and a pair of jeans – I desperately needed some "civilian" clothes in this city – I met up for a drink with my old comrade from the Gobi Desert, Taiichi, who had ridden in a couple of days earlier and was flying back to Japan the next day. We had last seen each other in Xi'an only three weeks before, but as we sat in a bar trying to make ourselves heard over the music, it felt like another era. A friend flew in from Tokyo and then another couple arrived the day after, and the last few days disappeared in a haze of bars, restaurants and sights. Shanghai was as expensive as Tokyo in many ways and the Shanghainese famously slick when it came to money; there would be no spontaneous displays of generosity here. Yet in contrast to all expectation I found the people friendly, outgoing and eager to interact.

All except one. The receptionist at my hotel had a permanent sneer and grumbled loudly and angrily whenever a guest made a simple request. She belittled them with snide remarks and barked orders like a drill sergeant. "You wait here!". "Pay me now!". "Move your luggage!".

And every day, carefully pinned in pride of place on her left lapel, she wore a badge of a large and well-polished smiley face.

Civilian clothes at last, Shanghai

CHAPTER 23

THE HIGH ROAD TO THE
FAR EAST

The ferry from Harwich to Holland had been packed full of bars, restaurants and a cinema, and I had been frantic to get my money's worth over the mere six hours it took. The next ferry I boarded had been half a continent away, the one that spirited me from Azerbaijan to the Republic of Turkmenistan overnight, where I tossed and turned in an uneasy sleep, dreaming of Middle Asian warlords pursuing me across the desert wastes. The ferry from Shanghai to an eminently civilised Osaka would take a leisurely two full days with just the basic facilities, showers and cafeteria, and no options for entertainment other than watching the horizon. I was looking forward to it; the laziness and lethargy would not be my fault.

Announcements over the tannoy were in Japanese, as well as Chinese, reminding me that the day after tomorrow I would at last be back in an environment which I knew something about. I would also have time to acclimatise to the sudden hike in costs – a can of coke from the vending machine was now the price of a night's accommodation in rural China. The passengers were a mixture of Japanese tourists, a few backpackers, and a large group of bewildered young Chinese women, cheap labour for the component assembly lines in Japanese factories.

"They are hired for their small hands", explained an old Japanese man who travelled this route regularly, "so that they can piece together intricate parts. Japanese don't really want to do such work nowadays."

They had been in the ferry terminal saying goodbye to their parents, their husbands and their children; it would be three years before they would meet again and the tears, the desperate hugs, the mothers clinging on to their children up to the very last moment... it was heart-breaking.

"You should see them when they do return", he said, "when they are reunited with their families. It is the happiest thing you will ever see."

At the port immigration desk in Osaka, in common with most of the land borders I had crossed to date, I was waved through customs with a cursory thirty-second baggage search while the backpackers next to me were having the contents of their toiletry bag emptied on the counter, and the tops of their toothpaste unscrewed. What is it that makes us cyclists so trustworthy?

The signs at first glance looked no different from Chinese signs, the high-rise buildings in the background like almost any view in Shanghai, and of course the vast majority of the faces I saw passing in front of me were oriental. The moment I was outside of the ferry terminal, however, it was obvious I was in a completely different country. Cars and busses followed the traffic signs slowly and obediently, people waited in a disciplined line at the bus stop and as I tried to manoeuvre my bicycle along the busy pavement, everyone was understanding and polite.

Taking a subway into downtown Osaka for some dinner, I was vaguely surprised that no policeman was shaking me down for bribes and bewildered at the orderliness of things, as people waited rigidly at pedestrian crossings for the lights to change and cars (without the accompanying eruption of horns and klaxons) used the proper lanes, rather than transitory gaps between vehicles. There were restaurants wherever I looked, just like any Chinese city, but with so much more variety in cuisine and some actual thought given to interior ambience, rather than a few chairs and tables on a litter-strewn concrete floor. I didn't care that everything was ten times as expensive!

Downtown Osaka

THE MOST DIRECT ROUTE FROM OSAKA TO TOKYO IS FLAT AND
straight and only five hundred kilometres; it follows the course of
the Tokaido, an ancient series of paths that were turned into a
proper thoroughfare in the early 17th century and linked the then
capital city of Kyoto with Edo (the old name for Tokyo).

However, the Tokaido has changed somewhat over the last few
hundred years: it is now the most heavily trafficked, concrete-
girdled transportation corridor in Japan, a continuous abomination
of multilane carriageways, congested city roads and dismal factory
and office buildings as far as the eye can see. If I rode this, I could
be finished within a few days - but it was no way to end things,
executing a sterile dash along main roads and through major cities
just to make a goal.

So, my plan was to travel only minor roads as much as possible
to the capital. Do it properly, deliberately, and in the process
perhaps understand what still draws me to this place. The going
would be tough; mountains form four-fifths of Japan's terrain and
they are almost all excruciatingly steep. But it is this inaccessibility
that makes them so attractive, a world apart from the plains where
the vast majority of the population live. My route would take me

from Kyushu (the southernmost of the four main islands of Japan) to Shikoku, where I would claw my way west to east along the spine of the island and then cut across the Kii Peninsula. From there I would re-join the mainland for the final push to Tokyo.

There was an overnight ferry bound for Beppu, a well-known *onsen* (hot spring) resort on the coast of Kyushu, and it was with an unexpectedly heavy heart that I joined the line of vehicles waiting to board. I had felt the full gamut of emotions over the last year but for the very first time, I felt a twinge of sadness. The end was now in sight. The year of planning and anticipation. The long months spent cycling through distant deserts and mountain ranges. The people I had met, and the exhilarating, if sometimes hairy, experiences I had been through. I couldn't believe that it would soon be over.

THE FERRY WAS PACKED WITH DOZENS OF TRUCKS TAKING A short-cut to the eastern flank of Kyushu and carloads of Japanese holidaymakers going to enjoy the hot springs. We docked mid-morning and the last hour was a hive of activity, with the youngsters occupying all sinks in the bathroom putting in contact lenses and preening themselves with *Nudy* hairspray and *Mandom* hair gel, while the older folks lined up ready to disembark in uniforms of identical track-suits, tennis shoes and baseball hats issued by their travel agent.

From aboard the ferry, I could see Beppu wedged between the ocean shimmering in the sunshine and a range of steep tree-clad mountains beyond, displaying dashes of the brilliant red and orange hues of autumn. The only way out of town was over these mountains and I couldn't quite believe that I was cycling in Japan once again. The last eight months already seemed like a dream.

I was headed for the nearby *onsen* town of Yufuin, situated in a pretty valley just below the twin-peaked mountain of Yufu-san. I had first come here almost a decade ago on my very first trip outside of Tokyo; there were far fewer tourists in those days, especially non-Japanese, and there were few of the trendy cafés and craft shops that Yufuin is now famous for. Back then I was invited to enjoy the private spa of a retired couple I had met on a walk, with the heights of Yufu-san towering up in front of us. Today I settled on an old bathhouse by the lake for a blissful two-hour soak in the hot, cloudy water. My thoughts were lost in the tranquil views of Lake Kinrinko, interrupted only by the occasional overseas tour group popping in to take photos, and me repeatedly scurrying for my towel.

At least I wouldn't be getting back into my putrid cycling shorts for a while, as a couple of old friends had offered to put me up in their house for a few nights. Jeff and Eri lived in the neighbouring prefecture of Fukuoka, their home an old Japanese farmhouse in a state of constant renovation with views of nothing but paddy-fields and mountains. While they were at work and their young son Hugh at playgroup, I spent the days warming myself in their kitchen, feeding logs into the stove, and musing on when might be a socially acceptable time to start the drinking by myself. Occasionally a neighbour would join me at the kitchen table, and we would stay that way, staring at each other for an hour or two. My hosts had originally told me I was welcome to stay as long as I wanted, but now they seemed worried that indeed I would.

Eri's parents had invited us all into the city to go out for a cele-bratory meal together and stay the night at their apartment. The last time I had met her parents was at their wedding and it hadn't turned out too well. I had prepared an impossibly embarrassing "best man" speech in best British tradition, which unbeknownst to me, was most definitely not a Japanese tradition. By the end, the only sound that could be heard were the quiet sobs of some aged relative, and the parents hadn't spoke to me since. All that unpleas-antness now seemed thankfully forgotten.

It was no real surprise that Jeff and I peeled off from the family for a quick nightcap. But returning in the early hours, befuddled by alcohol and foiled by the abundance of buttons and levers in the space-age toilet, I mistook the emergency cord for the flush. This triggered an ear-splitting alarm, set little Hugh off crying, and brought Eri's parents rushing out of their bedroom in a panic, just in time to see their son-in-law rush to the bathroom and thrust his head over the toilet bowl. It was probably time to move on.

I had a thumping hangover – my first since Uzbekistan I realised with some disbelief – and a certain unsteadiness on the bike after ten days of sloth. It was a terrible day of traffic as I threaded my way through the grim conurbations of Kita Kyushu. The occasional flash of green countryside and pleasant detours through small towns were marred by overwhelming tracts of concrete carriageway lined with dry cleaners, hairdressers, hostess bars and *pachinko* (slot machine) parlours strung along most of the 90 kilometres to the ferry port. This drab urban scenery was unfortunately typical of Japan's built-up industrial centres and something I planned to avoid as soon as I arrived in Shikoku.

Yufuin Onsen, Kyushu

"WE HUMBLY THANK YOU FOR YOUR KIND PATRONAGE OF OUR modest services. Please note that the ferry shop and restaurant will open in 60 minutes."

"We profusely thank you for your kind support of our services. Kindly note that the ferry shop and restaurant will open in 45 minutes."

The overnight ferry was headed to the castle town of Matsuyama and announcements annoyingly apprised the passengers of its progress in granular updates throughout the night.

"There are six hours remaining before we land in Matsuyama."

"Please remember there is no smoking other than in the designated areas."

"There are four hours remaining before we land in Matsuyama. Be sure to try our famous oranges during your stay."

"Please no jumping from the ferry."

"We have arrived in Matsuyama Port. Get up! Get up! Get up!"

It was early morning when the ferry docked and cold and dark outside, so I tried to get some sleep in the empty ferry terminal. As soon as I got comfortable over a couple of chairs, a miserable old port employee prodded me awake and told me to sleep upright like the guy three rows behind me. He was the only other person there.

Later in the morning I cycled into the city to meet Taiichi, my companion from the Gobi Desert. He was here visiting his parents and had offered to put me up for the night. It was wonderful to meet up and reminisce about our China crossing, as we relaxed in the famous spa baths of Dogo Onsen, a sprawling three storey bathhouse and the oldest hot spring resort in Japan. The water was too hot to enjoy, no doubt designed this way to get through as many tourists as quickly as possible.

He convinced me to go shopping for a bicycle helmet. After surviving some of the most dangerous roads in the world with my helmet hanging off the handlebars and eventually left on a street in Kyrgyzstan, I now felt compelled to don some head protection and not leave my fate solely in the hands of a few lucky charms. Japan was starting to have an effect.

It was a cold and overcast morning as I said my goodbyes and headed towards the first climb of the day, and a mild taster of what was to come. The roads were practically deserted, but in Japan a lack of traffic and rapid rural depopulation doesn't mean a lack of public works projects; I passed the gaping mouth of a monstrous tunnel under construction in the mountainside. According to my map, it would link this quiet overgrown lane to another quiet overgrown lane in the neighbouring valley.

I cycled past very old men and women, their backs bent double from decades spent working the land of their small farms, and I nodded hello to a figure dressed in white robes and a conical straw hat; he was leaning on his wooden staff taking a break, and greeted me as I approached.

"*Otsukaresma desu*", he said, "Well done."

I was not hallucinating: he was an *Ohenro-san* - a pilgrim - walking the 1,200 kilometre Shikoku Pilgrimage. You can find these white-clad figures all over Shikoku trudging between temples, across mountain trails, following miles of deserted coastline or along busy highways. There were 88 temples spread across all four prefectures of the island and it could take months to complete. The motivations for someone taking such a chunk out of their daily lives varied enormously: some were novice monks, but most were regular men and women from all walks of life, aiming to complete this undertaking once in their life. Many were walking for a loved one, hoping their prayers and dedication and might help them get over an illness, while a few walked simply for their own salvation.

Riding along Omoyo gorge the autumnal colours enveloped me as I rose above the river. The landscape was a sea of orange and yellow and the river below a turbulent ribbon of luminous blue. The ravine narrowed as I climbed higher, and the road frequently disappeared into dark, narrow tunnels hewn from the rock. I came to a small hotel and campground occupying a narrow ledge of flat land clamped tightly by steep dark cliffs on either side, but something stopped me pulling out my tent.

It wasn't terribly cold and looking at the wispy clouds above, it didn't look like it would rain either, but still I paused. Ten days of comfort in Kyushu had turned me soft. I turned my bike towards the hotel, looking forward to a warm bath, a full meal and a heated toilet seat.

IT WAS COLD THE NEXT MORNING AND, AS I CLIMBED A 1500 metre pass, snow was piled up high on either side of the road, the dusting of snow on the trees looking like frozen cherry blossoms. I was alone in savouring the views over the valley, noticing the fiery orange and gold trees still radiant below the snow line. Frozen sweat chilled me as I dropped the best part of a mile's elevation in a fast descent, and I caught sight of narrow tracks leading off the main road, shaded gateways into the unnerving stillness of the surrounding woods, like a Brothers Grimm fairy tale. Old Japanese *ryokan* inns nestled deep into the bosom of the forest with aromatic smoke rising in slow spirals from their chimneys, the warmth of their interiors tempting me to call a premature halt to the afternoon.

I lodged in Motoyama, a quiet rural town with an overwhelmingly grey-haired population. The ryokan I stayed in was a rambling old building of steep wooden stairs and cramped corridors leading off in all directions, mysterious doors and walls of *shoji* paper screens partitioning the rooms throughout. My room looked over the central courtyard where rows of elaborate terracotta roof tiles sloped down from each storey, overhanging a garden of persimmon trees. The only sound was the regular *thunk thunk* of a bamboo water fountain rebounding from a rock, and the woodpecker laugh of the gregarious owner emanating from somewhere on the ground floor.

If I thought I might lose myself in too much quiet contemplation, I needn't have worried; there was always Japanese television to drag me back. I tuned into a variety show of the format prevalent across almost all the channels here: a line-up of celebrities (mix of loud, leering middle-aged male comics, young and attractive aspiring actresses, and a token gay and/or foreigner), a studio audience of the lowest denominator, and a barrage of inane topics and bawdy jokes. The production team were on location in a zoo where an elephant was refusing to eat; he was apparently sad that his previous keeper Kenji had moved on. So, they had erected a life-size cardboard cut-out of Kenji and played a recording of his voice, until he started to swing his trunk around, caressing the picture and the tape recorder.

Meanwhile back in the studio, the TV personalities were crying away like babies, with the camera zooming in on the most emotional as each one tried to outdo the others with their blubbering, and I despaired for the future of this country.

Contemplating the next climb, Shikoku

AS A CYCLIST, YOUR INTERACTION WITH THE LOCAL POPULATION varies by region. On the one extreme there is Central Asia, where you – a westerner with odd-looking transport and a strained smile – immediately stand out as a person of interest, and the locals are not shy about stopping you to find out more. The experience is centred around people at every point, which is just as well because the miles of barren desert and desperately stark mountains offer few alternatives for distraction. The Chinese, in contrast, are decidedly less outgoing so you get some welcome breathing space, but still you find yourself the object of constant staring, like an exhibit in a zoo.

In Japan, your hosts are much more reticent, more so than in Europe, and you are generally left alone, no interruptions, no eye contact, no hassle; one less variable to account for, although such shyness may come across as being aloof. Your focus moves to the intimate scenery enveloping you. The mountain roads cloaked in moss. Sleepy hamlets, firewood piled high outside the farmhouses for the coming winter. Well-tended mountain shrines spotted through the undergrowth. Or a roadside verge punctuated with knee-high stone statues of *jizo*, the guardian of travellers, each wearing a neat red bib and with an offering of fresh flowers and a cup of *sake* at his feet. You might pass a laughing group of old ladies in one village, resplendent in their antique silk *kimono*, whilst in the next enjoy the haunting notes of a bamboo flute floating from a window, caressing you with a wave of melancholy.

My destination was the Iya valley, a region that until as recently as seventy years ago was only accessible by foot. Today there is a proper road carrying tourist traffic to the area's number one attraction, Kazurabashi, a suspension bridge built from wood and vines. The drivers of the cars and tour busses that passed me were careful and considerate; it was the occupants that were dangerous, as I was elbowed out of the way time and again by parties of late middle-aged women bustling for photographs in a flurry of pink and gold jerseys and pompoms.

Iya is known for its villages of traditional thatched-roof houses, perched on precipitous valley sides, and in the early afternoon I turned onto a steep and narrow broken road heading up to one of them for the night. With the rapid abandonment of rural living in Japan such houses are disappearing, and the Chiiori Project was one attempt to preserve a way of life that is in danger of being forgotten. A beautiful three-hundred-year-old restored farmhouse, it was in a commanding location and I surveyed the valley far below; this was one hell of a place to get to, and likely explained why I was the only guest that evening, outnumbered by its young volunteers by four to one.

They were all on a working holiday, staying anything from two weeks to two months, and the frosty response I got suggested a less than enthusiastic outlook on the "working" part of the deal. After a day of climbing I was starving but there was barely any food in, just some bread for breakfast the next morning; the snacks they served at a nearby hot spring barely stated me and I settled down for sleep with my stomach rumbling.

These houses were built for communal living and we all slept around the sunken *irori* fireplace in the middle of the house. It was only with the upmost care that I silently got up in the freezing pre-dawn darkness, scoffed all the bread while they slept, and got the hell out of there.

A vulgar grey sky oppressed me all day, dark clouds smothering the light, with an icy chill that cut to the bone. I passed through near deserted hamlets balanced precariously over fast flowing rivers or tucked in tightly at the forest edge; there were farmhouses built inaccessibly high up on the slopes of the other side of the valley, and fields of well-dressed scarecrows watching me watching them. An old lady was making painstakingly slow progress along a path; she paused on seeing me and politely bowed as I cycled past.

I rode over two major passes, one almost a mile high, following a narrow lane that alternately burrowed through forests, rose high above ravines, or threaded me delicately through small highland villages of just a handful of homes. Towards dusk, as I crested the last pass of the day, I had a peculiar feeling of being in harmony with everything around me. I descended swiftly down the darkening valley, passing old wooden farmhouses cloaked in shadow, the only sounds the whistling of the wind in my ears, the rapids of the river below me and the sharp squeal of my brakes at the approach to every corner, echoing from the valley walls.

There really are gods in these mountains.

Mountain Roads, Shikoku

THE KII HANTO IS THE THICK PENINSULA THAT LIES SOUTH OF

Kyoto and Osaka, and its less ventured mountainous interior is given little thought by the millions of overseas visitors to those cities every year. I was climbing the long road up to the temple complex of Koya-san as autumn foliage overflowed onto the tarmac and deep shadows crept slowly over paddy fields. A solitary farmer was in his field, picking late-season persimmons off heavily laden trees with a bamboo pole.

Koya-san is an important sacred mountain for Japanese Buddhists, and midweek in November it was packed full of tourists and pilgrims. This would be the third time I had ridden up here (there was some substantial atonement needed for past sins) but despite the crowds and the increasing commercialism I still liked to linger, and the temples and shrines emanated a genuine sense of tranquillity. For a while I took refuge in the grounds of the mausoleum of Kobo Daishi, the holy man who had established this place some 1,200 years ago.

A young monk in a brand-new imported Range Rover drove past me at speed, almost knocking me off the road, and I had just enough time to catch his look of distain. I recalled what the old Japanese traveller had told me on the ferry from Shanghai:

"Religion here is all about the money. People can bankrupt themselves paying the fees these damned people demand for blessings, funerals, remembrances and the like. Think about it - have you ever seen a poor priest?"

Making the most the remaining daylight, I continued past Koya-san and found a fabulous descent snaking down the eastern side of the valley. A clear blue river gushed over rapids on my left, a sharp granite rock face bore down upon me from the right, and everything was swathed in a dazzling mass of yellow, orange and red.

THE MORNINGS WERE GETTING COLDER, AND THE FRIGID AIR FELT like ice on my face. The well-kept villages I cycled through were refreshingly alive and bustling with small shops and activity, whilst timber-mills punctuated the spaces in-between, filling the air with the delicious scent of pine and cedar.

However, I had to be doubly wary of the drivers around here; I saw one woman carefully applying her makeup with a handheld mirror while crossing an intersection. Another one almost ran me into the gutter because she had to stop *exactly* before a sign which said, "Stop Here".

It was dark when I set up camp in a riverside park under a clear, star-lit sky, and I awoke to a landscape that had been brushed with a gossamer coating of frost. The day warmed up quickly as I made my way out of the hills and rode past villages with dizzyingly steep terraces of neatly trimmed hedgerows of tea. I was headed to Toba to catch a ferry across Ise Bay, but first I was to stop off at the famous Ise Jingu shrine, the spiritual centre of *Shinto*, Japan's animistic "old religion".

Dozens of tourist buses were parked outside the shrine, thousands of people milling around, tour guides shouting orders through loudspeakers and waving their flags. It was a busy public holiday and I would not be discovering much spiritual enlightenment today, so I attended to a more practical matter instead – my laundry. I stripped off and hid in the corner of a laundrette until the machines were done, like some poor man's Levi's jeans ad.

The ferry dropped me in Irago, at the very tip of Achi prefecture, and the sun flung up a thousand rays of light as it set behind the mountains of the Kii Hanto. I found a bed and breakfast where the friendly landlady fussed over me and my bike.

"Let's get a picture together. Is it okay if I put it on my home-page?" she asked and called across to her neighbour to take the photograph. "If only my daughter was here tonight, I would introduce you."

"Oh no you wouldn't", said her neighbour, "I'd introduce him to my daughter first!"

Neither of them introduced their daughters to me.

TODAY A JAPANESE DRIVER WAVED TO ME FOR THE FIRST TIME, the sun shone a little warmer, and the clock was rewound from early winter back to late autumn for a day. I was losing my battle with the coastal bike path that would deceptively tempt me along a scenic section of coast, only to suddenly dump me back on the main road, which was getting increasingly busy as the capital got closer. I reached Cape Omaezaki by sunset and stood there looking out across the Pacific Ocean for the longest time.

Tonight's television entertainment: a cooking program with an assortment of dairy products and ten young, attractive female *talento* (aspiring celebrities) in miniskirts animatedly watching the proceedings through binoculars three metres away. As they zoomed in on garnished omelettes and fluffy cheese flans, these once demure ladies competed with each other in the excitement stakes, bouncing up and down on their chairs and uttering squeals of excitement, the camera hovering over the most enthusiastic of them before the food was removed and they eventually calmed down, breathless but apparently satisfied. I despaired for the future of this country.

The road was thick with traffic as I cycled through the suburbs of Shizuoka city to meet up with some old friends. Jim and Teena had had a baby son since I had last seen them, so they took turns between supervising Hayden at home and supervising me in the local pub; I had no doubt as to which was the short straw.

The next morning it was a relief to turn off the busy coastal road and head inland for the mountains once more, and the remnants of a heavy morning mist cleared to tease me with views of Mount Fuji between the trees, the perfect cone of this 3,776-metre-tall dormant volcano capped with a brilliant white covering of snow. It was a long grind to Lake Yamanakako, the largest of the five lakes that lie at the foot of Fuji-san, and darkness had already descended by the time I got there.

In the off-season it was a lonely place and there were no obvious signs of accommodation available. The tourist information office was still open, and the lady sat behind the counter warming her hands in front of a gas heater, barely able to pull herself away from it to attend to probably her only customer that afternoon.

I would like a room, I said, with dinner if at all possible. Nothing fancy and anywhere around the lake was fine, I explained, as I could cycle there. She didn't look too confident and reluctantly rang a number.

"It's a foreigner", she said apologetically over the phone, and listened to the response at the other end, glaring at me accusingly.

"Do you speak Japanese?" she asked me in Japanese, and I

reminded her that was indeed the language we'd been speaking all this time.

"What about rice?" she demanded, "can you eat it?"

After enduring another half dozen such questions, assuring her I knew to take my shoes off in the premises, I would not be holding any noisy parties that evening and would certainly try not to set fire to the place, the cross-examination was over and I was allowed the privilege of paying for a room.

Things were improving. Five years ago, they'd have just told me to bugger off.

Approach to Mount Fuji, Shizuoka

THE MORNING PRESENTED INCREDIBLE VIEWS OF FUJI-SAN FROM across the lake before I took a forest road downhill for the best part of 50 kilometres until it stopped at a T-junction. Then with a single ninety degree turn, the tranquillity of the mountains was brought to a sudden halt and I was thrown into the maelstrom of cars and trucks making their way in the direction of the city.

Familiar areas of Tokyo started appearing on signposts - Hachioji, Shinjuku, Shibuya - and English newspapers were now available in the ubiquitous chains of convenience stores. Half the policemen ordered me off the road and onto the pavement, while the other half ordered me back. This final week had eased me gently back into the concrete jungle, so Tokyo was not a sudden shock to the system. However, a champagne reception, a large crowd of old friends and a hundred handshakes made me realise the finality of the situation: 18 countries, 16,000 kilometres and almost 8 months later, this little adventure of mine was over.

Well, almost over. As I was still coming to terms with seeing so many familiar faces once again, my bike was swiftly covered in colourful bunting and a cloud of oversized gold and silver balloons tied to the rack.

Congratulations!
Welcome Back!
Well Done!
Yet I still had five miles to go.

The final goal was Nihonbashi bridge, from where all distances to the capital are measured. If I had mentioned earlier that people in Japan don't give cyclists a second glance, then I had not been thinking of a cyclist with a dozen large and shiny helium balloons tied to his bicycle, making his way through the busiest business district in the world. It is not easy to remain nonchalant when an enormous gold and pink balloon is punching you repeatedly in the face, and the customary reticence of the Japanese breaks down into unrestrained pointing and laughing.

Parked alone on the bridge, as party balloons sashayed around my head in the very centre of Tokyo, I reflected on my fortune. It was a relief to no longer worry about where I was going to sleep, what I might find to eat, and whether I had enough water to make it to the next town. There was no need to stretch my imagination or perform facial gymnastics to communicate with the locals, and no more dealing with yet another policeman asking me for a "present".

Yet... I was already feeling a little lost, a little empty. In the day to day pattern of travel I was always preoccupied with what might be coming next, rarely stopping to reflect on what had come and gone, and I couldn't quite believe this was the end. The following week I would be on a flight back to London, and in 239 days less than it took to cover the same distance by bicycle, I would be back where I started in the UK, feet up on the sofa, cup of tea in hand. Wondering what on earth I was going to do now.

The End!

AFTERWORD

There was a sort of minor events circuit after I arrived back in Tokyo: a magazine article, a few slideshows and talks given to cycling clubs, adventure clubs, schools and colleges. I did them with bemusement, never quite understanding what all the fuss was about. What had once looked like a terrifying plan on paper had eventually become a day to day normality – and now that the whole thing was finally over, I couldn't appreciate that I had actually pulled it off.

My ten minutes of fame came and went. A flurry of emails from people I had met along the way died down, first through a lack of language skills (Russian, Turkish, Chinese...) then once I had started work again, a lack of time. A cyclist at one of my talks was inspired to try some of the same route himself, and I asked him to stop at the same restaurant in eastern Turkey where I had been nursed back to health. He sent me a photo of the place a year later; I recognised the murals on the wall, but the restaurant was in a state of disrepair and had long since been deserted.

Fourteen years later there is one tenuous link remaining; an email of season's greetings I receive without fail every Christmas Day, from a man I met for ten minutes in a yurt in the highlands of Kyrgyzstan. He sends a photograph of his family and always asks me where I am in the world. And I am quite content to give him the same answer every year: Japan.

ACKNOWLEDGMENTS

I owe a debt of gratitude to my editor Amanda Eaton for the comprehensive edits which make me sound considerably more cultured than I am. From floating the initial idea of a bike trip through to eventually writing this book, I must thank Padraig MacColgain for his constant and patient support. William Hay enthusiastically took up the role of beta reader and gave me invaluable advice on the first draft, as did Brad Corbet, Jim and Teena Smith, and Elicia La Valle – my grateful thanks for your help.

Only now that I have a son of my own can I appreciate the worry that goes into a walk to the bus-stop, never mind a bike ride around half the world, so I must thank my mother, Maura Tallon, who never wavered in her encouragement, and also Mark and Victoria Tallon who dispatched parcels of bike spares and maps throughout the journey.

Most of all, I am indebted to the many people who offered me their friendship, shared their stories and let me step briefly into their lives. The thing I could least plan for in this venture was the one thing crucial to its success; without the generosity of strangers this whole thing could never have happened.

Made in United States
Orlando, FL
25 March 2022

16144924R00181